D0437195

Wheel, Deal, and Steal

Deceptive Accounting, Deceitful CEOs, and Ineffective Reforms

FT Prentice Hall
FINANCIAL TIMES

Pearson
Education

Wheel, Deal, and Steal

Deceptive Accounting, Deceitful CEOs, and Ineffective Reforms

D. Quinn Mills

An Imprint of PEARSON EDUCATION
Upper Saddle River, NJ • New York • London • San Francisco • Toronto • Sydney
Tokyo • Singapore • Hong Kong • Cape Town • Madrid
Paris • Milan • Munich • Amsterdam

www.ft-ph.com

A CIP catalog record for this book can be obtained from the Library of Congress

Editorial/Production Supervisor: *MetroVoice Publishing Services*
Executive Editor: *Jim Boyd*
Editorial Assistant: *Linda Ramagnano*
Marketing Manager: *John Pierce*
Manufacturing Manager: *Alexis Heydt-Long*
Cover Design: *Nina Scuderi*
Cover Design Director: *Jerry Votta*
Series Design: *Gail Cocker-Bogusz*
Full-Service Project Manager: *Anne R. Garcia*

Publishing as Financial Times Prentice Hall
Upper Saddle River, New Jersey 07458

The publisher offers discounts on this book when ordered in bulk quantities.
For more information, contact
Corporate Sales Department,
Prentice Hall PTR
One Lake Street
Upper Saddle River, NJ 07458
Phone: 800-382-3419; FAX: 201-236-7141
E-mail: corpsales@prenhall.com

Printed in the United States of America

First Printing

ISBN 0-13-140804-6

Pearson Education Ltd.
Pearson Education Australia PTY, Limited
Pearson Education Singapore, Pte. Ltd
Pearson Education North Asia Ltd
Pearson Education Canada, Ltd.
Pearson Educación de Mexico, S.A. de C.V.
Pearson Education — Japan
Pearson Education Malaysia, Pte. Ltd

Financial Times Prentice Hall Books

For more information, please go to www.ft-ph.com

Business and Technology

Sarv Devaraj and Rajiv Kohli
The IT Payoff: Measuring the Business Value of Information Technology Investments

Nicholas D. Evans
Business Agility: Strategies for Gaining Competitive Advantage through Mobile Business Solutions

Nicholas D. Evans
Business Innovation and Disruptive Technology: Harnessing the Power of Breakthrough Technology...for Competitive Advantage

Nicholas D. Evans
Consumer Gadgets: 50 Ways to Have Fun and Simplify Your Life with Today's Technology...and Tomorrow's

Faisal Hoque
The Alignment Effect: How to Get Real Business Value Out of Technology

Thomas Kern, Mary Cecelia Lacity, and Leslie P. Willcocks
Netsourcing: Renting Business Applications and Services Over a Network

Ecommerce

Dale Neef
E-procurement: From Strategy to Implementation

Economics

David Dranove
What's Your Life Worth? Health Care Rationing...Who Lives? Who Dies? Who Decides?

David R. Henderson
The Joy of Freedom: An Economist's Odyssey

Jonathan Wight
Saving Adam Smith: A Tale of Wealth, Transformation, and Virtue

Entrepreneurship

Oren Fuerst and Uri Geiger
From Concept to Wall Street: A Complete Guide to Entrepreneurship and Venture Capital

David Gladstone and Laura Gladstone
Venture Capital Handbook: An Entrepreneur's Guide to Raising Venture Capital, Revised and Updated

Erica Orloff and Kathy Levinson, Ph.D.
The 60-Second Commute: A Guide to Your 24/7 Home Office Life

Jeff Saperstein and Daniel Rouach
Creating Regional Wealth in the Innovation Economy: Models, Perspectives, and Best Practices

Finance

Aswath Damodaran

The Dark Side of Valuation: Valuing Old Tech, New Tech, and New Economy Companies

Kenneth R. Ferris and Barbara S. Pécherot Petitt

Valuation: Avoiding the Winner's Curse

International Business

Fernando Robles, Françoise Simon, and Jerry Haar

Winning Strategies for the New Latin Markets

Investments

Harry Domash

Fire Your Stock Analyst! Analyzing Stocks on Your Own

Philip Jenks and Stephen Eckett, Editors

The Global-Investor Book of Investing Rules: Invaluable Advice from 150 Master Investors

Charles P. Jones

Mutual Funds: Your Money, Your Choice. Take Control Now and Build Wealth Wisely

D. Quinn Mills

Buy, Lie, and Sell High: How Investors Lost Out on Enron and the Internet Bubble

D. Quinn Mills

Wheel, Deal, and Steal: Deceptive Accounting, Deceitful CEOs, and Ineffective Reforms

John Nofsinger and Kenneth Kim

Infectious Greed: Restoring Confidence in America's Companies

John R. Nofsinger

Investment Blunders (of the Rich and Famous)…And What You Can Learn from Them

John R. Nofsinger

Investment Madness: How Psychology Affects Your Investing…And What to Do About It

Leadership

Jim Despain and Jane Bodman Converse

And Dignity for All: Unlocking Greatness through Values-Based Leadership

Marshall Goldsmith, Vijay Govindarajan, Beverly Kaye, and Albert A. Vicere

The Many Facets of Leadership

Marshall Goldsmith, Cathy Greenberg, , Alastair Robertson, and Maya Hu-Chan

Global Leadership: The Next Generation

Frederick C. Militello, Jr., and Michael D. Schwalberg

Leverage Competencies: What Financial Executives Need to Lead

Eric G. Stephan and Wayne R. Pace

Powerful Leadership: How to Unleash the Potential in Others and Simplify Your Own Life

Management

Rob Austin and Lee Devin
Artful Making: What Managers Need to Know About How Artists Work

Dr. Judith M. Bardwick
Seeking the Calm in the Storm: Managing Chaos in Your Business Life

J. Stewart Black and Hal B. Gregersen
Leading Strategic Change: Breaking Through the Brain Barrier

William C. Byham, Audrey B. Smith, and Matthew J. Paese
Grow Your Own Leaders: How to Identify, Develop, and Retain Leadership Talent

David M. Carter and Darren Rovell
On the Ball: What You Can Learn About Business from Sports Leaders

Subir Chowdhury
Organization 21C: Someday All Organizations Will Lead this Way

Subir Chowdhury
The Talent Era: Achieving a High Return on Talent

James W. Cortada
Making the Information Society: Experience, Consequences, and Possibilities

Ross Dawson
Living Networks: Leading Your Company, Customers, and Partners in the Hyper-connected Economy

Robert B. Handfield, Ph.d, and Ernest L. Nichols
Supply Chain Redesign: Transforming Supply Chains into Integrated Value Systems

Harvey A. Hornstein
The Haves and the Have Nots: The Abuse of Power and Privilege in the Workplace... and How to Control It

Kevin Kennedy and Mary Moore
Going the Distance: Why Some Companies Dominate and Others Fail

Robin Miller
The Online Rules of Successful Companies: The Fool-Proof Guide to Building Profits

Fergus O'Connell
The Competitive Advantage of Common Sense: Using the Power You Already Have

Richard W. Paul and Linda Elder
Critical Thinking: Tools for Taking Charge of Your Professional and Personal Life

Matthew Serbin Pittinsky, Editor
The Wired Tower: Perspectives on the Impact of the Internet on Higher Education

W. Alan Randolph and Barry Z. Posner
Checkered Flag Projects: 10 Rules for Creating and Managing Projects that Win, Second Edition

Stephen P. Robbins
The Truth About Managing People...And Nothing but the Truth

Ronald Snee and Roger Hoerl
Leading Six Sigma: A Step-by-Step Guide Based on Experience with GE and Other Six Sigma Companies

Jerry Weissman
Presenting to Win: The Art of Telling Your Story

Marketing

Michael Basch
CustomerCulture: How FedEx and Other Great Companies Put the Customer First Every Day

Deirdre Breakenridge
Cyberbranding: Brand Building in the Digital Economy

Jonathan Cagan and Craig M. Vogel
Creating Breakthrough Products: Innovation from Product Planning to Program Approval

James W. Cortada
21st Century Business: Managing and Working in the New Digital Economy

Al Lieberman, with Patricia Esgate
The Entertainment Marketing Revolution: Bringing the Moguls, the Media, and the Magic to the World

Tom Osenton
Customer Share Marketing: How the World's Great Marketers Unlock Profits from Customer Loyalty

Yoram J. Wind and Vijay Mahajan, with Robert Gunther
Convergence Marketing: Strategies for Reaching the New Hybrid Consumer

Public Relations

Gerald R. Baron
Now Is Too Late: Survival in an Era of Instant News

Deirdre Breakenridge and Thomas J. DeLoughry
The New PR Toolkit: Strategies for Successful Media Relations

Strategy

Thomas L. Barton, William G. Shenkir, and Paul L. Walker
Making Enterprise Risk Management Pay Off: How Leading Companies Implement Risk Management

Henry A. Davis and William W. Sihler
Financial Turnarounds: Preserving Enterprise Value

To Debbie and Sterling

Contents

Acknowledgments

I greatly appreciate the assistance of several people in preparing this book. Among them are Jeremy Cott, whose help was invaluable in the research, and Kim Davis, who read the book carefully and made numerous significant suggestions. I also benefited from the assistance of James E. Bayne, Henry A. Davis, John T. Dunlop, Deborah Folk, Robert R. Glauber, Robin Gregory, Torrence C. Harder, Paul R. Lawrence, Jay Light, Edward C. Johnson III, John H. McArthur, Andrew G. Mills, Shirley Mills, Lynn Sharp Paine, Steven Rosefielde, and Bruce R. Scott.

I also owe much to the excellent work of financial and business reporters who have uncovered much about corporate practices.

Thanks as well to Jim Boyd and Elisa Adams at Prentice Hall for their help with all aspects of this book.

Finally, I am grateful to the Research Division of the Harvard Business School for its support of my work.

All interpretations and any errors are my responsibility alone.

—D. Quinn Mills

1

What Happened to Investors' Money?

"America's investors have been ripped off as massively as a bank being held up by a guy with a gun and a mask."[1]
—Arthur Levitt,
former chairman of the Securities and Exchange Commission

"Some will rob you with a six-gun and some with a fountain pen."
—Woody Guthrie,
in his ballad about outlaw Pretty Boy Floyd

1 Why You Should Read This Book

On a bright late summer's day the islands off the northeast coast sparkle like diamonds set in a blue chain. A yacht swung on its mooring directly off a dock jutting out from the water's edge just below a newly renovated mansion. On board the yacht, so new that everything glimmered in the sunlight, maids in white uniforms hurried about their tasks, and the captain and crew were preparing to sail. The owner of the boat, the pier, and the house sat in his shorts, shirtless—his tanned chest dark in the bleached noonday light, his hands gripping the wheel of the ship; his new wife stood pert and pretty beside him, an admiring smile on her lips.

An English guest stood beside the owner; he wore slacks, a polo shirt, and a yachting cap. The owner grinned up at him. "This is how bankers live in America," he said, smiling broadly.

His guest smiled in return and cast an admiring glance around the boat, house, sea, and sun; he even took a peak at his host's wife.

In the distance was an even larger yacht. "Whose is that?" asked the visitor.

"That belongs to the CEO of one of our client companies," his host replied.

"Oh," responded the Englishman. "So everyone makes lots of money." He looked around again, as if searching for something in particular, and then asked, "But where are the investors' yachts?"

There was a sudden embarrassed silence. The beautiful wife looked away. The banker cast a suspicious glance at his guest and then, seeing that the man was in earnest, responded, "Well, you see, in America it doesn't work that way."

Many of us have lost money in stocks. I'm continually asked, "Who took our money? Is it true that some people got very rich off this? Why did that happen?"

People add, "I thought the system was supposed to protect investors—why didn't it? I thought CEOs of companies were supposed to make money if their shareholders did, and not make money if the shareholders lost. But it didn't work that way. Why not?"

And as they warm to the topic, they ask, "What's been going on in the market? Will it continue? Do I want to be in the market? If not, what else can I do to build a retirement nest egg? Is there a safe way to do it? Whom can I trust?"

Finally, the most important question of all: "Is there any way I can get any of my money back?"

These are the topics of this book.

Investors Aren't Primarily to Blame for Their Losses

It's common for the media and financial professionals to blame investors for their losses. Investors were greedy, they claim; investors didn't do their homework about the companies in which they invested; it was investors' own fault they lost so much. People could have done more and been less gullible, it's true, but still investors aren't primarily to blame for their losses.

Some of the arguments that make investors responsible for their losses begin by trivializing what happened in the stock market boom. "Bosses will always be greedy," wrote the editors of a major business magazine, "auditors will always be fallible, boards will always miss things..." It follows, goes this argument, that an investor must presume the worst and exert constant scrutiny and questioning, and by implication, if he or she loses, then it's his or her fault for being willing to "suspend disbelief and be fooled."[2]

But the evidence in this book will show that much more happened in executive compensation than is captured in the phrase, "Bosses will always be greedy." Evidence will also show that auditors were not simply fallible, missing some things, so to speak, but were actively engaged in long-term efforts to mislead investors; and that boards of directors didn't merely miss things, but supported executives in manipulating financial reports to enrich the executives and themselves. It was not business as usual, and it wasn't something from which an investor could protect himself or herself by more vigilance. There was (and is, for similar behavior continues today) generalized deceit and deception and wholesale self-dealing at the expense of investors. What happened was generally prohibited by ethics and by law, but neither self-restraint nor regulatory agencies were effective in preventing deception and self-dealing in order to protect investors.

Other arguments that make investors responsible for the bubble and burst are very sophisticated. For example, an analysis now making the rounds of investment banks begins with the assertion that investors have become more willing to accept greater risk, and from that assumption the analysis shows that markets will then behave differently—exhibiting more volatility and bubbles and crashes. Thus, it's investors' fault that the market crashed—investors began to seek more risk, and the bull market and crash were the result.

This argument turns the actual causality upside down. In fact, investment banks, brokerages, venture firms, and companies promoted rising stock prices in a variety of ways (including fraudulent accounting and technology hype) and thereby enticed more investors into the market at rising prices. It was the bubble that turned investors into speculators (just as had happened during the tulip mania, the South Sea bubble, and other speculative manias hundreds of years ago), not investors who suddenly became speculators and created the bubbles.

In recent years it was the failure of investors to realize certain things about American stock markets as a whole that was the source of their losses. Investors failed to realize that the deck had been stacked against them; that they were the turkey at a Thanksgiving dinner held by CEOs and professionals in the financial markets.

Investors didn't realize that CEOs would fake the financial reports of their companies—that banks would help CEOs do this and accountants would permit it. Investors failed to realize that government wasn't paying attention, and that Congress was helping dishonest executives. Investors failed to realize that stock market analysts whom investors consulted about their investments had major conflicts of interest that were not disclosed to investors and so misled investors intentionally. Finally, investors failed to realize that many mutual funds also had conflicts of interest that turned them against their investors. It was their failure to realize these things that caused investors the enormous losses they took in the past few years. This book tells how and why it happened, and it will help investors avoid being turkeys again.

The question of the degree of investor responsibility for losses is one of the most controversial that is tackled in this book. Many executives in the securities industry and their supporters in Washington and New York believe that investors are let off too easily. They insist that bubbles happen in part because investors are greedy and readily feed on the hype they are fed.

The answer given in this book is twofold: first, that there is a legitimate role for the securities industry—to bring investors and businesses together for the purpose of building economic value. But for securities firms, banks, and corporate executives to encourage and exploit the weaknesses of people (certainly there is some greed in almost all of us) for their private gain is by far the greater sin. Leaders in the securities industry are in much the same position as executives in the gaming industry—there is a legitimate role for gaming as entertainment, but when gaming executives exploit chronic gamblers, they cross a line. The same is true of the alcohol industry—there's a legitimate role and there's exploitation of human weakness.

Second, exploitation of investors by banks, brokers, and corporate executives as described in this book goes far beyond mere hype to intentional, considered, and long-going deception. It's akin to a gaming company not only enticing a problem gambler to gamble, but going so far as to insist that the odds are in his or her favor; it's akin to a liquor company insisting that there is no harm from excessive drinking of its products. That is, it's pure deception—intolerable in almost any business.

Further, as we'll see in many of the chapters that follow, it's quite a spectacle to watch executives of banks and brokerages condemning their customers for excessive greed.

Why is the question of investor greed and investor responsibility for the stock market bubbles so contentious? Because there is a great deal of money involved.

Most bankers, analysts, and brokers cannot make a substantial living in the investment business without resorting to systematic deception. The average investment return is modest; the economy grows at only about 3 percent per year, and so there's rarely a killing to be made in matching investors and companies. Yet the securities industry has for many years delivered outsized compensation to many people. For decades now a large portion of the graduating classes of the major business schools have gone to Wall Street and many have made fortunes. What about the securities business makes bankers and brokers rich? The answer is clear from the history of the stock market bubbles of the nineties—deception.

This is why it's so important to those who profit from the industry to insist that their customers are greedy and insist upon being deceived.

Power Is at the Root of the Corporate Financial Scandals

The theme of this book is that though today's corporate scandals appear to be limited to accounting fraud, they're really part of a fundamental clash between top executives of American corporations and investors. The problem goes far beyond a group of well-publicized scandals and involves the stock market crash as a whole. In this broad perspective, the crisis is about power as well as about money—the basic cause of the scandals is that CEOs used their enormous power in large firms to enrich themselves at the expense of investors. Shareholders are supposed to own American firms, and executives are supposed to be their agents in running them. In reality, executives used their power to make fortunes and used the fortunes to expand their power—and investors were left farther and farther behind in the process.

There's much in this book about accounting, because investors need to understand the techniques used to defraud them; but so-called "creative accounting" was only the mechanism of the theft—its roots lay in a shift of power from investors to CEOs, so there's also much in this book about power in today's

American corporation. The principal story this book tells is about the misuse of power on a large scale. CEOs initiated the misuse, but they were joined by institutions and professionals that investors trusted and that owed responsibility to investors—accounting firms, attorneys, and investment banks.

Since the securities market crisis is largely about power, it must be resolved in those terms or it will reoccur. From the point of view of investors, it's crucial to jettison the too-powerful CEO—the imperial CEO—in favor of a management team that will be more responsive to corporate boards of directors. It's equally important to change CEO compensation packages by providing the right kind of stock options. (An option is a legal contract between a company and an executive that allows the executive to buy stock from the company at a specified price. How to fashion options that will reward executives, but only for real performance and only when investors gain, is discussed in Chapter 14.) Also, because regulators have been largely ineffective in protecting investors from fraud, there's a need for a total overhaul of the system by which securities markets are regulated (the topic of Chapter 13). President George W. Bush reminds us often that at the heart of the scandals is a failure of ethical standards among executives. So this book says much about ethics and about how business schools might help improve business ethics.

The Internet Bubble and The Big Company Scandals

This book is not about the Internet bubble, which occurred in the so-called "new economy," but rather about the scandals that have cost investors trillions and undermined confidence in the heart of the American economy—the "old economy" of the blue ribbon companies.

This book supplements my previous book, *Buy, Lie, and Sell High*. Together they present a complete picture of the boom and bust in America's stock market during the late 1990s and early 2000s. *Buy, Lie, and Sell High* explains the bubble in technology stocks; *Wheel, Deal, and Steal* shows how investors lost out in other sectors of the economy. There were major differences in what happened in the two sectors. The Internet bubble was driven by a continual barrage of publicity about the promises of the new technology, but hype played a much less significant role in the old economy. Venture firms and investment banks were the principle source of the bubble in the Internet sector; large-company CEOs and accountants were the principal sources of the fraud among the blue chips, although the investment banks again played a major role. The method used to mislead investors about the dot-coms was to inflate expectations; investors were mislead about the blue chips by misrepresentation of their financial situations.

The titles of the two books reflect the difference between the two manias. To create and exploit the technology mania, venture firms bought into entrepreneurs' ideas to obtain significant positions in their companies; joined with investment banks and the business press to tout the Internet and the supposedly wonderful prospects of the startups that they then sold to the public; and sold out when investors had pushed the share prices to unjustifiably high levels. Hence *Buy, Lie, and Sell High.*

To mislead investors, executives in large firms had to develop compliant boards of directors and accountants, and banks prepared to support their efforts; then they had to do deals that would look good in their financials and get approval from auditors and boards for misleading financial reports. Finally, they had to cash in their options before the frauds and other misrepresentations were discovered. Hence the title of this book: *Wheel, Deal, and Steal.*

Not much of long-term value was created by the great bull market of the 1990s. This was not like the mania that occurred when canals first linked the East Coast and Midwest; nor like the mania that occurred when railways first tied the country together coast to coast (though Internet propagandists pretended that the many miles of fiber optic cable laid in the late 1990s rivaled the canals and railways in importance). Nor was it even like the repeated stock market booms and busts that accompanied the building of our great manufacturing industries or the market boomlets that accompanied each new generation of computer technology (though considering the Internet as a new generation of technology helped set off the Internet craze). Instead, this was primarily a financial bubble, like that of the late 1920s, not an element in the growth of the economy, but a sort of parasite upon it. These two books together constitute a complete, contemporary story of the manipulations that resulted in the great bull market. Probably a better label for the experience is the manipulated market, because manipulation is what happened. The investor excitement that is said to be the cause of the bubbles was in fact the result of careful manipulation undertaken by top corporate executives, boards of directors, and every element of the financial services industry.

In the course of the chapters that follow we will explore the American financial securities system as it's supposed to operate—in behalf of investors—and as it has operated in recent years in which conflicts of interest have been exploited by corporate executives, accountants, and banks at the expense of investors. Much of what is contained in the book is summarized in two diagrams that appear in the final chapter. Some readers may want to take a look at the two figures now—they allow readers to figure out the system and its abuses before going through the text.

For CEOs it has been wheel, deal, and steal. For investors it has been believe, buy, and bust.

The Decay of American Capitalism

How did American business stray so far from the powerful economic model that the world admires and that has served us so well in the past: private enterprise, investor-owned companies, honest accounting, clear reporting of financial results so that investors can choose where to put their money, and ethical responsibility of financial professionals to ordinary investors? In the past two decades honest accounting, transparency in reporting financial results, and ethical responsibility of professionals to investors went by the wayside, and the result is massive losses for ordinary American investors and a crisis of confidence in the system as a whole. How this happened is a fascinating story about two decades of evolution in American financial markets and how the markets became corrupted in the process.

This is not a book of outrage, but a calm appraisal that provides a picture of what's happening. It clarifies for the reader complex matters about which the press is often confusing. It begins with what happened and then turns to what to do about it—to reforming the system and getting restitution for investors. This book will tell you how and why investors lost so much money, why it's likely to happen again, and what can be done to try to stop it. This book will also tell you how you can try to get your money back. Finally, our financial markets require reform, which in turn requires an understanding of causes. Different causes require different responses. This book clarifies the causes and proposes remedies.

Many of the matters discussed in this book should not be the subject of ideological or partisan controversy. That the left might be affronted by corporate misdeeds is no surprise, but the right should be also. Economist Milton Friedman commented, "There is one and only one social responsibility of business—to use its resources and engage in activities designed to increase its profits, so long as it stays within the rules of the game, which is to say, engage in open and free competition without deception or fraud."[3] The issues here are deception and fraud, on a very large scale. As such, they threaten the utility of free markets, and should affront the right as much as the left, though perhaps for a somewhat different reason.

Where there is proper reason for ideological and partisan differences is with regard to what should be done to rectify the situation. The left is likely to prefer more regulation; the right more reliance on markets. In this book I've suggested responses of each type—not more but better regulation (see Chapter 13) and greater, not lesser reliance on choice in our markets (see Chapter 16).

Returning to a More Honest America

On the fourth of July, many Americans boast of the virtues of our great country—of hard work and commitment and honesty and free enterprise. These are real and significant virtues and they are admired in much of the world. But recent corporate scandals have shown that they are fast giving way to easy money, self-interest, fraud, and dishonesty.

As a young man I served the American public during the Vietnam War in a position of business regulation. At the time I came across some clear incidents of corruption—self-dealings and bribes—and couldn't understand why the perpetrators hadn't been taken to court and to jail. A senior official of the government, a man who'd served during World War II and the Korean War in positions similar to the one I was in then, told me that whenever one came across situations of longstanding corruption in business, it was always associated with corruption in the police and judiciary as well—otherwise, it couldn't persist.

And when I came across things that were unfair, things that should have been illegal but were in fact legal, he told me that they in turn were always accompanied by corruption in the legislative process—at the local, state, or federal level. That was how things that should have been illegal were made legal.

Over the years I've seen that he was correct. The well-recognized downside of democracy is that it has in it the seeds of corruption. The court system and the legislative systems are deeply implicated in the current business scandals. The courts because the system is so imperfect that investors cannot get quick and sure restitution of money taken from them by deception. The legislatures because they help the swindlers with favorable laws—both permitting actions that shouldn't have been permitted and lessening potential penalties for those unlucky enough to get caught.

The best way to end the securities market crisis is for the government to make investors whole for their losses, have federal and state regulators punish the corporate and financial leaders who caused fraud and benefited from it, and reform the system so that it doesn't happen again. This approach, championed in the chapters that follow, is a far better method of dealing with the crisis than is lengthy class-action litigation and limited regulatory reform, which we shall see is the method now being pursued.

There are many Americans now in the stock market, and if we are sufficiently upset about our losses, politicians and courts may act. Estimates are that the proportion of U.S. households that owned stocks or mutual funds has grown from 19% in 1983 to 49.5% in 2002; and the proportion of single individuals who own stocks or mutual funds has grown from 42% in 1983 to 84% in 2002.[4] If investors exert their potential influence, can we create a safer, more reliable, more honest America?

Talking Points

The bursting of the Internet bubble wiped out the savings of many American investors. But those who fell for the much-hyped promise of the high-tech stocks weren't the only ones who got burned. People buying shares in large, blue ribbon companies of the old economy also saw their nest eggs evaporate in the market meltdown.

When it comes to assigning blame for these huge losses, there's a tendency to find fault with the investors who are the victims. But was it really their greed-fueled desire to seek more and more risk that caused the market to crash? It's one thing to lose money through greed or irrational exuberance; it's quite another to be duped by people who were supposed to be on your side. The truth is investors didn't realize they were being systematically deceived by corporate executives who were supposed to be their agents but instead were masterminding schemes to pocket millions of dollars regardless of what happened to shareholders. Furthermore, when investors sought impartial investment advice, they were often misled by Wall Street professionals who had their own interests in mind.

This book addresses the key questions about the investment debacle: How did it happen? Why did a system that was supposed to protect investors fail them? Will investors regain their badly shaken confidence in the stock market? What can be done to help restore their trust? And last but not least, how can investors get their money back?

2 Scandals and More Scandals

The purpose of this chapter is to explain what has happened in the most publicized corporate scandals and to clarify the differences among the various situations in different companies. In Chapter 3 we explore what's common among the scandals. Because there's much that is common, we turn in Chapter 4 to the questions: Are the scandals only a matter of a few bad apples; if not, what needs to be fixed; and what is the significance of the scandals for the economy as a whole?

The Scandals in a Nutshell

We've heard the news reports but they're still difficult to believe. Below are a baker's dozen of the major corporate scandals, briefly summarized. They're presented in roughly chronological order, with a little bit more space given to the Sunbeam episode because in many respects it provided a model for later scandals.

Many of the companies included in the list below are unfamiliar names, but others are among the bluest of blue-chip American firms. Some of the actions described below are clearly fraudulent; others, which took advantage of flexibility in accounting rules, may be at the edge of legality. But all the actions described, whether illegal or not, had in common a basic objective: fool investors about what was really going on in the companies.

Sunbeam

The first in what became a flood of major scandals centered around Albert J. Dunlap, CEO of Sunbeam. Dunlap had a reputation as a cost-cutter—a corporate turn-around expert who idealized his mode of operation thusly: "to turn around a company at lightning speed. To focus on the best ... to eliminate what is not best. To protect and enhance shareholder value."[5] Before coming to Sunbeam, Dunlap had been CEO of Scott Paper and merged it with another firm. He added in his book, "Most CEOs are ridiculously overpaid, but I deserved the $100 million I took away when Scott merged with Kimberly-Clark."

When he was hired by Sunbeam in 1996, Dunlap was one of the first executives to get from the board of a major company a pay package consisting mainly of stock options. His was a closely watched performance. He took over as CEO, promising great financial performance by the company. Its stock rose accordingly, but when the financial performance didn't materialize, the company falsely inflated its sales and profits. In 1998, when the fraud was discovered, "Chainsaw," as Dunlap was known, was fired.

After Dunlap's departure, the company restated its financials for a year and a half. It reported that its profit for 1997 was the result of an exaggerated charge for restructuring the company that had been taken in 1996, premature bookings of revenue, and other dodges. Arthur Andersen was the company's auditor.[6]

"It appears that Sunbeam's board brought [Dunlap] in to radically restructure and streamline the company," commented Harvard researchers who studied Sunbeam, "not to grow it over time. That is, they believed Sunbeam needed radical surgery, not investment and a long-term growth plan. Either the strategy was wrong, or the strategy was executed poorly, or both."[7]

In fairness, Dunlap never exercised his options or sold any of his shares in Sunbeam. Had he done so at the peak stock price, he would have pocketed over $100 million from exercising his vested options alone, without even touching his stock holdings and new 1998 options. Why didn't he cash in?

Researchers at Harvard speculate:

> One possibility is that Dunlap believed that his restructuring strategy would eventually work. Another possibility is that he knew his strategy was not working but also believed that selling stock or exercising options at that high price would send a signal to investors that he thought the company was overvalued. If his strategy was to use accounting gimmicks to artificially inflate the price and make a quick profit, he executed that strategy very badly. Because of the additional decline in Sunbeam's stock price following his departure, Dunlap's options were all underwater [that is, without value] shortly after he departed.[8]

In the end, Dunlap not only failed to make any money for himself from the short-lived increase in Sunbeam's stock price, but he also lost a significant amount of money from his stock purchases. In addition, well after he was fired, Dunlap was sued by Sunbeam's shareholders and bondholders for accounting fraud and eventually settled the case (without admitting guilt) by paying $18 million out of his own pocket, $15 million to the shareholders and $3 million to the bondholders.[9]

But this wasn't all. In September 2002, Dunlap agreed to pay the Securities and Exchange Commission (SEC) a fine and to accept a ban on his ever serving again as an officer or director of a public company.[10] According to *New York Times* reporter Floyd Norris, there were also irregularities in accounting at Scott Paper, where Al Dunlap made his fortune, and at a company he'd run before that.

> Mr. Dunlap fooled investors for years. Had the SEC looked at Scott's books while he was there, perhaps he would have been stopped earlier. But he was not. He made his millions while fictitious profits were posted and investors lost billions. If he were charged, Mr. Dunlap would probably claim ... that he is not an accountant and had no responsibility if the accounting was wrong...[11]

Dunlap has not yet been charged with a criminal violation and may not be. Chainsaw's experience at Sunbeam had been well publicized in the late 1990s, but his failure didn't dissuade other CEOs from taking a similar path. If anything, they learned from his mistakes and carried their own efforts further. In particular, top executives and directors at other companies sold very large numbers of shares into the bull market at the top of the boom, took the money and, when their companies later collapsed, had their attorneys tell victimized investors that the executives had done nothing wrong—in effect thumbing their noses at investors and the SEC and taunting them that they couldn't get the money back.

Enron

Enron is an old gas pipeline company that turned itself into a darling of the Internet economy by claiming to make lots of money in energy trading and other new products of the computer age. Executives at the company used a variety of devices to inflate its earnings, including simply making them up. For example, Enron faked earnings when it got $110 million of financing (that is, a loan) from a Canadian investment bank for a new video-on-demand business—recording it as revenue. When Enron received this financing, in fact, it was just beginning to test the new business and had virtually no paying customers for it. Ultimately, the video-on-demand business produced nothing.

Executives inflated revenue by booking as sales transactions those that had little or no real economic basis—they were conduced for the purpose of inflating sales. Loans were kept off the company's balance sheet, so that the company looked stronger financially than it was, by the use of partnerships and favorable accounting interpretations. Company executives were partners in these off-balance sheet financing vehicles and profited greatly at the company's expense. The company concealed how it was allegedly making money—its business model—from investors via failure to disclose crucial elements of its finances. When a financial reporter finally insisted in the fall of 2001 that the company must disclose its business model, the stock began to collapse in value. As the stock fell, executives cashed out their holdings, but employees of the company, whose pension savings were largely invested in the company's stock, were forced to retain their holdings. Ultimately, the company filed for bankruptcy, employees lost most of their pensions, and investors lost most of the value of their shareholdings.

According to a report issued by a bankruptcy examiner, Enron raised almost $1.4 billion in cash from 1997 to 2001, all of which was reported as revenue from operations (that is, sales) or investments, but all of which was actually loans from banks to partnerships set up by Enron. The money was used to buy assets from Enron. But these transactions were not really sales. "Through a complex financial arrangement known as a total return swap, Enron retained all rights to any profits produced by the asset that was purportedly sold, and also assumed responsibility for paying the banks cash that equaled the total amount loaned to the partnership, plus a fixed interest rate. It would be as if an individual claimed to have sold his own house while remaining responsible for the mortgage, retaining the profit from any increase in value in a future sale, and continuing to live in the place to boot."[12]

Andrew Fastow, Enron's CFO, apparently made a fortune from running off-balance sheet partnerships, called special purpose entities (SPE), which hid the company's debt from its investors.[13] The original purpose of an SPE was to create a title to the specific assets involved so that they may be used as collateral for loans or can be insured. This is unobjectionable. But they've been used to hide debt from investors by taking it off the balance sheets of firms—a process called "financial engineering" and one which became the special expertise of CFOs and investment banks. According to a report of a bankruptcy court examiner, Enron used as many as 50 SPEs, which entered into hundreds of separate transactions on behalf of the company. The examiner looked at only six transactions in detail but determined that they had a dramatic impact on both the balance sheet and the income statement of the company.[14]

Secret agreements promised that Enron would shield the SPEs from losses, so that individuals and institutions that participated in the partnerships did so at no risk. Enron shareholders retained all the risk, yet the liability did not appear on the company's balance sheet. This was fraud.[15] That Enron's executives were intentionally looting the company is made evident by the fact that higher-ups accepted payments from their subordinates for letting the subordinates participate in the special purpose entities.[16]

Perhaps the most astonishing of the events at Enron was the board of directors waiving the conflict of interest restriction so that executives could manage partnerships engaged in prospective transactions with Enron. It's not unheard of for a board to waive a conflict of interest for an executive, but it almost always occurs in the context of a specific transaction the full details of which are known to the board at the time it acts. Enron's board waived conflict of interest for executives on a wholesale and prospective basis. This was a breath-taking lapse of judgment by the board. It was also of great legal value to the executives. It may mean that Enron's executives did not violate the law despite their deep conflicts of interest. Since it appears that the government will not prosecute Enron's board, it is likely to turn out that the board successfully laundered the executives without cost to themselves.

Finally, when the government at last got around to investigating Enron, a letter to the SEC from the Senate Governmental Affairs Committee accused the Commission of "systematic and catastrophic failure" in the Enron matter. "Investors were left defenseless," said the letter, noting that the SEC had failed to review any of Enron's post-1997 annual reports, particularly that of 1999 when the off-balance sheet entities first appeared.[17]

WorldCom

The chief financial officer and controller of WorldCom, according to federal prosecutors, worked backward from Wall Street analysts' estimates of what earnings per share would be at the company to determine the upper limit of expense WorldCom could have in order to meet the profit targets, then fraudulently misclassified expenditures to hide costs and increase profits. An objective was apparently to try to maintain the company's high share price in the face of the collapse of the Internet bubble in the stock market. WorldCom was one of the largest carriers of Internet traffic and was responsible for exaggerating the rate of growth of Internet traffic.

Massive accounting fraud involving billions of dollars in costs went on for several years. Chief financial officers were charged with falsifying WorldCom's books and records, providing misleading information to auditors, illegally manipulating company information in connection with buying and selling WorldCom securities, and filing false reports with the Securities and Exchange Commission. The chief executive officer of the company, Benard Ebbers, denies any knowledge of the fraud (a topic to which we'll return in a later chapter). One method used to exaggerate sales was referred to as "rolling revenue"—booking a single sale many times over, even if it meant paying multiple commissions to salespeople in the process.[18]

One especially interesting device used by WorldCom managers was to promote the notion that Internet traffic was doubling every hundred days. There's no other evidence of this than statements from WorldCom, one of the largest carriers of Internet traffic. WorldCom was in a position to know, but it lied and so distorted all the corporate and government economic planning in the United States in the 1990s, misleading investors in their millions. In fact, Internet traffic did double every hundred days in 1995–1996 at the start of the Internet boom, but growth quickly fell to one-tenth what WorldCom was reporting."[19]

The CFO centralized financial reporting to such a degree that only a handful of people in the company ever saw a profit and loss statement for the company as a whole. This made it possible for the CFO to manipulate the numbers, and to engage in large-scale fraud. Had the data been shared more widely among the company's many divisions and executives, then discrepancies would have been quickly perceived and perhaps acted on.

The vice president of internal audit at WorldCom supported members of her staff in uncovering accounting frauds perpetrated by her boss, CFO Scott Sullivan, and taking it to the board of directors, ultimately saw the CFO fired.[20]

Most of the accounting fraud at WorldCom is said to have occurred after the share price was down to $1 and after the CFO had cashed out most of his options, so, one argument goes, the motivation wasn't personal greed but an effort to save the company. But this seems unlikely. Had the company collapsed immediately after the CFO and others had cashed out, SEC and shareholder suits would have endangered the executive's take. The founder and other executives cashed out very large sums in stock while the share price was high, and then the company collapsed, leaving shareholders with nothing.

Global Crossing

Global Crossing used capacity swaps with other firms to inflate revenue, treating the swaps as if real transactions using money had occurred. The CEO, Gary Winnick, maintained he played little or no role in these transactions, but it seems that he approved such a deal only a few weeks before he and other executives sold large amounts of stock in the company.[21]

Global Crossing was sold in mid-August 2002, for some $250 million, well below its indebtedness of $12.4 billion and also below the $700 million or so that its former CEO took out of the company before letting it go bankrupt. The investors who hadn't jumped ship in time were left with nothing.

Tyco

Starting in 1992, CEO Dennis Kozlowski assembled Tyco, a $36 billion company in home security, electronics, finance, and medical products, all unrelated areas. It was an old-fashioned conglomerate. He and his CFO and the company's general counsel then proceeded to loot it—taking huge sums from the company for their personal use in a variety of ways. Federal prosecutors charged Kozlowski and another Tyco executive with a racketeering scheme, using the term "corrupt enterprise," which is usually applied to Mafia prosecutions.[22]

Prosecutors contend further that the CEO made sure the internal audit division of the company reported directly to him, and that he kept it from looking at the books of the unit he was using to take money from the company without reporting it to investors or the SEC. The CFO made sure he had control of the company's reports to the SEC, so that nothing would be disclosed about what the indictment calls the "top executives' criminal enterprise."[23]

In one incident, Tyco bought a stake in a small company at an inflated price so that Tyco took a loss on the transaction (the smaller company later went bankrupt), but Tyco recorded the purchase as a profit of more than $70 million and used it as a basis for paying executives more than $20 million in bonuses.[24]

It turned out that until he was indicted and resigned in June 2002, Kozlowski had received tens of millions of dollars more in loans from the company, which were later forgiven, and none of this had been disclosed by the company, in violation of SEC regulations.[25] Tyco itself alleged in a lawsuit that its former general counsel had received $35 million of undisclosed pay, which again was not reported to the SEC as required.[26] Furthermore, apparently the former general counsel was guaranteed a large severance payment even if he were convicted of a felony. The CEO had signed off on the severance agreement, which may have reflected the two men's understanding that what the general counsel was doing for the firm might well be criminal. A similar agreement may have existed with the company's chief financial officer, because Tyco agreed to pay a severance package of tens of millions of dollars to him while he was under investigation by a grand jury.[27]

There is controversy about whether or not the company's financial reports were misrepresented. Analysts who recommended the company to investors have pointed out that just because the top executives looted it doesn't mean the company misled investors. However, it's almost certain that Tyco has carried on a significant amount of accounting fraud involving restructuring and acquisition-related charges, the effect of which has been to make its earnings growth from year to year appear to be much greater than it really was.

Adelphia

Adelphia is the country's sixth largest cable television company. The company's founder, his family, and other company executives received enormous loans from the company that were not disclosed to investors. The disclosure drove the company into bankruptcy and wiped out the holdings of its investors. When the founder and members of his family were arrested, federal prosecutors accused them of treating the company as their own personal piggy bank.

In an indictment of the company's founder, two of his sons, and two other executives, federal prosecutors said that the five had operated a scheme under which about $2.5 billion had been misappropriated from the company. The executives drew down Adelphia's credit line to purchase stock for themselves and took more money later to meet margin calls on some of the stock. False documents were drawn up to make it look as though the founder and other family members had actually paid for the stock from their own funds.

Furthermore, the executives bought more stock in the company whenever it issued additional stock, keeping their proportion of all the stock unchanged, and to pay for the new shares they set up a credit line for the family, which the company guaranteed to the lender. According to a United States attorney, "The scheme charged in the indictment is one of the most elaborate and extensive corporate frauds in United States history." The government is seeking to recover the money taken from the company.[28]

ImClone

ImClone's chief executive forged the signature of its chief financial officer on loan applications, pledged the same collateral for different loans, and, when the company's stock was about to collapse because of an adverse decision by a government agency about its key product, sold much of his holdings in the company and had his relatives do the same. It's alleged that he also somehow notified a friend, Martha Stewart, to sell her shares. Stock sales based on information not yet disclosed to public investors are illegal insider trades. ImClone's CEO is also accused of destroying documents to impede an investigation by regulators.[29]

Qwest

Top executives at Qwest, a western telecommunications firm, made large fortunes selling company stock from option grants while releasing profit numbers that were greatly exaggerated and based on improper accounting.[30] Among other things, Qwest appears to have swapped telecommunications capacity with Global Crossing and other companies, treating the swaps as sales, which they were not, and counting the sales immediately while spreading costs over many years.

Warnaco

Warnaco went bankrupt, but former CEO Linda Wachner sued the company for tens of millions of dollars she claimed she was owed. A settlement of the suit provided her with several millions.[31]

It's tempting to put the companies that follow in a different category because of their long and respected history. It's very unfortunate to find them among the scandals, but that's where they are.

General Electric

General Electric derived almost half its profit in recent years from GE Capital, a unit of the company about which little could be learned from GE's books. At GE Capital, earnings from a variety of sources—interest payments, fees, sale of investments—could be treated in a variety of ways. GE was unwilling to divulge enough data about GE Capital to enable analysts to discover how the company actually earns its money. For years the company was successful in meeting analysts' expectations of steadily rising sales and profits via accounting that no one fully understood. With the retirement of its CEO Jack Welch, a master of this sort of earnings management, the share value of the company fell substantially and the new CEO began to provide greater financial information about GE Capital.

General Electric also covered some very expensive living costs for Welch, both while he was on the job and after he retired. The costs were not disclosed by the firm in ways that were intelligible to investors. After they were disclosed, Welch relinquished most of the perks. Nell Minow, a governance expert and the editor of *The Corporate Library*, once described GE's employment contract with its CEO as a model because it did not appear to include a huge number of benefits. After being told about the late disclosure filing, she was quoted as saying, "I would have thought that perks like this had to be disclosed, and they were not. There is really no justification to pay for any living or traveling expenses at that level, particularly now that he is in retirement."[32]

IBM

Several times in recent years IBM recorded substantial gains it realized from the sale of entire businesses not as gains realized from the sale of businesses but as offsets to overhead expenses, thus making its basic operations appear to be more profitable than they really were. (In 1999 it recorded $2.4 billion this way; in 2001 it recorded $300 million this way.) The $300-million gain IBM realized on the final business day of 2001, moreover, enabled it to beat Wall Street's consensus earnings forecast by the all-important penny a share (part of the standard game that has gone on on Wall Street in recent years).

Xerox

Xerox, one of the great business names in the history of American technology, discovered some accounting "irregularities" in its Mexican operations in 2000. It claimed, however, that this was due to a few renegade employees and was an isolated problem. As the SEC began to investigate this, however, the company's assistant treasurer, James Bingham, sent an e-mail to his boss, the company's treasurer, saying that the accounting problems went well beyond Mexico. According to Bingham, the treasurer told him not to distribute the e-mail, asking whether he "wanted people to go to jail." Bingham nevertheless sent the e-mail to the company's CFO and CEO, whereupon he was ordered by the treasurer's assistant to recall and "destroy" it. Soon after, he was fired.

The SEC eventually concluded that the accounting fraud at Xerox was widespread, had gone on for years, and had been directed by senior Xerox executives. Over the five-year period between 1997 and 2001, Xerox had misreported $6.4 billion in revenue and overstated its pretax income by $1.4 billion, or 36%. It did this by recording revenue from its leases of copier equipment prematurely, using "cookie jar" reserves to offset ordinary operating expenses, as well as other maneuvers. The SEC fined the company $10 million (the largest fine the SEC ever levied against a public company in connection with alleged financial reporting fraud), and the Justice Department opened an inquiry into the possibility of filing criminal charges.[33]

Allegedly, Xerox had defrauded investors with a variety of what the SEC called "accounting actions" and "accounting opportunities" to disguise its true operating performance. The company restated its financial results for 1997 through 2000 and adjusted its 2001 results to reduce its profits.[34]

Microsoft

In the mid-1990s Microsoft was involved in both understating and overstating income for the purpose of smoothing the company's reported earnings, because Wall Street gave considerable value to a smooth progression, quarter by quarter, of earnings increases. During this period, Microsoft's chief financial officer sent an e-mail to CEO Bill Gates regarding this issue. The company's CFO said to Gates: "I believe we should do all we can to smooth our earnings and keep a steady state earnings model."[35]

The SEC did not charge fraud, impose a fine, or require the company to restate earnings, in part because the financial statements for that period are more than three years old, SEC officials said.[36]

The SEC also told reporters that it didn't bring fraud charges because there was no evidence that improper bookkeeping misled investors "to their detriment," meaning the government did not find that the price of Microsoft shares was lowered by the underreporting or overreporting of earnings.[37]

But this was somewhat disingenuous of the SEC on two counts. First, the stock market in recent years has severely punished the stock of companies whose earnings are volatile, allegedly because such companies are perceived as more risky than companies whose earnings grow at a regular and predictable rate. So when Microsoft smoothed its earnings via illegal accounting, it was propping up its stock price in a significant way.

Second, the SEC should not use as a standard for deciding whether or not to bring fraud charges the fact that a company's share price didn't go down as a result of the fraud. It's very unusual for a company to violate accounting principles or the law in order to *lower* its stock price. The purpose of accounting fraud is the opposite—to raise the share price. If the government's standard for fraud charges is that the fraud has to lower share prices, then its unlikely there will ever be any fraud charges by the SEC. Companies could just invent earnings and thereby increase the price of their shares—but that's clearly a violation of the law—and is clearly fraud—even though so long as the fraud isn't detected, the company's share price is not lowered.

Why We Didn't See This Coming

Over the last few years a trickle of corporate financial scandals has become a stream. Many of the most serious cases revealed fraud that had been going on for years. Why didn't more people see this coming?

A key reason is that people inside companies who tried to blow the whistle were effectively squelched. For example, Roy Olofson was vice president of finance for Global Crossing. In August 2001, he wrote to Global Crossing's general counsel, James Gorton, alleging that some of the firm's accounting practices inflated the company's revenue. He was placed on paid administrative leave within a few weeks and fired a few months later.

In response to Olofson's accusations, Global Crossing stated that the 63-year-old Olofson was let go as part of a substantial reduction in the company's workforce. The company added that his accusations were investigated and eventually found to be without merit. It accused Olofson of bringing up unsubtantiated allegations in an attempt to win a multimillion-dollar settlement for wrongful termination.

In September 2002, after the company had become the subject of numerous investigations, Olofson and other former Global Crossing employees testified before an investigative subcommittee of the House Energy and Commerce Committee. They exposed many sham transactions the company had entered in 2001, which were designed to boost revenue. The deals kept the company's stock price high through the first part of 2001, although Global Crossing eventually filed for bankruptcy protection in January 2002.

Olofson told the subcommittee that Gary Winnick and other top executives pressured subordinates to make deceptive deals that gave a false picture of Global's financial health and that former CEO Thomas Casey routinely misled financial analysts. He said he twice heard Casey tell analysts that Global Crossing had not engaged in so-called swap transactions—in which companies swapped capacity on their network—when Olofson knew otherwise. "I became deeply concerned because I felt that the statement was inaccurate," said Olofson.[38] He added that he'd believed his bosses would investigate his concerns when he first suggested that the public wasn't getting a true picture of the company's fiscal health. "Instead, they fired me," he told the panel.

Among the other reasons why we didn't see the crisis coming are the following:

1. As long as stock prices were rising, investors didn't seem to care whether there were shenanigans going on.
2. The securities industry has a very substantial sales force, and they continued to promote stocks.
3. The securities industry employs analysts to study companies and advise investors whether or not to invest. As we'll see in Chapter 6, many analysts were knowingly giving investors falsely positive recommendations about companies.
4. The business press, later so vigilant, was for years promoting companies in which it later exposed wrongdoing.
5. Congress was supporting corporate efforts to restrict regulatory oversight of firms, and regulatory agencies were not looking closely at the financial statements and other activities of many firms.
6. Finally, investors found it very hard to be suspicious when no one else seemed to be, especially the professionals investors trusted—auditors,

> stock market analysts, brokers, and regulators. Investors thought, "With all those smart people who are professionals in the financial business saying good things about companies and their executives, things must be okay."

But they weren't.

Talking Points

We've looked at 13 American companies, including several blue chips, that were at the center of the most publicized corporate scandals in recent history. We've seen how CEOs and other top executives of those companies used various methods—from plain fraud to so-called "creative accounting"—to mislead investors.

Even though the methods of deception we examined differ in their level of sophistication and the extent to which they pushed—and often clearly overstepped—the boundaries of legality, their purpose was always the same: to enrich the perpetrators at the expense of investors. As a result, investors lost huge chunks of their savings and retirement assets, while the perpetrators amassed fortunes.

Some commentators or regulators saw this disaster coming. While it's possible to imagine how ordinary investors can be easy targets for corporate fraud, it's quite a stretch to believe that more professionals—auditors, stock market analysts, and brokers—didn't smell a rat. What was the role of securities industry analysts and others whom ordinary investors trusted? What is the government doing now to protect investors from dishonest companies? These are questions to which we'll now turn.

3 Systematic Deception

The previous chapter presented story after story about how corporate executives made money (or tried to make money) by misleading investors. It's a major challenge to investors to understand what actually went on in each company and how these situations are alike or different from each other. In some instances there's fairly simple dishonesty; in others there's very complex accounting fraud. In the most extreme cases, the complexity of the financial accounts is so great that even professionals are tempted to accept at face value the assertions of top executives that they themselves didn't understand what was going on in the company. It's an interesting defense, after all, when a CEO says something to the effect that "I was paid millions each year to run this company, but I didn't really understand it at all. I simply relied on the accountants and lawyers to tell me whether what we were doing was legal." It makes us wonder what the CEO was being paid for, and what in the world the board of directors was doing to protect shareholders, topics to which we'll return later.

But in some ways the most disturbing things are not the illegalities, but the actions of executives that were technically legal but outrageously unfavorable to investors. For example, it seems likely that many of the accounting choices made by companies like Enron that were intended to inflate earnings and/or to deceive investors were actually legal—on the borderline, perhaps, but not outside the line. These things are as important to identify and get rectified as are outright illegalities, because the companies belong to investors, and their interests should be protected but haven't been.

What Was Going On?

The big picture of what was happening in the American stock market during the 1990s is remarkably simple. For many years before the 1990s the total value of all corporate stocks (equity) traded on our stock exchanges grew at much the same rate as did our economy. The two grew at nearly the same rate because in the long term growth in the value of companies is likely to be similar to growth in the economy as a whole.

But beginning in about 1995 the value of stocks began to rise rapidly, and a gap developed between the growth rate of stocks and that of the economy. The gap was at its widest late in 1999, just before the stock market index peaked early in 2000, and began a precipitous retreat that by 2002 had brought the two quantities back together.

Stocks had gotten way out of line with economic reality. They came back to reality suddenly and as they did so trillions of dollars of wealth disappeared. Some of this was due to the bubble in Internet stocks, but not all of it. Nor can it be imagined that a bull market so strong was accounted for by fraud in the handful of companies we discussed in Chapter 2. Something much more significant was happening. But it wasn't happening in the economy, whose behavior was simply relatively steady growth during this period. Something had changed in the stock market—in what investors thought stocks were worth. That change, and how it occurred, is the topic of this chapter.

Corrupt Accounting

In the late 1970s, Edward Koch, the colorful mayor of New York City, was grappling with enormous problems in the city and would often go up to people on the street and ask, "How am I doing?" It became his trademark line.

"How am I doing?" is exactly what the financial reports of firms are supposed to tell investors so they can determine whether or not to make an investment. Without the information that financial statements provide, the stock market couldn't exist because risk would be too high for investors—an investor couldn't tell whether the promises of one set of executives about his or her company were any more reliable than the promises of another. So we have financial statements, but even then investors have to worry about honesty and reliability. Hence the work of auditors, which is meant to provide investors with a "reasonable assurance" that financial statements fairly represent the financial performance and condition of a company.

Unfortunately, in recent years companies have been manipulating what is on their financial statements so that investors have been badly misled.[39] This has been happening—and it continues today—because top executives want to exaggerate the performance of their companies, in part because they gain personally from appreciation of the stock. Executives are able to mislead investors because accountants, banks, brokers, and attorneys all benefit from helping CEOs do this. We will return to why so much has gone wrong with American financial reporting in upcoming chapters. But in this chapter we discuss how accounting reports intended to inform investors have been used instead to mislead them.

How widespread is the problem? In the first half of 2002, as the uproar surrounding evidence of auditing failures at Enron, Global Crossing, and other companies increased, various business executives and members of the auditing profession hastened to point out that, although these heavily publicized auditing failures were indeed bad, people shouldn't lose sight of the fact that 99% of audits were sound.[40] It is now evident that this claim simply isn't accurate. We'll never know for sure how many audits of publicly traded companies in the United States in the late 1990s and early 2000s were flawed, but because of restatement statistics we can be sure that far more than 1% of them were.

Restatements

In 1981, only three publicly traded companies in the United States had to restate their published financial statements. In 1997, there were 116 restatements. In 2001 the number was 270, a record high. In the five-year period between 1997 and 2001, there were 1,089 restatements.[41] This represents over 10% of the total population of companies, which is about 10,000. There's no reason to believe that all the firms that ought to restate their earnings have done so, since it's a process that is costly to the stock price of a firm and something most firms try to avoid at almost any cost. Hence the 10% figure is likely an undercount of the number of firms that should restate their earnings. Restatements have various causes. Sometimes they respond to the application of a new accounting standard, which is generally an innocuous event. (Fewer than 10 percent of the restatements in 2000, however, applied new accounting standards.) Sometimes restatements correct errors or misinterpretations. Sometimes they rectify serious misrepresentations or fraud. There isn't any exact breakdown of restatements on these dimensions. The figures for yearly restatements, however, are to some extent cumulative. That is, when a company restates its figures, it is usually doing so for a few years. Thus if a company makes a restatement in 2000, that restatement often adjusts its financial statements for 1997, 1998, and 1999. There are, therefore, more actual restatements than the 10% figure implies. Restatements are what companies do only if they take the initiative, if their auditors demand it, or if the SEC requires it. Companies that cook their books and get away with it don't restate anything.

CEOs Ask for Misrepresentation

So how many companies actually cook their books, and how often does this deception get by their auditors? At the beginning of 2001 the investing public believed that the financial statements issued by Enron, WorldCom, Global Crossing, and Adelphia, for example, fairly represented those companies' financial performance and condition. Their CEOs and CFOs had vouched for the truth of their statements. Their auditors had also vouched for it. But it wasn't the case for these companies, and likely for many more.

Some extraordinary data about what really goes on were revealed a few years ago. In October 1998, *CFO* magazine sponsored a conference at which it asked CFOs about financial reporting practices at their companies. Forty-five percent of those who responded anonymously to a survey said that they had been asked by senior executives in their companies to misrepresent their companies' financial results, and 38% of that number, or 17% of all of the CFOs responding, said that they had done so. (Larger numbers of people indicated that they had been asked to stretch accounting financial results within the framework of generally accepted accounting principles, and many of them said they did that as well.)

At a retreat sponsored by *Business Week* magazine in mid-1998 for 160 corporate CFOs, a similar survey was conducted. Sixty-seven percent said that they had been asked by senior executives in their companies to misrepresent their companies' financial results, and 18% of that number, or 12% of all survey respondents, said that they had done so.[42]

How many of these misrepresentations got by the auditors? We don't know, but the nature of the responses in these surveys suggests that most of what was done "worked," that is, it got by the auditors.

Hiding Relative Importance

It's not uncommon to hear in defense of the accounting profession that the number of flawed audits (due to negligence or fraud) is quite small compared to the total number of audits. The impact of flawed audits on investors in recent years, however, is much greater than that argument suggests. For investors, the auditing of a company with a market capitalization of, say, $100 billion is a lot more important than the auditing of a company with a market capitalization of $100 million. Investors, on average, invest a lot more money in large companies than they do in small companies; the large companies simply represent more of the stock market in terms of shares traded and total value.

A handful of companies that have almost certainly committed accounting fraud, or something close to it (Enron, Global Crossing, WorldCom, Qwest, Microsoft, Xerox, Waste Management) were together worth over a trillion dollars in stock market value at their price peak—equal, for comparison purposes, to the total stock market value of a thousand other companies whose accounting is proper. So if we were to give a figure for the percentage of bad audits in the whole population—assuming that the audits of these thousand other companies were sound—it would be less than 1%. But if we were to give a figure for the percentage of bad audits in terms of their impact on investors according to the amount invested, we would have to say it's more like 50%. It appears that bad audits have occurred in a disproportionately large group of the larger companies in America, creating a much bigger problem for investors than just the number or proportion of fraud cases suggests.

Just Like the Others

Notorious companies were in a variety of industries, were of a variety of sizes, were of a variety of ages, were located in a variety of geographical settings, and so on. They were a cross-section of the American economy. Much of what happened in these companies has been happening in others. It follows that the breakdown of checks and balances that allowed fraud to happen could have occurred elsewhere and could still happen again. This is the meaning of systemic failure.

Private companies have a small number of shareholders and tight oversight, so fraud by means of misleading information is difficult and rare. But the publicly held large corporation is a different animal. It's partly private (run by a small group of executives with a small board) and it's partly public (with many shareholders). Theoretically, and legally, the public shareholders own the company, and the board represents them and oversees management to be sure it acts as their agent. But from its inception, the public company has been bedeviled by a divergence of interest between executives and shareholders. Often shareholder oversight is weak, and executives are able to enrich themselves at shareholder expense. Many devices to do this were common at the turn of the 19th and 20th centuries and contributed to the Great Crash of the stock market in 1929.[43]

Americans thought we'd put this behind us with the new laws of the 1930s, including the establishment of the SEC. So it's a great surprise to see very similar scams on an enormous scale being played out in the 1990s. But nonetheless, 80 years later we see exactly that. "This type of looting really hasn't been seen in our lifetime," said Thomas Newkirk, the associate director of enforcement at the Securities and Exchange Commission, at the announcement of the indictments directed against the top officers of Tyco.[44] Today, just as decades ago in the bad old days, investors have been taken to the cleaners by the executives of companies in which they've invested.

The Common Accounting Dodges

Referred to as "creative accounting" by analysts, accounting tricks are used extensively to fatten financial statements. The three main financial statements—income statement, balance sheet, and cash flow—are snapshots of a company's financial status. The goal of an executive or a firm is to increase the apparent profitability reported in these statements. There are three ways to do this: inflate sales (revenue), deflate cost, and understate indebtedness.

Currently, there are numerous accounting dodges so widely used by American firms that they implicate almost every company in the deceptions. In general, their objective is to exaggerate sales, minimize costs, and thereby inflate profits. But they also serve to hide debt, to conceal how a firm makes money (so that investors can't predict its future), and to smooth the path of sales and profit growth.

Each of these dodges has been attacked by sophisticated investors for years. But companies persist in using them. These accounting rules that are used to give a veneer of legitimacy to the dodges were originally created to address certain economic situations faced by businesses. If used honestly, they can be beneficial to companies and investors. Unfortunately, these rules have also created opportunities for companies to exploit.

Each of the accounting devices listed below is intended to mislead investors as to the true state of a company's finances. These dodges are not arcane technicalities about which reasonable people might differ with no real effect on the outcome. These are big matters with big consequences; the issue is whether or not companies are allowed to mislead investors intentionally. Nor are these dodges completely hidden, so that there is a failure to report an overt fraud. Rather, they are intended to mislead the investors who are not professional stock analysts and who haven't the time and skills to disentangle a company's financial reports and then reassemble them in a different manner.

There are ways of keeping crucial items out of investors' sight by excluding them from the ordinary income statements and balance sheets and by trying to draw attention away from the traditional financial reports. In each instance the purpose is to make the company's current finances and its prospects look better than they are. Both the income statement and the balance sheet of corporations can be and have been manipulated. The key elements of misinformation are the following.

Managing Earnings: Cookie Jar Accounting Using Reserve Accounts

Companies use reserve accounts to set aside revenue against predictable future costs, such as unpaid bills or pending lawsuits. Companies have much latitude to reduce or increase those reserves, but they are not supposed to do it simply to make the growth path of sales and profits look smoother. A smooth and predictable course of financial improvement has been very much rewarded by investors, however, so managing earnings has become an important means for increasing stock values.

Managing earnings is also a large category of accounting fraud, just as making up earnings is another. Earnings can be managed, for example, by overaccruing certain expenses in one period (by restructuring charges or provisions for inventory write-downs) and then in a subsequent period reversing some of the expenses in order to pump up earnings in that subsequent period. Another example is slowing down the rate of depreciation on certain assets far more than is justified (this is one of the things that Waste Management did in cooking its books). These kinds of earnings management activities play tricks with the *timing* of earnings or revenues.

It is sometimes argued that there is no real harm in managing earnings. For example, consider a moderate-size company that may have 16 separate businesses. It has risks in each and estimates its possible losses in each. It then adopts a reserve in case of losses for each business. Suppose the firm decides to be conservative and sets aside 80% of the possible loss in each case. By doing this it has created total reserves perhaps as large as half or more of its annual profit. Wall Street provides a great premium to firms whose earnings rise in a predictable manner and amount quarterly. So when a down quarter comes, it's very tempting to the firm to decide to reduce some reserves to increase profit and conversely, when a strong quarter comes, to put more into the reserves and shave profits a bit. Where's the harm?

Generally accepted accounting principles in the United States definitely allow for the recording in income statements of reserves for certain expenses. These "loss contingencies" can be very ordinary items like estimates of noncollectable accounts, or less ordinary events like litigation pending against the company. Companies are in fact required to record expenses for these contingencies if two conditions are met: the losses in question are *probable* (not just possible), and the losses can be *reasonably estimated.* If just one of those conditions is met, the company cannot record the expense in its income statement, but it must disclose the situation in a footnote to its financial statements.

But a company is not allowed to record expenses based simply on estimates of possible losses in its various businesses, and it can't do so in some generalized way. The losses must be probable, they must be able to be reasonably estimated, and there must be some specific documentation to back the estimate up. A company is definitely allowed to be "conservative," however, in its estimate of the losses.

There is no limit to the size of an expense that the firm can record in a given year for a legitimate reserve or loss contingency: it could be more than 100% of what the company's profit might otherwise be. What is not legitimate, what is in fact illegal, is for a company to record an expense for a reserve that doesn't have the appropriate substance and documentation to back it up.

So, again, where lies the harm in a company's using loss reserves to manage its earnings? The most important reason it's wrong is that it can show a company experiencing earnings growth far greater than reality. For example, a company will record excessive "restructuring" or acquisition-related charges—and then, the following year, the company will announce fantastic earnings growth because it has already charged a lot of ordinary operating expenses in that second year to the fake restructuring charges taken in the previous year. The stock market cheers because it loves high-growth companies, and it bids up the price of the company's stock. In some instances a company will boost its earnings by reversing a previous restructuring charge.[45]

So managing earnings has a dark side for investors—it conceals from them the actual progression of sales and profits in a company. The entire purpose of cookie jar accounting is to mislead the markets into believing there is stable growth where there is not. That makes it a clear violation of the duty of disclosure of top executives of most American corporations under the incorporation law of our states (see Chapter 7 for a discussion of this legal duty). But that hasn't kept earnings management from becoming epidemic in American business because it helps to increase stock prices and reward executives personally via stock options, and it is not frequently discovered or punished by regulatory authorities. This list of reasons could, of course, be added to our discussion of each of the additional accounting irregularities listed below:

Not expensing options. Options are a large cost to the shareholders of many firms, but most companies don't count them as costs. Hence, profits seem higher than otherwise and large payments to corporate executives appear to have no cost to shareholders. According to Warren Buffett, "Options are a huge cost for many corporations and a huge benefit to executives. No wonder, then, that they have fought ferociously to avoid making a charge against their earnings. Without blushing, almost all CEOs have told their shareholders that options are cost-free."[46]

The importance of not-expensing options to some firms, especially technology firms that use options generously, is very great. For example, had Microsoft treated stock options as an expense in 2001, its net income would have been not $7.3 billion as it reported, but $5.1 billion, or 30% lower. Had Cisco Systems treated stock options as an expense in 2001, its net loss would have been not $1 billion as it reported, but $2.7 billion, or 170% lower. Had Siebel Systems treated the cost of options as an expense—as accounting rules encourage but do not require—its profits of 49 cents a share in 2001 and 24 cents in 2000 would have turned into losses of $1.02 and 29 cents, respectively.[47] In 2000, Sanford C. Bernstein Company has calculated the value of stock options granted by the largest 2,000 U.S. corporations to have been $162 billion.

Expensing options is an especially controversial topic because it can be argued both ways more convincingly than any other accounting issue with which we deal in this book. Ordinarily, it's fairly black and white, but not here. The reason is that stock options carry little or no direct cash cost to the company. Hence, why should they be expensed? The reason is that though options have little or no cash cost to the company, they have a very real cost to shareholders. Increasing the number of shares reduces the value of the shares of its current shareholders. This is a very direct cost and one that the company should somewhere recognize in its financial reports. Otherwise, a company would look no different to shareholders if it had few options outstanding than if it had many—and this isn't sensible.

Using one-time write-offs that occur year after year. Firms employ so-called one-time write-offs during the year to disguise ongoing problems in the cost structure of a business. They disguise operating expenses as nonrecurring charges to make the company's basic businesses look better financially.

Issuing pro-forma financial reports. Pro-forma earnings are a set of financial statements issued by a company that conform to no general set of accounting principles except their own, and that are always more favorable to the firm than would be statements conforming to general principles. They are issued in addition to more conventional financial statements, and allegedly remove or add items in order to give a more accurate view of the firm's financial position. They are to a degree creatures of the media, in that the business press will often seize upon pro-forma earnings and publish them, without regard to their plausibility. Analysts also are tempted to use pro-forma reports without doing the additional work necessary to more accurately evaluate a company. Pro-formas are, therefore, primarily another of today's attempts by executives to increase the value of the shares of their firms by misleading investors.

The problems with pro-formas from the point of view of investors are several:

- There are no standardized rules for pro-formas. Each company decides what it wants to include and exclude, and therefore there isn't any comparability among companies in this form of financial reporting.
- Companies sometimes exclude so many things that they become almost unrecognizable. For example, some established companies in recent years were excluding the entire (unfavorable) results of small Internet businesses that they were developing. A computer chip maker was excluding some of the depreciation on a factory that it said was "underutilized."
- Individual companies have sometimes been inconsistent in what they include and exclude. For example, they may include an unusual gain but exclude some unusual loss.
- Companies are suggesting via pro-formas to analysts and investors that everything that is excluded from pro-forma earnings has no relevance to the company's valuation—which is of course incorrect. In principle, a company could issue a pro-forma showing healthy profits one day and file for bankruptcy the next.

A focus on pro-forma earnings often leads—although it doesn't necessarily lead—to ineffectiveness on the part of boards of directors in the way they evaluate a company's performance and therefore establish compensation for the CEO. For example, in recent years the board of directors of Tyco used the company's pro-forma earnings to reward Dennis Kozlowski for supposedly great performance, even though the pro-forma earnings excluded over a billion dollars a year in supposed restructuring and acquisition-related charges.

In order to help investors and analysts better evaluate corporate financial reports, the SEC in January 2002 issued what it termed "best practice" guidelines regarding pro-forma earnings announcements. The guidelines had been developed by Financial Executives International and the National Investors Relations Institute. Later in the year, the Sarbanes-Oxley Act, at Section 401(b), specifically mandated new rules regarding pro-forma earnings, including their reconciliation to GAAP figures. Section 401(b) of the law required the SEC to implement these rules, and in late October 2002, the SEC issued proposed new rules for this purpose.

Calling Something What It Isn't

Transactions were misclassified to make the financial performance of a business look better—as, for example, when IBM recorded the sale of an asset as a reduction in expenses in order to make operating profits seem larger.

Misclassifying or Fabricating Revenues

A number of companies in recent years classified as revenue large amounts of money that had nothing to do with revenue. The money involved was simply financing (debt or equity) that they had received from outside investors. A good many companies did even better than that; they just plain fabricated revenues. "Round-trip revenues" (sometimes called "revenue swaps") became a common activity among energy and telecommunications companies: they sold network capacity to each other. The transactions cancelled each other out; they had no economic substance; and they produced no additional profit for anyone. But they enabled the companies to show significant "top line" growth, which stock analysts were particularly interested in seeing.

Recognizing Revenue Too Soon

There are all sorts of devices that companies can use to recognize revenue sooner than they should. For example, a number of software companies in recent years recorded, up front, all of the revenue from commercial software contracts even though they were obligated, as part of the contracts, to provide significant additional services to their customers in the future. "Bill and hold" accounting (sometimes called "channel stuffing") allows companies to record revenue from products long before their customers actually need them. Companies will ship products out to customers but tell them that they can take six months or more to pay for them. Alternatively, companies will simply ship products to third-party warehouses where the products will sit until customers actually order them. Another scam some companies use is to backdate sales contracts: for example, they may finalize a contract in January but backdate it to December so that sales for the just-completed year appear to be higher than they really were.

Creating the Appearance of Sales via Small Acquisitions

Acquisitions can be used as a major accounting dodge. When they're small enough, they don't have to be reported separately to investors, and the increased sales that come to the company via acquisitions can be allowed to appear to be increased sales to the original business. When there are enough small acquisitions, then sales can be artificially inflated by this device alone.

Creating Profits by Assumption from the Pension Fund

A company that must pay pension benefits to retired employees must maintain a pension fund. Companies have been making assumptions that gains on pension investments would be large and including these gains in their reported income. The result is to raise profits.

Warren Buffet identifies this deception with that of the nonexpensing of stock options as one of the most serious deceptions used by firms.

In calculating the pension costs that directly affect their earnings, companies in the Standard & Poor's index of 500 stocks are today using assumptions about investment return rates that go as high as 11%. The rate chosen is important because an upward change of a single percentage point will increase the annual earnings a company reports by more than $100 million on a large enough base. It's no surprise, therefore, that many chief executives opt for assumptions that are wildly optimistic, even as their pension assets perform miserably. These CEOs simply ignore this unpleasant reality and their obliging actuaries and auditors bless whatever rate the company selects. How convenient: Client A, using a 6.5% rate, receives a clean audit opinion—and so does client B, which opts for an 11% rate.[48]

The so-called revenues that come from assumptions about pension gains can be very important to executives. For example, if General Motors had had to account for pensions by what actually happened, losses in the pension account due to the bear market would mean that the company has had no profit at all since 2000.[49]

Recognizing Expenses Too Late

Companies minimized their operating expenses in order to reduce deductions from sales and thereby make profits seem larger. They used such devices as disguising operating expenses as capital expenditures in order to deduct only part of the expenses from sales.

Disguising Loans to the Company

CEOs loans were kept off their balance sheets by putting them into so-called special purpose entities or off-balance sheet vehicles.

A company's financial statements have thus become a complex and confusing mélange of actual cash transactions, assumed earnings, pretended earnings, mislabeled expenditures, and disclosed and nondisclosed items. Almost always these items are used to exaggerate the financial performance of the companies, misleading investors either by conveying incorrect information or by creating intentional confusion.

Fudging Cash Flow

While investors understood that companies were increasingly manipulating the income statement and balance sheet, they still believed that firms could not manipulate the cash flow statement. But there is now substantial evidence that some companies did manipulate cash flow inappropriately, and this is profoundly disturbing.[50] Executives at a large electronics company acquired by Tyco International took action to accelerate certain payments, at Tyco's request, to boost Tyco's cash flow after the deal closed, according to internal e-mails at the acquired company. The Bermuda-based conglomerate has routinely forced companies it acquires to prepay expenses and lower their earnings and cash flow just before they are melded into Tyco. Critics of the firm, who include short-selling investors who profit from a stock's decline, have said the practice is designed to enhance Tyco's post-acquisition financial results.

Companies accrue sales and costs independently of actual payments so that earnings statements and balance sheets can be filled with items that don't reflect actual cash coming into the company, or going out. But cash flow statements are supposed to reflect only cash and therefore be much less liable to manipulation. The idea is that companies compute earnings based on all sorts of funny accounting rules that they can play all sorts of games with. Cash flow, on the other hand, is the real thing; it's either there or it's not there.[51] Hence, there's a rule of thumb that reassures cautious investors who distrust income statements and balance sheets: "Cash flows don't lie."

Recent experience in the business world, however, has shown that this picture of things isn't accurate. Some companies in recent years manipulated actual cash flows. More often, they manipulated the way cash flows were classified. To take a simple example: say there are two companies, each of which has a million dollars of cash on hand. One company received the cash by selling its products to customers, whereas the other received the cash simply by borrowing it from a bank. We would be inclined to regard the first company as healthier than the second. If the second company, however, said that it received its cash by selling products to customers, it would be deceiving investors.

Companies sometimes manipulate cash flows in ways that have no impact on earnings; they just want to make their cash flows look better. More often, however, manipulating cash flows is closely tied to manipulating earnings; one is simply an offshoot of the other. Here's one example.

Tyco International involved itself in many different kinds of businesses. In the past decade it made huge numbers of acquisitions. It is almost certain that it manipulated its earnings through excessive restructuring and acquisition-related charges. In addition, however, it manipulated its cash flows.

When Tyco acquired a large electronics company named Raychem in 1999, for example, it got the treasurer of Raychem to maximize cash outflow from Raychem just before the acquisition was finalized. It did this by having Raychem pay out $55 to $60 million in cash to suppliers even though the bills weren't yet due. "The purpose of this effort," the Raychem treasurer wrote in a clearly angry e-mail to people in his department, was "at Tyco's request, to cause cash flows to be negative in the 'old' Raychem and more positive in the new company." The assistant treasurer of Raychem said she was "outraged" by what Tyco asked Raychem to do, adding that the actions were intended to "deceive."[52]

Here is a situation where cash flows themselves were manipulated; the problem didn't involve their classification. The manipulation also didn't affect earnings because the expenses had already been recorded. Tyco shifted the timing of the cash flows, however, so that its cash flows would look better after the acquisition was finalized.

Manipulating the Classification of Expenses

Over a period of 15 months in 2001 and 2002, WorldCom, a huge telecommunications company, paid $3.8 billion in cash for the use of other companies' phone lines and for ordinary network maintenance. In terms of basic accounting principles, these were operating expenses. But instead of recording them as operating expenses, WorldCom recorded them as capital investments. This accomplished two things. It inflated profits because operating expenses are deducted immediately from revenues, whereas capital investments are charged to expenses much more slowly ("amortized"), often over a period of many years. In addition, however, the maneuver also misrepresented cash flow. Instead of including $3.8 billion as a cash outflow in the "operating activities" section of its cash flow statement, the company recorded it as a cash outflow in the "investing activities" section of its cash flow statement.

Why is this significant? It's significant because "operating cash flow" is customarily viewed as an indication of a business's ability to generate cash from its core operations, whereas cash flows from a company's "investing" and "financing" activities, while very important, have a more long-term significance and often involve special business decisions. In fact, when stock analysts talk about a company's cash flow, they often mean its operating cash flow (or some variation of it). What WorldCom did served to inflate its "operating cash flow" numbers by huge amounts. Thus the cash flow at WorldCom was real, but the way WorldCom classified it wasn't.

Sunbeam, a consumer products company, manipulated the classification of other kinds of cash flows. In 1996 and 1997 it carried on a massive accounting fraud. One of the things it did was to capitalize a lot of marketing expenses. There are only very limited circumstances in which marketing expenses can properly be capitalized. Generally they have to be recorded as expenses immediately. By capitalizing marketing expenses Sunbeam not only inflated its profits; it also inflated its operating cash flow. As in the WorldCom example, the cash flow was real, but the way Sunbeam classified it wasn't.

Other Examples

Other kinds of cash flow manipulation are more complicated. In some respects they manipulate actual cash flows as well as their classification.

Disguising loans as sales. Enron used all sorts of partnerships to disguise loans as sales. The partnerships were supposedly separate from Enron, but they were largely controlled by the parent company. In one instance, Enron received $115 million in financing from a Canadian investment bank for a new video-on-demand business, then in its early testing stage. The financing was formally provided to an Enron partnership. The partnership then turned the money over to the parent company, and in the last quarter of 2000 and the first quarter of 2001 Enron recorded it as revenue. A few Enron employees said that when they learned that Enron was booking all this money as revenue they were "floored"; they "couldn't believe it." The project, after all, was in its early testing stage, with just a few hundred paying customers. The maneuver, however, enabled Enron to record $115 million in operating cash flow that had nothing to do with operations. It was simply financing, and everyone involved understood that the project would take a long time to develop at best. (As things turned out, moreover, the project never went anywhere.)

Other Enron partnerships borrowed money from banks in order to purchase assets from the parent company. Although the loans were guaranteed by the parent company, that fact wasn't disclosed to the parent company's shareholders. The partnerships turned the cash over to the parent company as supposed payment for certain assets, but the parent company retained the rights to all profits generated by those assets. Enron was thus able to record significant amounts of additional revenue along with significant additional inflows of cash as part of its "investing activities." In reality, it had just borrowed money from various banks. From 1997 to 2001 transactions of this sort boosted Enron's cash flow by about $1.4 billion.

Vendor financing of high-risk customers. Vendor financing is a legitimate business practice. When companies are in desperate circumstances, however, they sometimes apply it in extreme, deceptive ways. In the late 1990s, for example, Lucent wanted to keep the apparent boom in its telecom equipment business going, and so it lent $700 million to a very shaky telecom company (Winstar Communications), which then paid most of the money back to Lucent to purchase its products. Thus Lucent had a cash inflow of close to $700 million as part of "operating" activities, and a cash outflow of $700 million as part of "investing" activities. Not long thereafter, however, Winstar filed for bankruptcy, and Lucent had to write off $700 million.

Disguising compensation as loans. One of the worst abuses of corporate treasuries in recent years was insider loan programs. More than a quarter of large

U.S. companies had these programs, which lent large amounts of money to senior executives.[53] Years ago the practice may sometimes have had a legitimate purpose. In recent years, however, it spun out of control. Insider loans became, in most cases, a backdoor form of compensation.

Senior executives paid back some of these loans with company stock that they had acquired through stock options. In many cases, however, the loans were forgiven, for reasons that companies generally didn't make clear. What did it mean to forgive loans made to people who were very wealthy and who could obviously pay them back? (Some companies—like Global Crossing, WorldCom, Enron, Flagstar, and K-mart—forgave millions of dollars of loans to senior executives not long before the companies themselves filed for bankruptcy.)

When companies initially made these loans they recorded them as cash outflows as part of "investing" activities (for example, an increase in "Loans receivable"). When the firms forgave the loans, they simply wrote them off; there was no further cash flow related to them. Since in most cases, however, the loan forgiveness was a backdoor form of compensation, companies in effect made their "operating cash flows" higher than they really were. The money paid should have reduced operating cash flows; instead it reduced investing cash flows, and cash outflows related to loans that a company might occasionally make generally don't concern stock analysts very much.

SEC Oversight

How could fraud have been perpetrated in the accounts of so many large and prominent firms?

The ultimate watchdog of the financial reporting and auditing of publicly traded companies in the United States is the Securities and Exchange Commission (SEC). It is widely recognized, however, that the SEC has for years been seriously underfunded and understaffed. In July 2001—months before the scandals surrounding the auditing of Enron, Global Crossing, and other companies began to develop—the SEC said it had nearly 260 accounting investigations under way; 40 of them implicating Fortune 500 companies. "If we had nothing else to do," the head of the SEC's enforcement division said at the time, "the accounting investigations alone could keep us busy for the next five or ten years. The size and magnitude are crushing."[54]

The SEC has in recent years had a general policy of reviewing the annual reports of significant companies at least every three years. In early 2002, however, after the evidence of accounting fraud at Enron became news, SEC records showed that the last annual report of Enron's it had reviewed was the report for 1997. Enron's 2000 report had been scheduled for review, but the process was delayed because SEC staff knew that Enron's filings were complicated, and they didn't have the time.[55]

During the last few years investors in American firms have been despoiled by executives of companies on a scale unprecedented in our history. The SEC was supposed to protect investors. Has it been incompetent, or rather frustrated by an inability to address the crisis? The answer seems to be that two things have frustrated it: (1) A lack of Congressional support that showed itself in the placing of overt limitations on the SEC and chronic underfunding so that the agency lacked the resources to do its job; and (2) a lack of support from the financial community in the country, with executives, brokers, banks, accountants, and attorneys abandoning their responsibilities to investors in favor of their own pocketbooks.

On a nationally televised program in spring 2002 about the business and accounting scandals in the United States, a senior reporter at *Business Week*, John Byrne, was asked: "Is anyone protecting the public?" And Bryne answered: "You know, I think the SEC is trying to, but I think that the SEC is basically out of it...because they're understaffed. It's a major problem." "So the SEC is outgunned, outspent, outmanned?" he was asked. Byrne answered: "Completely. Doesn't have a chance."[56]

The anti-fraud legislation passed by Congress and signed by President Bush in July 2002 mandated a 66% increase in the SEC's budget. Even at that, a *Wall Street Journal* analysis of the change in stock trading volume, the number of investors in stock mutual funds, and the number of IPOs relative to changes in the funding of the SEC over the previous decade suggested that the 66% increase would be "just a drop in the bucket."[57]

The Criminal Mind

It has surprised some people that the former CEOs and CFOs who escaped from their companies with large sums of money haven't returned to work somewhere else. After all, they're allegedly Type A personalities who need action and achievement—how can they be hanging around the house, sailing their boats, attending party after party—with nothing of significance on their agenda? And people sometimes say that the real punishment for an executive who has lost his job due to fraud is the damage to his reputation—so it follows that he'd be anxious to get back to work as soon as possible in order to try to restore his reputation. Instead, the former executives seem content to enjoy their riches in their mansions and various playgrounds of the well-to-do.

Why aren't they struggling to get back to the mainstream? This question betrays a misunderstanding of the criminal mind. Every Hollywood robbery film depicts one or a group of thieves who devote lots of time and careful attention to planning and carrying out the heist, but they're not active in legitimate pursuits before or after. Rather, after a successful piece of larceny, they sit by the beach enjoying the fruit of ill-gotten gains, and enjoy life. Why should executives who are crooks be any different? So it's no surprise that the top officers of many firms who made off with bundles of money now do nothing but sit inactive, keep a low profile, and count their loot.

Should you run into one of these people on your vacation and sit beside him or her in a bar, don't expect that you'll get to talking about business or the scandal or the executive's role in it. Quite the contrary: he's unlikely to say anything at all or to voice any opinion about the matters. Why not? The answer is that if his former company is bankrupt, then his attorney has a firm lock on his mouth, and if his company is not bankrupt, then his company has him under an agreement to say nothing at all about any topic of importance, because the company knows that both the former executive and the firm itself are vulnerable to prosecution by federal authorities or to suits by disgruntled investors. So he keeps silent and enjoys his spoils.

Talking Points

We've seen that CEOs and their accomplices did many things that were illegal to mislead investors. But it's equally disturbing that there were and still are many actions the law deems legal even though they are unethical and extremely hurtful to investors.

When stock market indices took a dive, trillions of dollars of wealth evaporated. It turns out that much of it was never real in the first place. Corporate financial statements, which are intended to help potential investors make informed decisions, were systematically doctored to exaggerate company performance. Many companies manipulate their financial reports and are able to get away with it, which has a negative impact on investors. Different companies use different accounting dodges to help executives increase the apparent profitability of their companies by inflating sales, deflating cost, and understating indebtedness. What's common among the dodges is the same objective: all methods are designed for the purpose of enriching the top executives at the expense of shareholders.

The type of looting of investors that led to the stock market crash in 1929 has happened again, despite the establishment of the federal regulatory agencies after the earlier crash. The key agency, the SEC, has been chronically underfunded and lacks the resources to protect investors from fraud on today's massive scale.

4 More Than a Few Bad Apples

"The System has not failed us, but a few have failed the system."

—Donald L. Evans,
Secretary of Commerce of the United States.[58]

"There are a few bad apples, the dirty little piggies."

—Muriel Siebert[59]

A Lot of Dirty Little Piggies

In Chapter 2 we described a group of companies in which there have been significant financial scandals. From media reports, each situation seems quite distinct—a different set of schemes and a different group of people. From these apparent differences it has been argued that each of these situations is unique, unrelated to the others, and that each therefore represents a bad apple in a barrel of otherwise well-behaved companies.

But this isn't the case. In fact, the differences among the firms are largely superficial. We saw in Chapter 3 that in each of the scandals certain underlying influences were at work, all sharing the same objective—to create wealth on an enormous scale for executives, if necessary by transferring it from investors to corporate executives. The problem for investors wasn't only newer companies like Tyco and Global Crossing that were involved in frauds; the accounts of blue chips like GE and IBM also were almost unintelligible to investors and cost them considerable losses. It is this generality of confusion and deception that proves there is a problem with the system, not merely a problem of a few bad apples. Many publicly held companies in the United States have engaged in financial deception—though some in a different class (involving illegalities) than others, and some on a grander scale than others.

Bad Actors but No Scandals

In most instances in which corporate executives have enriched themselves while investors were left with devalued stock, there were no headlines, no well-publicized scandals, but merely victimization of shareholders. About the mainstream of corporate leaders Warren Buffett has written, "For many years, I've had little confidence in the earnings numbers reported by most corporations. I'm not talking about Enron and WorldCom—examples of outright crookedness. Rather, I am referring to the legal, but improper, accounting methods used by chief executives to inflate reported earnings."[60]

This is an especially significant comment because Buffett is a sophisticated and successful investor who is in a position to know about the quality of corporate earnings reports, and because of his blanket condemnation, which goes far beyond the "few bad apples" scenario. "Recently," he added, "a few CEOs have stepped forward to adopt honest accounting." This is a startling statement, for it implies that only a few CEOs do honest accounting. Buffett continued, "Most [CEOs] continue to spend their shareholders' money, directly or through trade associations, to lobby against real reform. They talk principle, but, for most, their motive is pocketbook."[61]

The story this book tells is about the greatest failure of business leadership in American history—a failure occasioned by a rejection of leadership responsibility to shareholders in favor of the pursuit of the leaders' own personal financial interests. It's ironic, because the current failure followed one of the great successes of American business leadership—working in the 1980s and early 1990s with employees, unions, and the government to restore American competitiveness in both our domestic and the international marketplace against the challenge of Japanese competition. But the contribution made by business leadership to American society in that difficult contest (which still continues to a degree today) has been pushed into the background by the scandals that have accompanied business leadership's shift of focus to its pocketbooks.

During the 1990s the American people entrusted the leadership of the nation to its top business executives. Polls showed the people's trust in business leaders to exceed the trust they had in political, military, educational, religious, labor, media, or other leaders. Business leaders were respected and emulated. Yet they used the nation's respect primarily to make themselves rich. Today they are at the bottom of public respect—mistrusted and the butt of jokes.

In defending pay packages that make a CEO wealthy, CEOs often refer to the high earnings of athletes and motion picture actors and actresses in America. For example, speaking to a reporter, Louis Gerstner, former CEO of IBM, argued, "The American people have no problem paying great athletes and great actors lots of money if they're the best and if they perform well."[62] If athletes and actors are the proper comparison, then we can admire CEOs' talents in running a business, rather like the talents of any athlete or actor, while deploring their lack of character—including greed, selfishness, ruthlessness, manipulation, and lack of feeling for others.

At the conclusion of an article titled "Does the Rot on Wall Street Reach Right to the Top?", Gretchen Morgenson, a financial reporter for the *New York Times*, pointed out the previous scandals on Wall Street had not impoverished small investors, because so few had been in the market, and asked a question in the minds of millions: "Why is it so hard for smart people," specifically naming the chairman and top analyst of Citibank, "...to see that if the road to instant gratification requires taking a wrong moral turn, such a turn is inadvisable?" She added as an afterthought, as if disillusioned by the behavior of leaders of American banks, the plaintive plea, "I really and truly want to know."[63]

Few Prosecutions Doesn't Mean Few Violations

In 2000 the Justice Department charged 226 people with securities or commodities fraud.[64] That number seems to be up somewhat in 2001 and 2002. The Securities and Exchange Commission has brought about a dozen cases in 2002 in which it seeks court approval to seize executive's ill-gotten gains, and this is as many as it brought in the preceding 18 months.[65]

These are not many prosecutions, and an investor might conclude from this record that deception is uncommon in American companies. But the case is just the opposite. The conclusion must be that the legal system is completely failing to control the problem. Congress has played a role. It has kept the SEC underfunded; has intervened to stop regulators from tightening key rules; and in 1995 passed a law making it much harder for trial lawyers to win cases of corporate fraud. On a smaller scale, Congress pressed energy regulators for favorable treatment for Enron before the scandal broke.

A survey taken by the KPMG found that 60% of employees had observed violations of law or company standards at least "sometimes" during the previous twelve months, and that 37% had observed misconduct that they believed could result in "significant loss of public trust" if known. The same survey found that only 64% of employees believed that their CEOs or other senior managers would respond appropriately were they to become aware of misconduct, and only 62% believed that their CEOs or other senior manager wouldn't authorize illegal or unethical conduct to meet business goals.[66]

Investors Made Too Little, and CEOs Too Much

Chapter 2 demonstrated that very bad things have been happening to investors; and Chapter 3 demonstrated that these were not a few isolated cases but were part of a widespread pattern and practice. The system's failures are twofold. Investors have made too little from their investments, and CEOs and their helpmates in the accounting firms and the banks have made far too much. Investors have not gained appreciation that would be expected under a fairly functioning system; and executives and financial service professionals have gained from the system out of any and all proportion to their contributions. The system has been rigged to benefit some at the expense of others.

Financial services hold fiduciary responsibilities by which professionals and executives are expected to subordinate their own interests to those of investors, but this obligation has been violated on a massive scale. Our system is designed to protect the investor; but it has in fact operated in a very different way. Many people in the financial services industry broke the rules, gamed the system, and concealed realities from investors. These things occurred not in isolated instances, nor in the unusual case of technology startups, but in the mainstream of the economy—the so-called "old economy," the big economy, the economy we thought we knew.

To use an odd but poignant expression that has been circulating among disillusioned investors, for fortunate pension investors 401(k)s became 301(k)s; for most pension investors 401(k)s dwindled to 201(k)s; for the less fortunate 401(k)s dropped to 101(k)s (they lost 75%); and for a final large group 401(k)s are today only 001(k)s (they lost more than 90%). The stock markets have wiped out about $5.5 trillion in wealth, about 39% of the stock market's value at its peak, and somewhat more than 55% of the nation's GDP in 2002.

Changes in CEOs' Attitudes Led to a Decline in Investors' Trust

Subtle changes in attitudes among key players in American business and financial markets have resulted in an unexpected crisis in security markets. These changes in attitudes are about ethics, executive compensation, and disclosure. Attitude changes have occurred slowly over several years and in the end have had a surprisingly large impact. There were no important external changes that caused the current crisis in our equity markets, but they are the consequence of internal developments.

Investors are no longer certain they can trust the system. This suggests that sending a few executives from a few companies to jail isn't enough to restore confidence. Much deeper and more serious things have been occurring than a few instances of larceny instigated by a few bad apples among corporate CEOs. These deeper things, if not addressed, will undermine the whole edifice.

There's a crisis in American capitalism similar to what occurred in the 1920s. As a result, investors need a new level of protection; the way companies are run needs to be reformed: Government has to redefine its role and that of the markets; and we have to look hard at ourselves as a society and see why it is that some of those who were our most admired leaders and institutions have felt themselves free to defraud millions of their fellow citizens of their savings and pensions.

Business Isn't Only to Blame

There's no implication here that business alone exhibits unacceptable behavior. If it's true that more than a few businesspeople have engaged in unethical and often illegal behavior, then it's also true that more than businesspeople are implicated. The problem is systematic, but not just in the business community. During the period of the corporate scandals, Congress failed each year to pass campaign finance reform legislation. Leading political figures were denouncing the campaign finance system but saying that as long as the rules weren't changed, they themselves would continue to raise money in a way widely recognized as corrupt. The President of the United States was named in a sex scandal that soon turned to questions of perjury. One of the nation's great churches was engulfed in its own sex scandal.

Furthermore, not only were other institutions engaged in their own questionable conduct, they were happy to glorify corporate executives in order to try to get money from them. Our great universities, our museums, and our churches were actively soliciting gifts from the very executives who were soon to be immersed in scandal. They all wanted to dip their hands into the buckets of dollars the executives were filling, and CEOs were the gatekeepers.

Business executives didn't wake up one day and decide to become absolutists while their boards let them. Instead, they were flattered into the position by those who sought money from them, including many of the leading people in our society. Corruption is not limited to business but is a deep issue in our society. Still, whatever the context, many business executives gave in to the temptation to defraud investors and thereby created the scandals. It's not only business that is broken in our society.

Corruption has two different types of effects on us. First, it causes an unjust transfer of wealth and income from some people to those who are corrupt. Second, it reduces the efficiency of our economy and so reduces the well-being of all of us. These are the reasons we have laws that attempt—poorly, it will be seen in later chapters—to prevent corruption: because it's unfair and it's inefficient. There's no reason why criminalizing fraud should be viewed as impairing the legitimate managerial pursuit of shareholder profits.[67]

Not a Great Depression—Yet

Though they are important, investment markets are not the entire economy, and it's important to keep this in perspective. Investment markets are only one part of America's financial markets, a smaller part of its business sector, and an even smaller part of the economy as a whole. So although the investment markets may be in disarray—and though this may adversely affect the rest of the economy—having a mess in the investment markets doesn't mean that the rest of the economy is equally messed up.

Today seems to be unlike the days after the Great Crash of 1929. Soon after the Great Crash, the American economy dipped into a recession and then into the Great Depression, which reached its bottom four years later. But this time the market's crash has not yet turned into a depression (although around three years have passed since the stock market peaked in the spring of 2000). The American economy isn't broken today in the same way that it was a few years after the 1929 crash, and this gives us an opportunity to fix the investments markets, which are broken, without having to struggle with the economy as a whole.

The American Economic System Is Not Broken

The American economy is not broken. Economic indicators are rising. The economy is growing. In the 1930s the Fed tightened the supply of money and reduced consumers' and investors' ability to buy. That helped cause the great depression.

But this time the Fed has done the opposite and the economy is recovering from a brief recession.

The recession that followed the stock market decline in 2001 was the shortest and least severe on record. Americans continue to work; unemployment is not very high, nor has it risen very much since the stock market turned down—certainly not by the standards of the Great Depression, in which 25% of our workforce was unemployed. Today about 6% of American workers are unemployed.

Our economy is enormous by world standards and still growing—it's worth about $10 trillion, approximately one-third of world economic activity, generated by about 5% of the world's population. Although we have economic problems and must continually address them if the economy is not to deteriorate, our situation today is not bad. This is all good news.

The Business System as a Whole Is Not Broken

At 88% (by dollar volume), private business remains the core of the U.S. economy. It is dynamic and functioning to provide goods and services and jobs, and it is competing in the international economy. It may seem strange to argue that the business system isn't broken, while at the same time recognizing that most CEOs of most large companies in most industries were deeply implicated in the financial shenanigans that defrauded investors. In effect, we're saying that the financial side of the business house is a mess, but the non-financial side isn't so bad—the leader of both is doing things that are not at all acceptable on one side of the house but doing an acceptable job on the other.

Yet this is true. In part, it's true because most CEOs don't actually run the operations of their companies—this task has been delegated to a new executive position in American companies, the COO, or chief operating officer. It's the COO who oversees the business, freeing the CEO to concentrate on four things: the company's financials, including its stock price (where the CEO is closely assisted by the company's CFO or chief financial officer) and executive compensation (where the CEO is closely assisted by the company's chief human resources or personnel executive); the company's external relations; the company's key customers; and the company's strategy. In all these areas the CEO is usually in close contact with the company's board of directors. So, in fact, in recent years the CEOs of American businesses have relinquished close oversight of operations. And although some companies have major operational problems, and all companies have some operational problems, for the most part the day-to-day business of America is being conducted by private business organizations in fairly successful fashion.

During the slow buildup to the current financial scandals, significant progress was being made on many business issues. Even during the dot-com bubble we learned much about how to manage in the Internet era.[68] And during the difficult years of the main Japanese challenge to our manufacturing companies, much improved in American leadership and teamwork.[69] While the business system as a whole isn't broken, some elements of large, publicly held American corporations definitely are, most importantly, the CEO function. The role has been perverted from being an agent of the shareholders to being an agent of the CEO's own self-interest.

The Finance function is broken because it has been corrupted; the Personnel function is broken because it has also been corrupted. Both have been turned to the pursuit of the CEO's personal interest rather than that of the shareholder. The proper role of the Finance function is to increase shareholder wealth via honest numbers and disclosure to investors of all material information. The proper role of the chief personnel officer is to increase shareholder wealth via motivated and satisfied employees. Unfortunately, CFOs have been corrupted into financial engineering, the objective of which is to confuse and deceive investors; and CPOs have been corrupted into designing compensation packages, the purpose of which is to enrich the CEO and the other executives and directors. And, of course, the boards of directors are broken, corrupted by the same compensation system (options), and driven by the same insider information that permits CEOs to prosper even if their companies don't.

How these elements of the American corporation came to be broken and what might be done about them to the advantage of investors is the subject of the rest of this book.

The Financial System as a Whole Is Not Broken

Mortgages are being written, homes are being built, consumers are getting credit, and parents are getting loans to send their children to college.

Financial transactions of these sorts are 8% of the U.S. economy as a whole.

The Securities Industry *Is* Broken

But the securities industry is badly broken. It represents 3% of the U.S. economy as a whole, and about one third (specifically 38%) of the financial services sector as a whole. This is what's broken.

How badly the securities industry is broken can be judged from what is likely to be the greatest economic surprise about the booming 1990s—that while the economy did well, the profits boom that fueled the great bull market in stocks was largely an illusion.

A key argument for the stock market boom of the 1990s was that American companies were more profitable than those abroad, so American firms should have higher share prices than those abroad. Partly on this basis much foreign investment was attracted to American equities and American investors were encouraged to pay high prices for shares in American companies. The financial reporting of American firms certainly said that American firms were more profitable. During the mid and late 1990s American manufacturing companies reported themselves more than twice as profitable, measured by return on equity, as did firms in Germany and the United Kingdom. American service firms reported themselves as more than twice as profitable as German firms, and about a third more profitable than British firms in the same period.

But this was not the whole story. When compared on the basis of return on total assets in a company, American firms were less profitable than those in Britain, about as profitable as those in Japan, and more profitable than those in Germany—a much less favorable picture for American firms than that given by their own reports.[70]

How did this happen? In part American companies had more debt in their total capital structure so that their return on equity was higher, but they were not better managed and their return on assets invested (whether financed by equity or debt) was not better than other significant national business groups. But in part the higher profitability American firms awarded themselves was simply a result of the imaginative accounting being done in America, which did not reflect real returns to shareholders, but instead inflated sales and concealed expenses.

So the securities industry is broken—it's sending fundamentally flawed signals to investors and causing them to lose great amounts of money, while it's making corporate CEOs and financial professionals rich. What should be done about it?

One point of view holds that we must not get further into revelations of financial scandals, this for fear public confidence will be irretrievably shaken, and that the financial system will collapse, taking with it the business system and the entire economy—rather like a house of cards tumbling down. To avoid disaster, goes the argument, it's best to deal with a few extreme cases of financial malfeasance, and to make somewhat minor adjustments to the regulatory system, in the expectation that the current crisis will blow over and the attention of the public will move on to other things. Even many investors who have been badly hurt by the scandals share this viewpoint, fearing that further revelations of scandal will wipe out what value remains in their investments.

But this fear is overblown. The securities industry is important, but not so important that the rest of the economy hangs on it. The fundamentals of today's economy are strong enough to permit us to rectify the difficulties in the investment markets without undue risk to the economy as a whole or to the value of remaining investments.

We don't have to fear that in recognizing that the securities industry is broken and fixing it, we will wreck the nations' economic system, or its business system, or its financial system as a whole. The problem in the financial system is significant, and it adversely affects the financial system, the business system, and the economic system, since it's a part of each. But it's not the whole of each, nor even the majority of each. To recognize that there's a serious problem in the securities industry will not undermine confidence in the other systems—in fact, it hasn't done so despite all the adverse publicity of the past two years. So we can go about fixing the securities industry without fear that we will wreck larger and more important elements of our economic system as a whole.

Conflicts of Interest: The Core of the Problem in the Securities Industry

"Wall Street had become an awful money machine. We were competing on an uneven playing field, one that favored us all the way against the small investor, the 401(k) saver, and the pensioner."[71]

—An investment banker

"Shut up and delete this e-mail."

—An October 2001 message about Enron between colleagues at J. P. Morgan Chase.[72]

The American securities industry is rife with conflicts of interest. We've examined the conflicts as they apply to many of the central players in the scandals that drained investors' pockets, and we summarize them here. Chapters that follow will look at the accountants and the banks in greater detail.

The CEOs: Benefiting Not with but without the Shareholder

The core of the conflict of interest that did and still does face CEOs is that while they are legally agents of the shareholders of the company, they are able to profit themselves at the expense of shareholders, and often do so. CEO pay packages ordinarily include stock options, which, if the share price of the company's stock rises dramatically, are likely to be extraordinarily lucrative to the CEO. The temptation is therefore enormous to move the share price up by any means possible, even if in the end the company collapses and shareholders are impoverished. Hence they resort to fraud in order to exaggerate sales and profit figures and thereby cause the share price to rise rapidly.

Furthermore, because options give CEOs such huge personal stakes in the companies they run, selling the company can be very lucrative to them—even though it may not be in the best interest of shareholders. In a review of research on merger and acquisition activity, Joseph Bower of Harvard criticized studies that "treat mergers made in the 1960s as if they were similar to mergers made in the 1980s and 1990s. They often ignore the huge personal gains available to U.S. executives of selling organizations that have large stock option packages."[73] Option packages distorted the entire merger and acquisition market during the 1990s in ways that, as Professor Bower points out, have not yet been fully appreciated.

But there's more. CEOs have also used their economic muscle with investment banks (via the fees companies pay banks for services) to obtain allocations of shares in the initial public offerings (IPOs) of companies brought to the public market by the banks. Since the stock of new companies often rises dramatically in price after an IPO, the CEOs thereby profit personally. These are both conflicts of interest because they subordinate the interests of the shareholders to the personal interests of the CEOs.

Members of Boards of Directors: Scratching the CEO's Back

Conflicts of interest are common in the boardroom. Board members are also tempted to sell out shareholders for the executives in a company. Often the sellout takes the form of excessively generous pay or severance packages. At other times it's more direct. For instance, at IBM the CEO of American Express sits on the compensation committee of the board; but American Express has a multibillion dollar contract with IBM.[74] The opportunity to trade out investors in favor of the two CEOs in a situation of this nature is very great.

Accountants: Doing Audits and Consulting for Clients

The major accounting firms have been operating both auditing businesses and consulting businesses. The audit function is supposed to be at arms length from the client company and is intended to be objective. The consulting business is supposed to be close to the company, subjectively for the client's gain. In trying to get consulting business, the accounting firms have an incentive to deliver the sort of audits a client wants, thereby undermining the objectivity of the audit, much to the disadvantage of investors.

Investment Banks

America's investment banks are the only major financial institution that played a key role in both the Internet bubble and the accounting scandals of the old economy. This may be a surprising statement, but the evidence for it is very strong. In the Internet bubble, while all elements of the investment industry played a role, venture firms and the IPO process of the investment banks were the most important factors. In the accounting scandals of the old economy, while once again all elements of the investment industry got in on the feeding frenzy that occurred at investors' cost, it was CEOs, auditors, and the loan (or deal) and analyst functions of the investment banks who played the key roles.

In the big company scandals, the banks had great conflicts of interest. Banks competed to provide loans to corporate clients that were disguised to fool the investors. Analysts at the banks knew the securities were of little value but recommended the shares of companies to investors in order to win or hold banking business for the banks. Generally, neither dealmakers nor analysts at the banks disclosed their conflicts of interest to investors.

Mutual Funds: Dealing on Their Own Account

Mutual funds gain influence with brokers from the large orders they place on behalf of their customers; but they use the influence to buy shares for their own accounts (not the accounts of the mutual funds owned by their customers). In attempting to get attractive investments for themselves, the funds may put their investors into less than attractive shares. This happened on a large scale during the dot-com bubble.

Managing Hedge Funds and Mutual Funds

Some mutual fund companies operate both mutual funds—which buy only for appreciation in value of the shares they buy—and hedge funds (see Chapter 21), which buy for appreciation but also sell short for gain. Hedge funds may therefore be speculating with the intent of driving down the prices of shares that the company's mutual funds may own. Thus the hedge fund is undercutting the mutual fund investors. Some mutual funds do not operate both types of funds, however, since the largest ones have seen that this conflict of interest is evident to outsiders and have avoided it.

Brokerage Houses

A long-standing conflict of interest is built into the core of the brokerage business, which often works to the disadvantage of clients. The brokerage house has a fiduciary responsibility to its customers (under NASD regulations) but also has a need to buy and sell shares—hence the continuing recommendations of brokers to their clients to buy and sell, and sometimes even the churning of accounts.

Public Officials

Senators, representatives, and the President oversee the nation's securities regulators and have obligations to the American people, including investors. But politicians are also dependent on individuals and corporations for campaign donations. During the bull market, campaign contributions rose enormously, and elected officials in turn passed legislation favorable to companies and restrained regulators, especially the SEC and the Financial Accounting Standards Board, in ways that facilitated the deception of investors. Election financing reform, while merited on many bases, is also crucial to protecting investors.

Awards for "the Best" in Corporate America

Recounted below are a series of awards given to executives by major business magazines in recent years. Not many months later, some of the recipients would be in handcuffs. It is not merely using hindsight to look back on these awards and see an unpleasant spectacle. What we've learned in recent years was in fact already discernible when these awards were given out. The awards were the work of a large number of people, supposedly expert in business and leadership, who evaluated corporate executives from different points of view—these were not isolated and idiosyncratic selections. Furthermore, the evaluations didn't concern matters like stock prices that are subject to the vagaries of the marketplace but instead were supposed to reflect underlying quality in business practices.

That these awards were given to people who so little deserve them reflects the general nature of the delusions in the business world about what corporate leadership means today. Investors have been misled not only by the companies themselves but by people who are supposed to be expert at assessing corporate performance.

CFO Magazine's "Excellence Awards"

- 1998 CFO Excellence Award in the "Mergers & Acquisitions Management" category: Scott Sullivan, CFO of WorldCom
- 1999 CFO Excellence Award in the "Capital Structure Management" category: Andrew Fastow, CFO of Enron
- 2000 CFO Excellence Award in the "Mergers & Acquisitions Management" category: Mark Swartz, CFO of Tyco International

CFO magazine has given out these awards to recognize "excellence in finance" for years. Each year there is an initial pool of about 100–120 candidates, nominated by senior executives in different companies. That initial pool is then narrowed down to about 40 finalists, from which winners are selected in about 10 categories (e.g., "Mergers & Acquisitions Management," "Capital Structure Management," "Cost Optimization," "Risk Management"). The judging is done by a panel of about seven people who are senior executives of major businesses; one of the judges is the editor of *CFO* magazine. (The awards are announced in September or October of each year.)

In announcing the awards, *CFO* magazine says that the winners "exemplify the highest levels of achievement in finance" (1998 awards), "are truly in a class by themselves" (1999 awards), have "broken through the traditional boundaries of finance, creating value in innovative ways and delivering it on a consistent basis" (2000 awards).

Scott Sullivan of WorldCom. In giving the award to Scott Sullivan in 1998, *CFO* magazine described him as "a whiz kid." It quoted an analyst from A.G. Edwards who said that Sullivan "is one of the brightest CFOs I have ever met. Not every CFO is cut out of that mold. He just gets it." It also quoted Bernard Ebbers, CEO of WorldCom, who said that Sullivan "has no peer in his ability to earn the trust and confidence of the investment community."

The magazine described Sullivan's excellence in all sort of deals. "But it is the MCI deal," it said, "that has become the stuff of legend" (even though the deal was just closing when *CFO* magazine announced this award). The magazine said: "Sullivan found that a WorldCom/MCI combination could offer two to three times the synergy of [a competing] proposed deal," and that, the magazine said, was what enabled WorldCom to offer a very high purchase price.

In a recent article in the *New York Times*, a WorldCom executive who was involved in the internal review of the MCI deal is quoted as saying, "MCI was purchased at an unbelievably inflated price." The article also cites a number of

WorldCom employees who say that the company, in making all its acquisitions, regularly carried on accounting fraud via acquisition-related charges. "The boost from post-acquisition accounting was like a drug," a former WorldCom executive says. "But it meant bigger deals had to come along to keep the ball rolling." And as for synergy, another WorldCom executive says: "Don't think of WorldCom the way you would of other corporations. It's not a company, it's just a bunch of disparate pieces. It's simply dysfunctional."[75]

Andrew Fastow of Enron. In giving the award to Andrew Fastow in 1999, *CFO* magazine said that much of Enron's growth has been "fueled by unique financing techniques pioneered by Fastow." It quotes a director of the credit-rating agency Standard & Poor's: "Andy has made it clear that maintaining the credit quality of the company is job one." This S&P director said that Fastow "has successfully financed billions of dollars in a manner that has held credit quality. And that is not an easy thing to do. It is a testament to Andy's focus on cash flow and his ability to think outside the box."

Mark Swartz of Tyco. In giving the award to Mark Swartz in 2000, *CFO* magazine said: "The award reflects a recent flurry of deal making that no other company can match. Tyco's tightly structured acquisition approach has been an unqualified success, one having no need of smoke-and-mirrors accounting."

Each of these three CFOs is now under indictment and his company the object of fraud investigations.

Chief Executive Magazine's Awards

- 2000 awards named Enron's board as one of the five best boards of directors in the United States.
- The 2002 "Chief Executive of the Year" award given to Sandy Weill of Citigroup.

Chief Executive magazine has given out the awards for the "best boards" for years. The awards are based on assessments done by Boris Yavitz and Robert W. Lear, in cooperation with the consulting firm Korn/Ferry International. (Boris Yavitz is dean emeritus of Columbia Business School. He currently works as a governance consultant and is a partner of Lear, Yavitz & Associates. Robert W. Lear, formerly the CEO of F&M, is chairman of *Chief Executive's* advisory board and a partner of Lear, Yavitz & Associates.)

The evaluations are said to involve all public corporations of sufficient size to be listed on one or more of the major stock exchanges. Evaluation criteria are established and board characteristics are assessed on the basis of published data, mainly annual reports, proxy statements, and a variety of directories.

In its introduction to the 2000 awards, the magazine stated the following:

> What makes a "Best" board this year? All five of our best board choices come very close to fulfilling the hallmarks of a good board that we began posting nine

> years ago. All five are successful, progressive companies, working in apparent CEO/director harmony and respected in their industries and communities for their policies and position. Each has also made an extra effort to accomplish something important on the corporate governance front and, therefore, stands as a role model for other corporations to follow.

The magazine also stated:

> Dramatic improvements in corporate governance have swept the American economic system in recent years.... A do-nothing or captive board has difficulty hiding from its shareholders, the press, and prospective investors.

And further:

> Today's boards evaluate their CEOs in hard-nosed fashion.

Enron. In October 2000, Enron's board was named one of the five best boards of directors in the United States.

The specific citation for Enron described it as "A Board That Runs Deep": "a fast moving, innovating energy and communications firm. It calls itself a 'New Economy' company. As such, its board—a big one, with 18 directors—works hard to keep up with things." The citation then described the supposedly good attendance record of board members at various meetings and the compensation paid to board members. It said that the board "uses working committees with functional responsibilities in the more complex and recurring areas where disinterested oversight is required."

Unfortunately, Enron's board was one of the least effective in corporate America.

Chief Executive of the Year Sandy Weill. The magazine has given the "Chief Executive of the Year" awards for years. The selection committee for the 2002 award consisted of 10 people: seven CEOs of major businesses, two heads of venture capital firms, and the president of the Center for Creative Leadership. The award to Sandy Weill was announced in the magazine's July 2002 issue.

John Alexander, president of the Center for Creative Leadership, said of Weill: "He's met just about every challenge a CEO could meet head-on and handled himself well. It was the total picture, the cumulative effect." Aart de Geus, the chairman and CEO of Synopsys, said of Weill's work: "A systematic, well-executed strategy; consistent, strong, demonstrable results; and commitment to the community." James Kilts, the chairman and CEO of Gillette, said: "He is an outstanding CEO with the total package of skills, demonstrating hands-on leadership."

The magazine itself said: "In an age where image is everything and honesty seems harder than ever to find, it appears to be the very genuineness of Weill's emotion, whether positive or negative, that fosters trust among his troops.... His reputation for honesty has also helped Weill complete major deals and recruit top talent." Former Treasury Secretary Robert Rubin, when he was considering joining Citigroup, was told that, with Weill, "there was zero question of integrity."

Yet Weil is directly involved in misleading investors via the reports of investment analysts in Citicorp's investment bank.

Fortune Magazine's Awards

- In 2000 Enron was named the "Most Admired" company in the country in terms of "Quality of Management." In 2001 Enron was named the second "Most Admired" company in the country in terms of "Quality of Management," just slightly behind the frontrunner.
- In 1996, 1997, 1998, 1999, 2000, and 2001, Enron was named the "Most Admired" company in terms of "Innovativeness."
- In 2000 Enron was named the second "Most Admired" company in the country in terms of "Employee Talent."
- In 2002 Citigroup was named one of the "Top Ten" most admired companies in the country in terms of overall characteristics.

Fortune magazine has given out the awards for "America's Most Admired Companies" for many years. It describes its list of America's Most Admired Companies as "the definitive report card on corporate reputations." The winners are chosen from the 1,000 largest U.S. companies (ranked by revenues) and the 25 largest U.S. subsidiaries of foreign-owned companies. The selection process is based on a survey that Clark Martire & Bartolomeo (CM&B) does of 10,000 executives, directors, and securities analysts. There are awards for the most admired companies in terms of overall characteristics and there are also awards for the most admired companies in terms of what *Fortune* calls several "key attributes of reputation" (e.g., Quality of Management, Innovativeness, Employee Talent, Financial Soundness).

Enron. *Fortune* didn't say anything substantive about the awards to Enron for "Quality of Management" and "Innovativeness." In 2000, however, it highlighted the fact that the quality of Enron's management was rated even higher than that of General Electric.

Enron has turned out to be one of America's most significant corporate frauds.

Citigroup. In 2002 Citigroup was named one of the "Top Ten" most admired companies in the country in terms of overall characteristics. *Fortune* cited various supposedly excellent qualities that Citigroup has, and it quoted a few people (including Sandy Weill) who said how outstanding the company is. Spencer Stuart Chairman Tom Neff, for example, called Citigroup "an extraordinary company."

Fortune acknowledged that the company "is also collecting some criticism. Allegations that the brokerage side of Citigroup sold convertible Enron bonds to institutional investors when Citi's lending side knew that Enron was in trouble were brought to light after our surveys were in. But it remains to be seen whether those allegations will be enough to hurt Citi's reputation."[76]

In fact, internal company documents obtained by Congress have shown that Citigroup executives knew all along that securities they were selling not only for Enron but for other energy companies as well would be defrauding investors and deceiving credit-rating agencies. Citigroup's stock research group has been corrupt for years and is under regulatory investigation. Yet when star analyst Jack Grubman left Salomon in August 2002, he was given tens of millions of dollars in severance, including forgiveness of a $19 million loan. The company's consumer finance business was engaged in "abusive and predatory lending practices" for years (quoting the Federal Trade Commission). There are charges that Citigroup was engaged in recent years in illegal "tying" arrangements between its commercial banking and underwriting businesses.

In the current state of business practice in America, what was going on in these companies, singled out for praise by these magazines, seems either to have escaped people who profess to be expert, or not to matter to those who give out awards for corporate leadership. It should, however, matter to investors for whom ethical corporate leadership is crucial, if they are not to be cheated out of their investments.

Talking Points

As much as we'd like to think that accounting fraud is limited to a few bad companies led by a few bad executives, the truth is much grimmer. Sadly, most publicly held U.S. firms have been engaging in some form of accounting shenanigans. The legal system, designed to protect shareholders, has been essentially ineffective in preventing, rectifying, or punishing securities fraud on the large scale on which it's been perpetrated.

The good news is that the American economic system is not broken and our business system as a whole isn't either; but some parts, especially the financial securities industry and the leadership function in large public companies, are definitely broken. Moreover, although the American securities industry is in shambles, it can be fixed. At the moment, however, it's rife with conflicts of interest. Most importantly, though CEOs are legally shareholders' agents, they are faced with opportunities to create enormous wealth for themselves at the expense of their shareholders, and they don't hesitate to do so. Boards of directors, auditors, investment banks, mutual funds, and brokerage houses are the willing accomplices of executives when they can participate in the gains.

Business can be a noble profession. It fuels economic improvement, advances knowledge and understanding, and enhances personal development. But too often in recent years those who are among the most successful in business have been anything but noble.

II *Infectious Greed: Who Got the Money?*

"I took a job in a jewelry store at the Mall where a good friend works. It's part time, but I did not realize how boring it would be... nor that the pay was about zip! The only good thing is I can make some commissions. I guess with the hit we all took in our retirement accounts, I decided to work a while; but I should have gone for something better and with regular hours. Now I'm really stuck, because the guy I work for is refusing to pay the commissions I've earned until the end of the following month—so I have to stick around each month at a tiny hourly rate of pay to get my commissions, and if I leave I know he won't pay me the commissions he owes me. It really makes me mad. I had a nice retirement nest egg and those guys in the stock market stole it."

—Woman in her mid-fifties in the southeast

5 Shareholders versus CEOs: The CEOs Make It Big

"You had highly promotional CEOs saying things were great yet selling just massive amounts of stock. It's virtually impossible to reconcile those two things."[77] According to Harvey Pitt, former chairman of the Securities and Exchange Commission, stock options gave CEOs "perverse incentives to manage earnings, distort accounting, or emphasize short-term stock performance."[78]

—"The CEO Crime Wave"
(CNBC, an item in a poll for viewers, September 20, 2002)

No matter how investors made out, CEOs profited enormously from the great bull market in stocks. For years banks and accountants knowingly joined CEOs, CFOs, and corporate boards of directors in undermining the fundamental principles of the American system of public investment by substituting concealment for disclosure, and opacity for transparency. Working together they sought to confuse and blind investors in order to make money for themselves.

The Fed, close overseer of the big banks, either knew about this and didn't care, or didn't know, in which case it would seem to have been negligent. The SEC, which is supposed to protect investors and prevent fraud, was in the same position as the Fed—though with the SEC there is strong evidence that its inaction was due to Congressional protection of the banks, accounting firms, and the companies. During the bull market this is what we offered to the rest of the world as a model financial system—one based largely on cronyism, concealment, and fraud.

This chapter is about how executives got large amounts of stock and cashed them in, no matter what eventually happened to shareholders' wealth. Stock options were the path to fortune for many top executives in the bull market. A rising market lifted almost all stocks, and the cost of options to a company, while deductible for tax purposes, was not treated as an expense that reduced profits reported to shareholders. Instead, options diluted ownership, which reduced returns to shareholders.

The dilution of ownership was mainly a result of executive compensation packages that stressed stock options. These packages were originally defended as aligning executive and shareholder interest, but their details and the way they rewarded executives when companies didn't perform well have led to a current view that they were a mechanism by which CEOs used their power in companies to get unearned rewards (economists call it rent).

In the 1990s, another phenomenon emerged that would further compromise investors' interests. Theoreticians had urged that corporate executives should have the same incentives to see a company's share price increase as did investors. A unity of interest was sought. The method chosen was stock options for top executives. Although stock options had been available since 1950, their widespread use in executive compensation did not begin until the bull market of the late 1980s and the 1990s. In 1993, Congress passed section 162(m) of the tax code barring companies from taking over $1 million in executive salary tax deductions, but permitting variable pay based on performance to be fully deductible. Options, therefore, became a preferred method of payment to executives in big corporations, for reasons spelled out below. They also led directly to the scandals now being revealed.

Companies began to give executives large option packages, and these gave top executives a strong incentive to raise the share price. One way of accomplishing this is to take steps to increase the long-run value of the company. Indeed, this is the main objective of such incentive plans. Unfortunately, high-powered equity plans—particularly those with short vesting windows—can also motivate executives to attempt to raise the share price by illegitimate means. That is, executives can attempt to fool the market by taking measures that raise profitability in the short run or, worse, by falsifying profitability numbers through shady accounting. Thus, high-powered equity incentives create incentives for value creation, but, at the same time, can also put pressure on executives to take short cuts to impress investors.

The most egregious cases occurred when executives cashed in big via stock options when their companies were exaggerating sales and profits before going bankrupt. The second most egregious cases occurred when executives got substantial severance (walkaway) packages as their companies were failing or not succeeding in increasing shareholder value.

CEOs Made Fortunes without Building Companies

In his book about the 1929 stock market crash, John Kenneth Galbraith thought about a potential clash between the interests of investors and those of corporate executives. He labeled it the approved contradiction of investor-owned capitalism. Since the economic theory of markets (so-called neoclassical theory) called for individuals to maximize their own welfare, Galbraith mused, why should executives be honest in the shareholders' interest?[79]

As it turns out, they weren't honest in the 1920s, and they weren't honest in the 1990s. Every so often, when boards of directors and government regulators look away, the approved contradiction turns on investors and despoils them. Yet it wasn't old-time CEO ruthlessness in business, which many think may be necessary to building great business empires—such as Standard Oil, U.S. Steel, the great railways, the Morgan banking interests—that occurred in the 1990s. No new business empires were built, although some companies did emerge and survive—so the excesses that occurred cannot be justified as necessary to building something important. What occurred was primarily deception—the executives at the center of the scandals of the 1990s aren't robber barons, they're just robbers. Even if only a few bad apples engaged in large-scale fraud, most engaged in accounting intended to deceive, not provide transparency; and almost all received generous compensation for improvements in share prices, which had little to do with their efforts, and which proved ephemeral for shareholders.

Aligning CEO and Investor Interests

So how did this occur? In the 1930s Gardiner Means and Adolf Berle pointed out the difference in interests that existed between top executives and investors in companies.[80] Instead of maximizing shareholder wealth, executives were shown by behavioral studies to be satisfying or trying to balance the interests of various constituencies—employees, customers, and shareholders. Means saw this result as benefiting the executives in retaining their positions, but doing little for shareholders. Studies also showed that executives in large, publicly held firms drew their compensation from salaries and bonuses and owned few or no shares in the company. Having no shares themselves, the theory went, CEOs didn't care about increasing the value of investors' holdings.

During decades of indifferent corporate performance, the notion gained adherents, and people tried to determine how to better align the objectives of CEOs and shareholders. The solution that came to earn general acceptance was that the CEO should own a substantial body of stock in a company he or she headed so that his or her dominant interest was the same as that of shareholders—to enhance the value of the company's stock. Hence was born the executive stock option, which, buttressed by favorable accounting treatment, was supposed to cause CEOs and shareholders to have the same objective—to enhance shareholder wealth by raising the price of the common stock of a company.

Shifting to Options

By the late 1990s, options had appeared in most CEO pay packages. When two economists asked in an important and influential article whether CEOs were then being paid like bureaucrats, they announced that the evidence said the answer was no.[81] They said further, "CEO compensation is highly responsive to firm performance." Lest there be any confusion about the point, the authors restated it, "The fortunes of CEOs are strongly related to the fortunes of the companies they manage." This was an important conclusion because it suggested that the objects of the CEO pay revolution were being met—that CEOs were benefiting when investors benefited—that an identity of interest between CEO and investor had been created by the option pay package.

Also, the authors found that "The relationship between pay and performance is almost entirely driven by changes in the value of stock and stock options." In fact, the authors reported, stock accounted for 98% of the tie between CEO compensation and the performance of the share price of their companies. This was also important because it suggested that the mechanism that had become the favorite of the CEO pay revolution, the stock option, was also functioning properly.

From 1984, when data began, to 1999, the proportion that executive holdings of stock and options provided of executive pay rose from none to about 60%. Even in 1990, just before the start of the bull market, equity holdings made up only 4% of executive pay. By 1999, as we've said, it was about 60%.[82] Equity holdings, especially options, were the way executives cashed in during the bull market.

But there was something seriously wrong with these conclusions. That these positive conclusions might be true only in the short run and only during a stock market bubble, so that CEOs would get rich while investors saw their wealth collapse, was not foreseen. CEOs, however, probably saw their opportunity from the start. A CEO almost always receives stock options at the current market price. If the stock price went up, he cashed in. If it went down, he received new options at the lower price. "The main reason executives are paid this way is that it gives them an almost sure thing—unless the stock falls steadily, sooner or later an executive who keeps getting options at the current price sees a rise in the market price of his company's stock and makes a lot of money."[83]

The heart of the story of the current scandals is how the apparently sensible notion of giving stock options to executives to tie their interests more closely to those of investors backfired on investors, and how, armed with share options, CEOs got rich and left shareholders holding the bag. This surprising result, very much unforeseen and unintended by the theoreticians who sponsored executive stock options, occurred because options caused CEOs to have an interest in the short-term increase in share value, while shareholders were often longer-term investors. Or, it might be said, executives and traders (short-term investors) had a very different interest than that of longer-term investors in a firm, and they effectively got money up front for what often turned out to be no long-term value creation.

The Failure of the Theoreticians

Theoretical analysis of the new compensation packages, especially options, was useful and technically imaginative, but naive because it failed to detect the conflicts of interest that later created the scandals. Option packages were adopted and then exploited by CEOs. Theoretical analysis became a rationalization, and academics, sometimes unwillingly, became instruments of the enrichment of virtually all CEOs at the expense of most investors.

Stock Options Begin to Dominate CEOs' Pay Packages

Why use options instead of stock itself? Both would presumably align the interests of executives and shareholders—that is, the executives would benefit when shareholders did, and vice versa. The primary reason for choosing options and not stock itself lay, and lies, in the accounting treatment. And why did option-based pay packages take off like a rocket? Because of consultants and egos.

Preferential Accounting Treatment

Under current accounting rules, if the number and exercise price of options are fixed at the time they are granted, option costs do not need to be expensed on a company's income statement (although they are listed in a footnote to the balance sheet). On the other hand, with stock itself restricted as to when it can be sold, the grant-date value is spread over the vesting period and expensed under fixed accounting rules. Hence, companies can increase profits by minimizing expenses when they use options, and so they generally prefer granting stock options to stock. Hence, our accounting rules encouraged companies to give options to executives and permitted the company to ignore the costs when reporting profits to investors.

Consultants, CEO Compensation, and CEO Egos

In the early 1990s, the SEC required companies to inform shareholders about executive pay in greater detail. Intended to give investors more information with which to evaluate companies, this requirement also allowed CEOs to discover what their counterparts in other companies were being paid. Quickly an industry of consultants arose to contrast and compare CEOs' salaries. The compensation committees of boards of directors received data from the chief human resource officer of each company, which was drawn from consultants reports and which showed how each CEO compared to those in allegedly comparable companies. A ratchet took effect—that is, when one CEO was behind another, the board raised his pay, and then the other company's board tried to reassert the original lead its CEO had. This is an old technique of unions in negotiating pay packages with employers, and it was ironic to see it applied to CEOs.

Most Americans think that there are two major types of causalities in the economic sphere: free markets and government direction. The first involves a large number of people each acting independently; the second involves one or a few people directing the actions of everyone else. But there is a third major type: the herd mentality. We often ignore it, but it is very powerful in exactly the two areas of the economy in which we've had recent problems: investments and executive compensation. Nor is herd-like behavior limited to American markets. It's been recognized and researched among large financial institutions in international capital markets.[84]

It's powerful in part because economic research in the area of herd mentality has been unfashionable in recent decades, so many otherwise intelligent observers were blind-sided by the magnitude of the current corporate financial scandals. The great bubbles and the bull market generally were an example of herd mentality; so is the mechanism by which CEO pay has become racheted to such a high level. Neither involves the operation primarily of a perfect market (lots of small buyers and sellers operating independently) or of a centrally directed economy. Both are instead about market leaders and the psychology of following what everyone else does.

There's a confused notion that if human psychology is a factor, then the economy must exhibit irrational and manic behavior. This is not the case. There is logic to group psychology just as to other causal factors. What is ordinarily left out in discussing group psychology and economics is the crucial role of leadership—of those individuals or institutions that set the path.

It is because people respond to leadership that markets can be manipulated, and often are. It's why irrational buying can be touched off by very rational leaders who know just what they're doing; and why irrational heights can be obtained for pay packages by people who know how to exploit a leader–follower phenomenon over a number of years.

There is nothing surprising about these effects—it's just that American economic thinkers are temperamentally and ideologically disposed to ignore the herd aspect of our economic life. This disposition can be clearly traced in American economic writing, and periodically, as now, it results in an unexpected disaster.

With respect to CEO compensation, the herd mentality has been much like a conspiracy of employment contracts. Every CEO takes the most favorable features of other CEO's employment contracts and submits them on his or her own behalf to the board. The board approves them, arguing that it is following a "market" process. Consultants urge the process along for their CEO clients. They send proposals to boards pointing out new provisions of CEO contracts at other companies and offering to prepare adjustments in compensation and other terms that keep up with the benchmarks. The system forces CEO compensation to ever-higher levels.

It is sometimes argued that pay packages received by chief executives of U.S. corporations, although enormous by most people's standards, accurately reflect the extraordinary financial performance of those corporations, and therefore the executives deserve what they receive. The facts, however, don't bear this out. From 1991 to 2001:

- Profits per share of large companies (the Standard & Poor's 500) increased 55%.
- Total after-tax profits recorded for all U.S. corporations by the U.S. Department of Commerce increased 67%.
- The Standard & Poor's 500 index had a total return of 233%, which reflected the bull market's increase in stock prices.

From 1990 to 2000, however, the average compensation paid to chief executives of U.S. publicly traded large corporations increased 511%, to about $14 million per person. In 2001, after the market had begun its dramatic decline, CEO compensation declined only slightly.[85] A study by *Fortune* magazine found that from 1999 to mid-2002 there were 1,035 U.S. companies with market values of at least $400 million whose stocks fell 75% or more, but CEOs and other executives at those companies were able to cash in $66 billion of company stock for themselves. At 25 of those companies, insiders took out $23 billion (For example, Gary Winnick, of Global Crossing, realized $730 million from his exercise of stock options not long before his company went bankrupt. Kenneth Lay and other senior executives of Enron realized over $1 billion from their exercise of stock options not long before their company also went bankrupt.)[86]

Even in 2001 when the stock market and corporate profits both declined, CEO compensation at many companies went in the opposite direction. For example, compensation paid to the CEO of Cisco Systems increased to $154 million even though Cisco's stock price went way down. Compensation paid to the CEO of Capitol One increased to $100 million even though Capitol One's stock price went down. Compensation paid to the CEO of SBC Communications increased to $89 million even though SBC's stock price went down. Compensation paid to the CEO of Coca-Cola increased to $74 million even though Coca-Cola's stock price went down.

There is another dimension to this disparity as well. From 1990 to 2000, while the average compensation paid to chief executives increased 511%, the average compensation paid to ordinary workers increased 37%. Thus the ratio of the average compensation of chief executives to that of ordinary workers has risen from about 55:1 in 1980 to 130:1 in 1990 and to 580:1 in 2000.[87]

Peter Drucker has suggested that the ratio of CEO to average employee compensation should be no higher than 20. Beyond that, he said, a society makes a mockery of the contributions of ordinary employees. "What's absolutely unforgivable," he continued, "is the financial benefit top management people get for laying off people. There's no excuse for it. No justification. No explanation. This is morally and socially unforgivable, and we'll pay a very nasty price."[88]

CEOs are overpaid. When consultants compare pay levels of CEOs at various companies to try to establish the proper pay at another firm, all the comparisons are overblown. There is no competitive market to rely on. All the rates are inflated by a process that depends on cronyism and what economists call "rent-taking," that is, the exploitation of a power base without a corresponding increment to value.

Circumstances of this type are common in economics. Forty years ago when unions were stronger than they are today, rates of pay for various occupations were racheted upward on the basis of comparisons among them. Economists who studied the process referred to it as "orbits of coercive comparison"; public discussion labeled it "cost-push inflation."

When investment bankers were trying to price IPOs in the heat of the Internet bubble a few years ago, they looked to similar companies for guidance. The resultant valuations were huge—far beyond any real economic value—though it took about two years for this to become obvious to everyone. The point was that the whole scale was distorted—so that comparisons within the scale made no sense except in relative terms.

So it is today with CEO pay. And a similar resolution of the matter must occur as it happened with cost-push inflation and with the Internet bubble. In those instances price levels collapsed—wages fell and dot-com prices tumbled. CEO compensation is poised for a similar tumble—probably by seeing standard options severely restricted in CEO pay packages. But the tumbles don't happen automatically. Employers and the government worked for years to squeeze out cost-push inflation; and some observers pointed to the bubble in Internet stocks for years before it burst. A decrease in CEO pay hasn't happened yet; and it will take considerable effort by the investor community to see that CEOs finally come to be paid only for actual performance, and on a proper scale. Most CEO compensation, of course, is now received in the form of stock options. Options go mainly to top executives, not other employees (though this is less true in young technology companies than elsewhere), and companies giving the largest option grants to executives ordinarily perform more poorly for shareholders than those with smaller option packages.[89] This suggests that standard options are not a way to enhance shareholder wealth, but rather a means of enriching executives. It follows that almost all stock option plans in the United States are poorly designed and therefore have very little to do with actual performance.

As we shall see below, indexed options would link pay to performance better than conventional, fixed-priced options do. However, indexed options are virtually nonexistent in this country. In the stock market boom of the late 1990s, therefore, countless numbers of executives with stock options got a free ride. One study indicates that over 70% of stock option gains in recent years were attributable to favorable economic conditions over which CEOs and other company employees had no control.[90]

Repricing and recisions of options are described below. Here we should note that hundreds of companies in recent years have repriced their stock options. Stock options are awarded to executives with a certain exercise price. If the company's stock price declines, the company lowers the exercise price. In most cases this negates the purpose of the whole program.

Even worse is the practice of stock option rescissions at some companies. If a company's stock price goes down after employees have exercised their options, the company will allow them to return the stock to the company and get their money back. This is the ultimate "can't lose" strategy.

Much of the compensation paid to executives hasn't rewarded any sustained performance in the shares of their companies, but rather short-term price increases, and that has often been tied to the manipulation of the timing or substance of earnings announcements.

The Company as the CEO's Piggy Bank

Stock options are the primary means by which CEOs got rich during the bull market, but not the only one. Another method was direct loans to top executives, many of which were later forgiven. We've seen in Chapter 2 how the top officials at Adelphia and WorldCom borrowed enormous amounts from their companies. In the case of Adelphia, prosecutors claimed that executives had treated the company as their own piggy bank.

Another method was life insurance policies that benefited executives. So-called "split-dollar" policies were paid for by the corporation, and upon an executive's death these arrangements paid benefits to the company and to the executive's beneficiary. But it was also possible for executives to cash in the policies for substantial sums. The premiums paid by the companies arguably are a form of loan to the executives, and may now be outlawed with other loans to executives by the Corporate Responsibility Act of 2002.[91]

A fundamental cause of the financial scandals has been that CEOs interests and those of investors have dramatically diverged in recent years. Much of the divergence is due to the recent prevalence of stock options in executive pay packages.

Behind the Executive Pay Explosion

In theory, options are a form of variable pay that executives might not receive if the company performed poorly or a bear market developed. The risk to an executive of receiving pay via options is therefore said to be much greater than receiving a salary. It follows that options should be larger than a salary increase, since they are more uncertain.

However, options are complex financial instruments to which it is difficult to attach certain values. This makes their size and nature less transparent than is the case for salaries and invites abuse by those who can benefit by them. For example, when one set of options doesn't pay off, companies have commonly issued other sets of options that do. Where is the supposed riskiness of options for an executive?[92]

Ironically, the use of surveys was encouraged by rule changes in 1993, which required companies to more fully detail the pay of their top executives in company proxy statements. This expanded the already pervasive practice of using surveys to determine pay, since the collection of accurate and complete executive pay data was made easier. One of the hopes of the new rules was that greater disclosure would slow the increase in executive pay, as publicity regarding high pay would curb abuses. But instead of being embarrassed by publicity surrounding large pay packages, many executives seem to have begun to compete vigorously to make the most money.[93]

In fact, it is sometimes argued that it wasn't the fault of top executives that they were overpaid; instead they were victims of temptation offered when boards and investors pushed standard options on them as part of their compensation packages.[94]

This wasn't the case at all, but rather many influential CEO's, who were also chairs of their boards of directors, stacked the supposedly independent compensation committees of their boards with directors who, though they were not executives of the company, were doing business with the company or its CEO, or were even members of the family of the CEO. A study by the *New York Times* discovered that of the 2000 largest American firms, more than 20% had compensation committees with directors of the firm who had business ties or other relationships with the company or its CEO, and were therefore not independent. These were the companies that had disclosed such ties to the public. Probably many other firms had not disclosed them.[95] In these situations, it can be no surprise that executives were granted outsize compensation packages.

But, it might be asked, if only 20% of the companies had stacked boards, why didn't the other 80% have more reasonable compensation policies for top executives? The answer lies in the process by which other firms set CEO compensation, a process in which consultants looked at other firm's CEO compensation packages, and provided recommendations which raised the pay and determined its form (standard options) by copying the leading firms, which were those with non-independent compensation committees. It was a dynamic which via cycle after cycle over time pushed executive pay in America into a netherworld of riches almost regardless of what happened to company performance and shareholder wealth. It's a dynamic very similar to that used by craft unions to drive up pay—a strong local union gets an outside pay package, and other locals in their bargaining with management point to it as the basis for pay raises of their own.

Why Options Pay Off When Companies Don't

People who supported the use of options to align the interests of executives and shareholders now have to explain a result in which CEOs got rich while shareholders suffered. The explanation—which was offered by Chairman Greenspan of the Fed to Congress in the summer of 2002—goes as follows: The theory of linking CEO and shareholder interests via stock options given to executives presumes that the financial system works perfectly—that there is honest financial reporting and full disclosure of material facts by the companies. But this isn't necessarily the case. It didn't matter much when CEOs were paid via salaries, because they had no big incentive to cheat. But when CEOs suddenly got options, then they could get rich if they could only get share prices to rise. This was like putting rocket fuel into an engine that had in the past had only gasoline. CEOs, their engines now full of rocket fuel, looked for ways to pop up the stock price and found them in the imperfections of the system—reporting false financial results and concealing important facts (like the amount of debt a company had and conflicts of interest) from investors. The objective was to raise share prices long enough for executives to cash in, even by means that ensured that the share price would ultimately collapse. Still, options were supposed to link CEO pay to stock performance for the longer term. Why did this crucial link fail?

Stock Options and the Link to Performance

The link of options to company performance is crucial—it's this link that makes options tax-deductible to the corporation (not to the executive). Congress passed legislation in the early 1990s stipulating that compensation to corporate executives in excess of $1 million per year would be tax-deductible to companies only if it were performance based. In most cases, however, stock options haven't succeeded in linking pay to performance. The following are some reasons why.

Indexing

Virtually everyone who talks about indexed options says that they would link pay to performance better than conventional, fixed-priced options do.[96] The reality, however, is that indexed options are virtually nonexistent. (Level 3 Communications is the only company in the United States that indexes its stock options.) In the stock market boom of the late 1990s, therefore, countless numbers of people with stock options got a free ride. One study indicates that over 70% of stock option gains in recent years were attributable to favorable stock market conditions over which CEOs and other company employees had no control.[97] Indexing is a technique that favors investors—it prevents executives from benefiting from stock options when it's a generally rising stock market, and not the company's own performance, which drives up the price of the stock.

But there are other techniques for manipulating options that favor not the investors but the executives. For example, what happens to options when the share price falls? During the bear market of the past few years, this has happened to many companies—sometimes the share price has declined by more than 90%. Most options granted to executives were at prices of the companies' stock that had long since been passed on the way down. The options were now underwater—that is, the price at which they could be exercised by the executives was far below the market price, so there was no value in the options. To deal with the so-called "disincentive" effect of options being underwater, companies have come up with a variety of devices. Some of the more important are described below.

Follow-Up Option Grants

Probably the primary mechanism through which companies protect executives from a falling share price that renders options valueless is to provide the executives with much larger option packages the following year. According to researchers, who note that options are a fragile form of compensation—that is, that they don't always pay off for executives—"approximately 40% of all stock-induced incentive declines are offset by larger-than-average option grants in the following year. Thus, we have uncovered the primary mechanism through which companies mitigate the problem created by option fragility—larger option grants."[98]

Reissuing

If a company's share price goes down so that options are worthless, it may issue more options, and then more, each at a lower price, until at some price the options have value. Large companies like General Motors and General Electric do this, accepting the very large dilution of stockholder equity that may occur in the process.

Repricing

Hundreds of companies in recent years have repriced their stock options—that is, lowered their exercise price after the stock price declined. Repricing options contradicts their supposed link to performance. A new accounting standard (Interpretation 44, issued by FASB in 2000) was meant to discourage the repricing of options, but many companies have exploited a loophole in the new standard to get around it. Interpretation 44 says that if a firm cancels stock options and replaces them within six months, it must institute "variable accounting" for them—that is, record an expense for them in the firm's income statement. If the options are replaced within six months and one day after they've been cancelled, however, there is no such requirement. Thus many companies have implemented what are called "six and one" plans. The big unknown with these "six and one" plans is what the price of the stock will be six months and one day later, which is when the new exercise price will be established. Thus, as Floyd Norris of the *New York Times* nicely puts it, these plans serve to align the interests of company executives with those of short sellers.[99]

Rescinding

An even more blatant contradiction of the supposed rationale for stock options is the practice at some companies of allowing for stock option rescissions. If a company's stock price goes down after employees have exercised options (that is, bought the stock from the company), the company will allow them to return the stock to the company and get their money back along with the original options. This is the ultimate "can't lose" opportunity for the executives—the company has acted to prevent them from losing money on the options they had already exercised and has also started them over in the options game with a new grant.

Hedging

A fair number of CEOs and other company insiders who own huge amounts of company stock hedge their positions. Stock options represent more than half the compensation that CEOs at large companies receive. One problem that results from this, however, is that they then have most of their wealth tied up in a single stock; they aren't well diversified. So some CEOs hedge their positions and then borrow against the hedge, thus diversifying their portfolios.[100] This has a few advantages over selling the stock outright. For example, one is able to defer the tax on the capital gains. More significantly, these transactions generally aren't disclosed to the public. As *Business Week* points out, "Many executives who hedge do so with shares they were awarded as a way to tie their pay to the performance of the companies they manage.… Hedging can undermine the purpose of performance-based pay, since it cuts the risk of ownership."[101]

Rigging

A fair amount of the bull market in the second half of the 1990s was rigged by company insiders. Much of the IPO market was directly rigged.[102] Companies that engaged in accounting fraud, or something akin to it, rigged the market in somewhat less direct ways. Auditors helped with this. Stock analysts who issued glowing recommendations about companies as a springboard to obtain investment banking business also helped. Because of rigging and other reasons (such as the Internet mania), many company stocks achieved valuations that had no connection to actual company performance, but company insiders were able to cash in their stock options while the going was good. As Sarah Teslik, the executive director of the Council of Institutional Investors, says, stock options turned many companies into Ponzi schemes in which the money put into a company by later investors is used to pay off earlier investors (in this case, the current executives who are being paid via share options).[103]

Reloading

Executives are sometimes permitted to exercise options when the share price is high, and then provided more options with the old expiration date. This lets executives profit from volatility in share prices, although the overall trend for investors in the share price is flat.

David Leonhardt of the *New York Times* has illustrated the failure of options to align the interests of executives and shareholders in graphic terms:

> Executives do not always prosper most by making their companies great. They can often profit more from creating unrealistic expectations. Consider two companies. One has a stock price that has appreciated slowly, starting at $20 five years ago and gaining $2 a year, to $30 today. The second company's stock also started at $20 five years ago, then zoomed to $100 after a few years but has since fallen back to $20.
>
> By any reasonable measure, the leaders of the first company have done a better job. Their share price has grown 50 percent, and they have avoided making grandiose predictions that cause Wall Street analysts to set silly targets. The second company has a stock that has under-performed a savings account over the long run, and scores of workers and investors have been burned by false hopes.
>
> Yet if the top executives of both companies had received similar amounts of stock and both sold their shares on a regular schedule, the executives of the second company would actually be ahead. They would have made so much money selling the stock when it was trading near $100 that they would be multimillionaires despite the humbling decline. This is the Enron model of pay for performance, and it has become common.[104]

Slow vesting of stock options was supposed to minimize this problem. Companies generally specify various circumstances, however, in which the vesting of options is accelerated. Moreover, stock option grants in many companies are so extravagant that even a temporary spike in a company's stock price can leave executives set for life. Public investors, meanwhile, are generally in the dark about what is really going on. Experience with stock options in recent years—the failure to index options, the prevalence of repricing and rescissions, the hedging that some executives do, the rigging of the market—demonstrates that the alignment that stock options supposedly establish between the interests of company executives and the interests of public investors has been mostly fiction.

It's important to note that this discussion has been limited to options provided for top executives. Similar problems of options going underwater occur for lower-level executives, managers, professionals, and in some companies rank and file employees. These are people who were in a very different position than top executives—because top executives know the risks that attend the stock price of a company and have the power to directly influence the share price via their own actions. This is, in fact, the logic of providing stock options to top executives—that it will cause them to take actions to benefit shareholders by increasing the share price. But lower-level personnel have neither the deep understanding of the risk involved nor the ability to directly influence the overall performance of the firm. Hence, it follows that options are a more normal part of their pay packages, not intended to reflect personal performance (bonuses are used to do this), and adjustments of the type described above that are intended to maintain or restore the value of options when the stock price declines, and that are inappropriate for top executives, may be appropriate for other employees.

Shareholder–CEO Alignment in Tatters

Shareholder primacy, which became a mantra of investors and executives during the 1980s, insisted that executives are agents of shareholders and have a sole responsibility to them (rather than a broader responsibility to customers, suppliers, employees, and communities); and share options had supposedly established an identity of financial interest between top corporate executives and investors. Yet today, this system lies in shambles—instances of fraud and self-dealing by executives are being revealed daily and the entire gain in the major stock market price indices of the so-called boom of the late 1990s has evaporated. Executives have profiteered greatly and shareholders have lost out.

Why didn't the system—CEOs tied by stock options to the same interest as investors in increasing the value of the company—work to shareholders' advantage? For two reasons. First, it was too short-term oriented—CEOs compensation was tied to short-term share price, so that when a bubble began, CEOs rushed successfully to take advantage of it, leaving investors holding shares when the bubble burst and share prices tumbled. Second, it wasn't really performance related. CEOs found ways to get rich without the company performing well. CEOs who were asked to leave firms because the companies weren't doing well were nonetheless given large severance packages. Furthermore, CEOs who could fool their boards used accounting fraud to get large compensation awards, and then left as the true stories came out and the companies collapsed. Again investors were left holding the bag.

In summary, what appeared to be a unity of interest between top executives and shareholders created by performance-based stock option grants wasn't that at all. The actual incentive was for top executives to get rich by manipulating a company's performance so that its short-term stock price rose and his/her options could be cashed in for a fortune. What happened to the company afterward was of no interest to the executives.

Is Alignment of CEO and Shareholder Interests Possible?

During the 1950s, 1960s, and 1970s, the interests of CEOs and shareholders were not aligned, it had been charged. The ownership of the corporation by investors, their exercise of oversight through a board of directors elected solely by shareholders and with the power to hire and fire CEOs, was insufficient to create an identity of interest. So a major change took place in executive compensation in order to create proper alignment. Instead of oversight by a board of directors, reliance was placed in a new sort of compensation package for top executives. What oversight by a board of directors couldn't do, incentives were intended to accomplish—an identity of interest between CEO and shareholder. And the result? As the 21st century opens we are again experiencing CEOs enriching themselves at the expense of shareholders. We are back to square one. In more than 50 years of effort, we have two false starts and still haven't gotten it right. Is it not possible to align CEO and investor interest?

Talking Points

The flood of corporate scandals was occasioned by incentive stock options for executives that began to be widespread in the late 1980s and 1990s in large, publicly held companies. Large option grants gave CEOs and other top executives strong incentive to raise the share price not by increasing the long-term value of their companies but by manipulating its short-term stock performance.

Many executives were cashing their options in the bull market and amassing fortunes, knowing that their companies were in bad shape. Others were given substantial severance packages, even when their companies were going bankrupt. Executives were making fortunes whether their shareholders won or lost.

The intentions behind stock option-heavy executive pay packages seemed reasonable. Theoreticians urged that giving generous stock options to executives would align executive and shareholder interests: if executives had a substantial equity stake in the company, they would want to get rich and would do things that would also make the investors rich. But it didn't work that way. Investor proponents of the system didn't foresee that a generous stock option package would cause CEOs to have a very different interest than investors—nudging up the price of a company's stock in virtually any way possible for a short period during which the executives could cash in. What happened to investors was then no longer a matter of interest to them.

The intent was that incentive options in executive pay would reward a CEO when the shareholders of a company did well. Instead, executives devised numerous means by which options paid off regardless of what happened to longer-term investors in the companies. Included among these devices were failure to index options, rigging of the market, and the prevalence of repricing and rescissions. In the recent stock market boom and bust, top executives made themselves winners, often at the expense of investors.

6 Osama Bin Andersen: The Role of the Accountants

MODERN FINANCIAL DEFINITIONS

EBIT—Earnings before irregularities and tampering
CEO—Chief embezzlement officer
CFO—corporate fraud officer
NAV—normal Anderson valuation
P/E—parole entitlement
EPS—eventual prison sentence

One of the most unexpected results of the current turmoil in the financial services sector is the sudden public prominence of a profession long regarded as staid and uninteresting by most Americans. According to a widely told story, Osama bin Laden sadly told his confidants, "If I'm to do real damage to America, I've got to give up terrorism and become an accountant."

Why has this happened? In brief, it's because during the past decade America's top accounting firms have abandoned investors and instead supported their corporate clients in deception. Accountants have ignored accounting irregularities, helped conceal irregularities (destroying important documents; instructing employees to comply with client management's wishes, whatever they are) and made favorable interpretations for clients at the borderline on accounting issues.

It appears that the basic objective of accounting changed during the 1990s from revealing to concealing. What had been a control in the system to ensure shareholders that employees were acting honestly and that financial reports were complete and accurate ceased to function reliably. Instead, CEOs found their accountants to be allies in the attempt to exaggerate companies' financial performance.

Accountants used to try to be honest scorekeepers; during the 1990s they instead became players in the game. They set special purpose entities to help companies hide debt from investors; they helped firms devise effective tax strategies to funnel more money into cash flow and thence into executives' pockets. As players, they sought more of the winnings from the game, and in the process lost their credibility as scorekeepers.

It's possible to mislead so readily with financial statements because, despite the implication in the public discussion that accounting is a fairly precise discipline, it is in fact a sequence of judgments. There is much less precision than the notion of audits suggests to most investors. Because of the complexity of business, broad latitude is granted by accounting rules. American accounting rules aren't the rigid set of specifications they're ordinarily portrayed to be—at least not entirely. Instead, they have the flexibility needed to accommodate a changing business environment, while always seeking first to inform and thereby protect the investor.

Managers must provide a basic set of accounts and backup information, but they have much discretion in choice of accounting method, what to disclose, what voluntary information to provide, and whether to disclose the firm's economic status honestly or to portray it in a more favorable fashion than the truth justifies.[105] But the purpose of the latitude given managers and their accountants is to provide as much accurate information to the investor as possible—not to provide as little as possible or, even worse, to mislead. Somehow in the past two decades accountants have switched sides and joined with executives and banks to mislead investors. Once this happened the necessary discretionary power of accounting procedures worked against investors.

There are some surprising guidelines in the accountants' "Code of Professional Conduct" and in federal case law covering what auditors can and cannot sign off on when they audit companies' financial statements. U.S. accounting standards are rule based, such that companies like Enron can engage in hypertechnical compliance with GAAP while still misleading investors. Section 203 of the "Code of Professional Conduct," however, states essentially that this isn't acceptable. Auditors, the Code says, must on occasion depart from GAAP if that is necessary to avoid misleading the public. Floyd Norris of the *New York Times* calls this perhaps the most ignored rule in all of accounting. Furthermore, an important ruling issued by Judge Henry Friendly in the U.S. Court of Appeals in 1970 said essentially the same thing. Judge Friendly found three auditors guilty of fraud for certifying financial statements that technically complied with GAAP but that were nevertheless misleading to investors.[106]

There are problems with GAAP (including, for example, the current accounting for executive incentive stock options) that we've discussed, but the guidelines as a whole are not so much flawed as they are improperly interpreted and applied. Why did accountants switch sides—and go from being professionals whom companies were required to engage to give investors confidence in the companies' financial reports, to being collaborators with management in misleading investors? The answer must be complex, but it appears to consist of three principal elements:

- Opportunities for financial gain
- Competition for business
- A decline in professional ethics

Specifically, in the past two decades consulting has emerged as a major business in America, and each major accounting firm has a large consulting unit. Not surprisingly, large corporations are potential clients for both auditing and consulting services. Accounting firms offered both services to their clients and developed lucrative consulting practices. That this arrangement created a potential conflict of interest—that accounting firms might be tempted to do favors for their audit clients in order to get their consulting business—didn't seem to bother either the accounting firms or their clients.

And for a variety of reasons, auditing services became more competitive. Accounting firms saw audit fees falling and price competition increasing, so that to get audit engagements, valued for both their own fees and for the opportunities for consulting contracts that accompanied them, firms were willing to humor client requests for creative solutions to accounting issues. That these accommodations by auditors to corporate clients were at the expense of investors didn't seem to bother the accounting firms or their clients.

Finally, riches seem to have overwhelmed ethical considerations at accounting firms. As a profession, accounting is largely self-regulated. Yet during the bull market accountants accepted conflicts of interest and questionable accounting decisions as routine. They lobbied strongly in Washington on behalf of these practices and gained a reputation as arrogant, stubborn, and unethical in support of their own interests.

Peer Review

And what about the auditing profession? Does it try to monitor itself? From 1977 to 2002 the auditing profession in the United States had a self-policing system, called a "peer review" system. Once every three years each of the firms that audited publicly traded companies was to be reviewed by another auditing firm. The reviews required an assessment of whether the auditing firm in question had proper quality control procedures and whether it followed them. (Practically speaking, the peer review system covered only a handful of auditing firms. In recent years almost all publicly traded companies in the United States were audited by the so-called Big Five: Arthur Andersen, Ernst & Young, PricewaterhouseCoopers, Deloitte & Touche, and KPMG.)

During the 25 years of its existence, the peer review system didn't produce a single negative report on any auditor. In December 2001, in fact, a report on Arthur Andersen's work (for the year ending August 31, 2001) was submitted by Deloitte & Touche, and the report concluded that Andersen's system of auditing quality had "been deemed to provide reasonable assurance of compliance with professional standards" following what Andersen called "the most extensive peer review in the firm's history." In early 2000 the SEC's chief accountant examined a review that PricewaterhouseCoopers had done of KPMG and found numerous violations of auditing standards by KPMG. He wrote to the head of the peer review's Oversight Board about this. He noted that the Oversight Board's staff had told SEC officials "the findings of the KPMG peer review were the worst results from a large firm peer review it had seen in 15 years." Nevertheless, the PricewaterhouseCoopers report had given KPMG a clean bill of health.[107]

Clearly, the peer review system of the auditing profession in this country hasn't worked. As a result, Congress replaced it in the summer of 2002 with an oversight board to be appointed by the SEC.

Deceiving Investors Legally

So far we have talked about outright violations of accounting and auditing standards. There are other things companies do, however, that strictly speaking don't violate the law but nevertheless misrepresent their financial performance and condition. It is well known that many companies "manage" their earnings—for example, by over- or underaccruing for various expenses on the grounds that accruals are based on estimates anyway. Much more serious is the practice of devising technically intricate ways of getting around the rules.

For example, one of the devices Enron concocted with its auditor worked to set up various partnerships or "special-purpose entities" that allowed the company to keep debt off of its balance sheet. Some of these arrangements turned out to be illegal, but some of them, strictly speaking, complied with the law, even though they served to deceive investors. Lynn Turner, who was the chief accountant at the SEC in the late 1990s, has described very plainly what goes on behind the scenes. Turner abhors the games that accountants play, but he nevertheless knows the world where they go on: for years he was a partner at one of the major auditing firms, and he has also served as chief financial officer of an international manufacturer of computer products. In spring 2002 Turner was interviewed on a nationally televised program about the accounting scandals being uncovered.[108]

Turner said that what happened in recent years was that "a relationship developed between Wall Street and the accounting firms whereby, just as soon as a new rule came out—for example, what you have to show on your balance sheet as debt—Wall Street and the accounting firms would get together and see if they couldn't figure out…a way to get around the rule: not break it, but yet certainly not comply with its intent" and thus "hide things from investors." The interviewer asked him (in italics below with his response following):

> *What kinds of things were being done when you were working on Wall Street for an accounting firm?*
>
> "All of the Big Five accounting firms have a group of accountants kind of like a financial services group, and that group of accountants works with Wall Street. In my prior life, we actually had a retainer arrangement with each of the major Wall Street investment banking firms under which we would help them financially engineer or structure hypothetical transactions for finding financing, keeping it off balance sheet, making companies look better than, quite frankly, they really were."
>
> *You mean doing the kinds of things that Enron and Andersen did?*
>
> "Yes. Exactly."
>
> *So there's a whole system that does this?*
>
> "A system that turns around and does it. Without a doubt."
>
> *And all of the big accounting firms have that?*
>
> "Yes. Every one of the big accounting firms has such a group…."
>
> *So, in Enron, we haven't just stumbled into something that may have happened. We've run into something that is a fairly common practice?*
>
> "This is day-to-day business operations in accounting firms and on Wall Street. There is nothing extraordinary, nothing unusual in that respect with respect to Enron."

An Insidious Dynamic Develops

In the wake of the collapse of Arthur Andersen, however, some people have a hard time understanding why those in charge there would have allowed the firm to become complicit in accounting fraud at so many companies. The same question probably applies to the other big auditing firms as well. One would think that senior managers of a professional services firm would understand that having a good reputation is crucial to the business.

Indeed, leaders in the investment community have argued in recent years that any problem with the quality of audits in the United States would be self-correcting. Alan Greenspan, the chairman of the Federal Reserve, for example, admitted that his view had always been that "accountants basically knew, or had to know, that the market value of their companies rested on the integrity of their operations, and that indeed [the] signature that they put on an audit form is where the net worth of the company comes from. And that, therefore, their self-interest is so strongly directed at making certain that their reputation was unimpeachable, that regulation by government was utterly unnecessary, indeed, most inappropriate."

In the summer of 2002, before a Congressional committee, Greenspan added: "I was wrong. I was really, deeply distressed to find that actions were being taken which very clearly indicated a lack of awareness of where the market value of accounting is."[109]

Greenspan and many other people failed to understand how deeply the culture of American business had changed and how the decline of ethical standards in American business had accelerated. In early 2002, an Arthur Andersen competitor provided one possible explanation of why Andersen had tolerated incidents of accounting fraud in one company after another in recent years. When Andersen agreed to pay some tens of millions of dollars in fines for its involvement in accounting fraud at Sunbeam and Waste Management, for example, this observer surmises that its accountants didn't view that as a serious problem or think that it would hurt them in the market. On the contrary, they probably viewed it as good business strategy: The fines weren't a lot of money for a firm with $9 billion a year in revenue, and news about the illegality attracts other clients who also want a soft touch from their auditor.[110] Plus, people in the accounting firms no doubt believed that in most cases they could get away with this sort of thing.

Another reason for the decline of the ethics of auditing standards is a big change that took place in auditors' monetary incentives. For decades major auditing firms had an image of probity, associated with their fundamental task of providing investors a reasonable assurance of the quality of financial information that companies published. "Auditor independence" was a critical part of this assurance. In the 1990s, however, the lure of greater financial gain took over. The auditing job came increasingly to be seen as a kind of commodity that could be used to leverage all sorts of other commercial possibilities.

The most significant of these new commercial possibilities was consulting services. Increasingly, the major auditing firms provided their clients not only with an audit of their financial statements but also with consulting services related to taxes, information technology, business valuation, mergers and acquisitions, and human resource management. Large, publicly traded companies in recent years paid their auditors, on average, three times as much for consulting services as they did for auditing work. (In 2000 Sprint paid Ernst & Young $2.5 million for audit work and $63.8 million for nonaudit work; Motorola paid KPMG $3.9 million for audit work and $62.3 million for nonaudit work; J.P. Morgan paid PricewaterhouseCoopers $21.3 million for audit work and $84.2 million for nonaudit work.)[111]

One auditor who rose quickly in the ranks at Arthur Andersen would give rousing speeches to his subordinates, designed to inspire them to sell all sorts of nonaudit work to their audit clients. (In one speech he had a violinist accompany him as he told auditors to think of themselves as "maestros.") In 1998 he implemented what he called his "2X strategy," which meant that audit partners were supposed to bring in two times their audit fees in nonaudit work, and auditors were judged against this "2X" standard in their performance reviews. He also told auditors how to "empathize" with their clients.[112]

Thus an insidious dynamic developed. Auditors said to companies, in effect: "We'll give you what you need most—a blessing on your financial statements—if you give us what we are most interested in—a lot of money for consulting work." The big drugstore chain, Rite Aid, for example, engaged in massive accounting fraud in recent years. (It had admitted overstating profits by more than $1 billion over two years.) A shareholder suit claimed that the company's longtime auditor, KPMG, identified numerous deficiencies in the company's accounting. In one incident the company's CEO and president allegedly met with two senior KPMG officials as questions about the company's accounting practices were mounting: The CEO said to the KPMG officials, "I'll do whatever you need to make things work out OK," and gave the firm $1.5 million of new consulting work. KPMG gave the company a clean opinion as to the accuracy of its financial reports.[113]

In early 2001 Arthur Andersen executives strongly considered dropping Enron as a client because they were concerned about serious accounting irregularities and conflicts of interest for executives in the company, but they decided not to break off the relationship because they felt they could manage their "engagement risks" and because they saw the potential for Enron to become a $100 million account. (In 2000 Enron was a $52 million account for Andersen: it paid Andersen $25 million for audit work and $27 million for consulting work.)

In 2000 the then-head of the SEC, Arthur Levitt, tried to eliminate this conflict of interest between auditing and consulting. He sought passage of a new rule that would prohibit auditors from doing consulting work for their audit clients, but he was frustrated by an intense lobbying effort that the major auditing firms mounted in Congress. (The major auditing firms gave $23 million in campaign contributions to members of both parties in Congress in recent years.)

Other Commercial Ventures

Other kinds of commercial ventures have also compromised the principles of auditor independence. Auditors aren't supposed to invest in the companies they audit. In 2000, however, the SEC found that large numbers of the audit partners at PricewaterhouseCoopers were doing just that. The SEC then asked the auditing profession's Oversight Board, in 2000, to review systems in place at all the Big Five auditing firms to ensure that they don't invest in audit clients. In spring 2002 the chairman of the Oversight Board said that it hadn't yet been able to complete the task due to stalling by the Big Five firms.[114]

Auditors naturally shouldn't be doing business with a company they audit. Ernst & Young, however, for years had a partnership with one of its audit clients, PeopleSoft, to develop and market payroll and tax withholding software. As many as 1,000 of Ernst & Young's employees were installing PeopleSoft products at other businesses, many of which were themselves Ernst & Young audit clients. Arthur Andersen did the same thing with SAP, a German software company whose securities were traded in the United States. Andersen employees not only installed SAP software at other businesses; they also toured the United States with SAP sales representatives to help promote it.[115]

The "Integrated Audit"

At Enron, starting in 1993, Arthur Andersen pioneered what it called the "integrated audit," which enabled it not only to be Enron's external auditor but also to do a lot of Enron's internal auditing, while at the same time also providing Enron with all sorts of consulting services. An Andersen partner began traveling to Andersen offices all over the world promoting the concept of the integrated audit.

Auditor independence, the ability of external auditors to provide a reasonably unbiased assessment of companies' financial statements for investors, went by the boards.[116] Over 100 Andersen auditors and consultants had permanent offices at Enron's headquarters in Houston. Andersen people attended Enron meetings and helped shape new businesses. They shared in office birthdays, lunchtime parties in a nearby park, and weekend fund-raisers for charities. They wore Enron golf shirts. They even went on Enron employees' ski trips to Beaver Creek, Colorado. "People just thought they were Enron employees," said one Enron employee who worked in accounting. "They walked and talked the same way." An Andersen auditor who worked in Enron's offices said: "Out here we don't call audit, audit." Jeffrey Skilling, Enron's president, said in a videotape recorded a few years ago: "I think over time we and Arthur Andersen will probably mesh our systems and processes even more so that they are more seamless between the two organizations."

An Andersen employee said his firm handled things the way it did at Enron because there was a lot of money to be made. Besides, he said, the other major auditing firms would have done the same thing.

Widespread but Not Ubiquitous

The important qualification to all this is that there are a good many certified public accountants in and out of the large accounting firms who are as angry about what has happened with auditing practices in this country as are investors.

A Scapegoat

Arthur Andersen was one of America's longest-lived and largest accounting firms. It was, however, the auditor for Enron, WorldCom, Global Crossing, and Sunbeam. When the Enron scandal broke, Andersen destroyed records that the government alleged were relevant to its investigation of the company. It charged Andersen with obstruction of justice, took the company to trial, and won a conviction. In the aftermath of its conviction, Andersen collapsed.

Each of the major accounting firms was involved in the subordination of accounting standards to the goal of deceiving investors, but only Andersen has been significantly punished. There is a legal explanation that is illuminating without being sufficient. It is that alone among the firms Andersen had already been convicted of several violations of securities laws and was operating under consent degrees to stop such actions when it destroyed records at Enron. After its trial, Andersen was the only firm to have been convicted of a criminal violation, not a civil one. But this is an answer relying on technicalities.

The fact is that the surviving large accounting firms were nearly as much if not equally involved in the same kinds of conflicts of interest and efforts at corporate concealment, but they've been punished little if at all, and in fact have benefited from Andersen's demise by raiding its former clients and personnel. Once a well-respected firm, Arthur Andersen changed greatly in ways that led to its collapse in the midst of several scandals. What happened at Andersen is likely suggestive of what has happened at other accounting firms, though they've yet to pay the penalty Andersen has paid.

Becoming an Arthur

Like all accounting firms Arthur Andersen was a partnership, not a corporation, the structure growing out of investors' insistence that auditors take personal responsibility for their assurances that the financial records of clients were accurate. Until the late 1970s it had a strong culture. People in the firm referred to themselves as "Arthurs," and spoke of themselves as having a "rich uncle"—the firm. Andersen was also a highly integrated firm. It hired graduates of midwestern schools, preferring them for their strong values and hard work, and training them itself rather than seeking perhaps better-educated people from eastern schools. Individuals were encouraged not to stand out but instead to fit into a large and well-functioning organization.

But by the 1980s Andersen had begun to change. It dropped "hard work" from the official list of company values. It set up incubators for Internet startups, believing that they would provide financial gains and help the people in the company become more innovative and less conservative. Its audit partners drew very close to their clients, helping them with their desires to inflate sales and profits and conceal debt in order to retain clients and add consulting work. In all this Andersen was transforming itself to participate in a more competitive market for audits and to make financial gains in nontraditional ways.

Talking Points

During the past decade America's top accounting firms have become willing participants in a widespread deception of investors, and of themselves too, which is both ironic and significant sometimes extending to overt fraud. Instead of ensuring clarity and accuracy of financial reports, they have aided executives in exaggerating their companies' financial performance. Motivated by financial gain and competition for business, accounting firms have largely abandoned their responsibility to investors and the ethics that supported it. They've been able to do so partly because the peer review system the auditing profession had in place didn't work.

In addition to outright violations of accounting rules, many corporations found "creative" ways to deceive investors without actually breaking the law. With the help of their auditors, they devised intricate schemes to keep debt off their balance sheets or do other things to manage their earnings and mislead investors about the true status of a firm's finances.

III The Failure of Checks and Balances

I grew up in a small rural town called Williamson, New York.

I am a descendent of slaves. This is my story. I have worked 31 years at the phone company. I raised two children all by myself and I never asked assistance for one penny, because I didn't have to. To me, $86,000 to supplement my pension was like having a million dollars. I was so proud of myself. I thought for sure with Global Crossing buying Frontier I would reach my goal of $100,000 so that my retirement years would be comfortable years, and I even could leave something for my children. That's why I held on, believing the statements a Global Crossing executive made when the stock was failing. Tom Casey sent an e-mail telling us the company was fully funded for two years and could weather the storm. Joe Clayton sent an e-mail saying that the *Wall Street Journal* was wrong about Global Crossing's debt. The company filed for bankruptcy in January 2002, leaving us shareholders holding the empty bag. Now, I have sadly lost my entire retirement money. Shattered are my dreams of having a modest retirement in Florida in a lovely retirement community called The Villages, where I had visited and had looked at a model home.

—Testimony of Lennette Crumpler, a 31-year employee of the Frontier phone company, which Global Crossing acquired in the 1990s (Hearing of the Oversight and Investigations Subcommittee of the House Energy and Commerce Committee, October 1, 2002, Federal News Service)

7 Neither Prevent nor Punish

"Do you want to hear the bad news first, or the very bad news?"

—Call from a broker to an investor

"The US system of corporate governance presumes that directors, accountants, equity analysts, investment banks, accountants, and regulators are all independent of both management and each other. During the past decade this independence was replaced by a rather incestuous relationship..."[117]

—Richard Katz

The extensive checks and balances that exist in America's financial system did not work in the scandals cited in Chapter 2. Is it likely that they worked in the cases of all other corporations? Certainly not. But if not, how did it happen?

Once-trusted institutions—accounting firms, banks, brokerage houses, and law firms—that used to be able to put their imprimatur on what corporations told the public so that investors had confidence in financial reports, failed to meet their responsibilities, and so today are increasingly discredited. Their default on their responsibility is the result of what is rather like a conspiracy—tacit though it may be in many instances—of the major leaders in the securities industry to benefit themselves rather than investors. And as private institutions failed to protect investors, they persuaded government regulators to look the other way.

Rubber Stamps—Boards of Directors

Often corporate boards of directors failed completely to restrain executives from misleading investors and enriching themselves. Some directors joined in, making fortunes, others good fees, while investors did poorly. To a degree boards acted as rubber stamps for CEOs; they failed to exercise close oversight of management; and they curried favor with CEOs by approving exorbitant executive pay packages in order to retain their positions as directors.

In some of the major scandals reviewed in Chapter 1, board members denied being aware of the various accounting and compensation gimmicks that are now at issue. But as further investigation proceeds, it is turning out that generally boards or their appropriate committees were fully aware of what was happening. For example, although Tyco's board initially denied knowing about the CEO's pay package, which included loans from the company and which was later described by prosecutors as looting of the firm, it turns out that the board's compensation committee was aware of the relevant details.[118]

The point is that CEOs normally didn't have to conceal from corporate boards actions that benefited themselves, because the boards were ready to comply with whatever the CEOs wanted. In case after case, the boards were aware of CEOs' actions but permitted the executives to enrich themselves anyway. The means by which CEOs keep board members supine include perks such as plane rides, fees, support for their favorite projects, flattering attention, consulting fees, and so on.[119] The boards were in the hands of the CEO and were not effective checks and balances for shareholders.

Perhaps boards were compliant because what benefited CEOs was apparently benefiting directors as well. All through the bull market boards paid themselves with stock options. Even in 2001, a year after the bull market had ended, boards paid themselves primarily with stock grants (21% of directors' pay packages) and stock options (41% of directors' pay packages)—a total of 62% of directors' pay packages.[120] In 2000 and 2001, in the midst of the collapse of the bull market, boards raised their average compensation by about 15%.[121] Directors also found other ways to profit from their roles. For example, "Frank Walsh, a former director of Tyco, took home a 20 million dollar fee for brokering its purchase of CIT."[122] A U.S. Senate subcommittee report issued in early July 2002 concluded that the Enron board was derelict in its "paramount duty" to safeguard shareholder interests.

Since accounting subterfuges were at the heart of many corporate scandals, the audit committee of each board was the place where investors should have found protection from deception. Generally, audit committees are made up only of outside directors. They can and should be a major check and balance on management. The audit committee usually receives a report from the company's auditors, and meets with the accounting firm partners who do the audit for the company. The company's CFO usually attends this meeting. Then the audit committee ordinarily meets separately with the partners from the accounting firm (without any company executives present). The committee asks two questions: First, how effectively is the company's finance and internal audit function staffed and operating, and second, is there anything else the audit committee should know about the company, its finances, other activities, the executive team, the accounts, the audits, and so on. This confidential meeting should be the key to discovering any fraud or questionable practices in the company. Following this procedure, an audit committee doesn't have to know everything about a company and can be a very effective check on management.

However, when an accounting firm's audit team is in cahoots with the company's management, as in the case of Enron, it's tough for an audit committee of the board to ferret out what's going on. The auditors in this situation give management a clean bill of health about the company's financial reports and, when given the opportunity to blow the whistle privately on any misdoings, say nothing.

It's possible that the complexity of accounting regulations and of some aspects of modern business transactions make accounting judgments debatable. But these should be talked out between a company's audit committee and its accountants. When both company directors and company auditors are trying to provide full disclosure to investors, these sorts of issues are not that difficult. But where there is an intent to conceal, then complexity becomes an excuse for decisions that are to the disadvantage of investors. This has been happening on a very large scale in American business.

Protection for Deception: The Role of the Attorneys

Much has been revealed by the scandals about how the companies they own operate, which investors didn't understand. Among the biggest surprises is that attorneys in firms routinely advise clients on how to hide information from regulators that could reveal violations of law and often go further to assist top executives when they get into legal difficulties. At Enron, an internal memo to destroy documents was found by a jury to constitute obstruction of justice, but to the surprise of many legal professors who defended the practice as routine.

Thus investors got a small peek into the role of attorneys in a large, publicly held American corporation. It's standard practice for attorneys to write memos to executives in a company advising them how to evade the requirements of the law in ways that can be made arguably, technically legal. Furthermore, attorneys advise executives to destroy files, to not put things in writing, to change words that might reveal too much—all in the interest of doing business not within the law, but without being caught by the law. Since much of the law that executives are advised to evade is regulation intended to defend shareholders from fraud, this is a disturbing revelation to investors. In fact, these practices by attorneys are at the core of what's wrong with today's corporate culture—it's one of legalistic deception instead of being one of openness, disclosure, and compliance.

In a book published in the mid-1990s bemoaning the decline of ethics and trust in America's legal profession, Sol Linowitz noted that attorneys once thought of themselves as keepers of the corporate conscience. But following a long, slow decline in the profession's standards of ethics, rationalized in part as providing ever better service to its clients, the American Bar Association in 1992 modified its model rules to prevent attorneys withdrawing from representing their clients even when the client was acting in violation of the law, "except when the action was likely to result in substantial injury to the organization." Thus, it would seem that if the client company is likely to get away with its crime, then its attorney must assist it.[123]

Some American corporations hire attorneys not to help them understand the law in order to abide by it, but rather to help them twist the law so that they can evade it. They hire attorneys not to defend them with the truth when they are falsely charged, but rather to defend them with lies when they are justly accused. This is true unfortunately in all American institutions today. This is especially inappropriate since corporate attorneys represent the company and its owners, the shareholders, rather than corporate executives. So when attorneys assist executives in committing fraud they are failing to represent their true clients, the shareholders, and may not even be protected by attorney–client privilege with respect to their communications with executives. The chairman of the SEC forcibly reminded attorneys of this at a session of the American Bar Association in summer 2002.

There's more to it than this. A corporate prospectus today is hardly more than a dozen pages listing the risks associated with investing in the company. This is the case because the attorneys who prepare the documents are trying to protect the firm from possible shareholder suits. And when a company files its reports, it tries to give good news and say as little more as possible, again trying to avoid suits. The result is that companies give less disclosure than our investment markets require if investors are to make intelligent choices.

It's a vicious circle. Investors get defrauded so they sue; companies try to avoid suits by providing less information. With less information, investors make poorer investment decisions, and then feel compelled to sue; and companies clam up further. Attorneys are now woven so deeply into the relationships between companies and investors that they are dictating much of the dialogue. They will continue to do so as the current wave of shareholder suits occasioned by the scandals and by enormous investor losses makes its way into the courts.

The Failure of the Regulators

It's disturbing that American law neither prevented nor punished the corporate excesses that so damaged investors. America has a large body of law and a plethora of governmental and private organizations regulating our financial markets. Among them are the SEC, the Fed, the Treasury Department, the Labor Department, the Attorney General, the attorneys general of the states, the stock exchanges, and others. Furthermore, Congress itself looks at financial markets in what is sometimes astonishing detail—either via legislation or by stopping regulatory initiatives. It's very discouraging that investors were unable to rely on any of these organizations to protect them from a decade of scandals. How this happened should be the subject of a book in itself. Here we point to only a few of the most striking failures of the system.

Broadly speaking, regulators are able to protect investors in two different ways: either from specific actions of fraud, such as occurred at Enron, WorldCom, and other firms, or from the overall situation in which frauds take place, as for example in the stock market bubble as a whole. In deflating a bubble, regulators protect investors in two ways: by lessening the incentives for executives to mislead investors, and by lessening the temptation for investors to jump into what appears to be a market that is growing without limit.

What the Prosecutors, Courts, and the SEC Didn't Do

It's peculiar that regulators didn't do more to protect investors since American law prohibits much of what occurred, including the most egregious of the scandals—the very large compensation some CEOs received via stock options, salaries, and bonuses from companies the share price for which later collapsed.

Corporate law in Delaware, the state in which most American companies are incorporated (though for that matter the corporate laws of most states are very similar to Delaware's) spells out top executives' fiduciary responsibility to shareholders and implements that responsibility via three duties, or in legalese "equitable limitations" upon the actions of executives and directors. The three are as follows: First, a duty of care requires that executives and directors read documents and, in effect, do their homework. Second, a duty of loyalty requires that executives and directors not prefer their own interests to those of a company or its shareholders, so as not to enrich themselves at others' expense. Third, a duty of disclosure requires that executives and directors tell shareholders of all material facts. A failure of any of these duties is a failure of fiduciary responsibility—a failure of equitable action.

CEO compensation is subject to two tests under the duty of loyalty. First, is it reasonable compared to what is paid CEOs in similar-sized firms in the same industry? Second, is it related to and reflective of performance by the CEO? In many recent instances CEO compensation was far beyond what others received and was paid despite the company's failing. Furthermore, because the CEO often appointed the outside board members who made up the firm's compensation committee, was a friend of each, and was in a position to reward each, there was not the arms-length relationship that gave a likelihood of legitimacy to grants of compensation to the CEO. Hence, when CEOs enriched themselves at the cost of the investors in a company, a violation of the CEOs' duty of loyalty to the company and its shareholders apparently had occurred.

Insider trading would seem to be illegal under the duty of loyalty. Privileged information is the property of a corporation, and its executives and directors are not permitted to use the property of the firm to enrich themselves. The misleading accounting that has become so common is apparently prohibited by the duty of disclosure, which requires honest reporting to shareholders.

The Security and Exchange Act of the United States at Section 10B5 prohibits executives and directors of firms from deceiving shareholders. The exchanges, particularly the New York Stock Exchange and the NASDAQ, have listing regulations—that is, a firm can't be listed for trading on the exchanges unless it complies with regulations that provide for standards of corporate governance. Under criminal law it is illegal to use the mail or wires to defraud (that is, to send false information intended to deceive investors via the post office or by fax). Finally, it is illegal to make false filings with the SEC.

In essence, most of the actions of the leaders of firms that became fuel for the scandals of the past few years are arguably violations of existing state or federal law. But corporate leaders chose to skate at the very edges of the law, hoping that investors would not notice what they were doing, or that their actions could either be defended in court or made prohibitively expensive for shareholders to challenge.

And while share prices were rising in the boom of the late 1990s, few investors were likely to quibble with what executives and directors were doing. If we review some of the scandals recounted in Chapter 2, we'd see that:

- At Enron, the company's off-balance sheet entities benefiting executives of the firm were a violation of the duty of loyalty. Misreporting of revenue was a violation of the duty of disclosure.
- CEOs and directors insisting that they didn't know what was happening at a company was a violation of the duty of care.
- At Adelphia, secret loans of more than $3 billion made by the company to executives were violations of the duty of disclosure.
- At WorldCom, misreporting operating expenses as capital expenses in order to inflate reported profits was a violation of the duty of loyalty and the duty of disclosure.

- At Global Crossing, enormous CEO compensation in a company on its way to bankruptcy was a violation of the duty of loyalty.
- At ImClone, insider trading before bad news sunk the company's share price was a violation of the duty of loyalty.

As to the criminal acts of individual corporations and executives, the law tries to prevent fraud, but its enforcement is ultimately in the hands of men and women—regulators, prosecutors, and politicians—and often the laws are simply not enforced. For example, the SEC didn't review Enron's books for three crucial years before the scandal broke.

Regulators are sometimes constrained by budget limitations, sometimes by provisions of the law about gathering evidence and the attitude of the courts to white-collar crime, and sometimes by elected officials who protect corporate malefactors. Our political system permits officials to solicit campaign contributions from business executives, and it's no surprise that many of the executives who did the most to defraud investors were also among the most active contributors to politicians.

Warren Buffet has pointed to the links between accounting scandals and the federal government:

> Indeed, actions by Congress and the Securities and Exchange Commission have the potential of creating a smoke screen that will prevent real accounting reform. The Senate itself is the major reason corporations have been able to duck option expensing. On May 3, 1994, the Senate, led by Senator Joseph Lieberman, pushed the Financial Accounting Standards Board and Arthur Levitt, then chairman of the SEC, into backing down from mandating that options be expensed. Mr. Levitt has said that he regrets this retreat more than any other move he made during his tenure as chairman. Unfortunately, current SEC leadership seems uninterested in correcting this matter. I don't believe in Congress setting accounting rules. But the Senate opened the floodgates in 1994 to an anything-goes reporting system, and it should close them now. Rather than holding hearings and fulminating, why doesn't the Senate just free the standards board by rescinding its 1994 action?[124]

Some senators still attempt to protect anything-goes executives. In spring 2002, Senator Phil Graham, husband of an Enron director, tried to kill the Corporate Reform bill in the Senate and almost succeeded, voicing astonishment when other senators, reacting to an outraged public, passed the bill, which he then supported.

But in fairness it must be said that a *Wall Street Journal* investigative team looked into who on Capitol Hill had received shares in hot IPOs from investment banks and came up with a list of three senators and three representatives. If this is accurate, then it seems to be a remarkably small group from the almost 600 senators and congresspersons.[125]

The New York Stock Exchange and the National Association of Securities Dealers are also important regulators of honesty in corporate reporting. But in an environment in which there was so much dishonesty, it's not surprising that key figures in these organizations were also involved. For example, the chairman of the New York Stock Exchange was a board member of Computer Associates, a company that produced misleading financial reporting, and failed to disclose his ownership of deferred stock in the company.[126]

What the Fed Didn't Do

It was striking in recent years that the scale upon which corporations misled investors became so great that the entire system suffered. The great stock market bubble of the 1990s was not just a matter of investor enthusiasm, it was also inflated by misleading financial information from corporations generally—so that the nation's entire equity markets were distorted. That there was an unjustifiably high valuation in the stock markets was evident to almost all by the mid-1990s, almost four years before the market peaked, and yet those in charge of the nation's economy did nothing about it. They were urged to, but they didn't act.

In the aftermath of the crash, with the economy slowly emerging from one recession and teetering on the edge of another, Chairman Greenspan found it necessary to explain why the Fed had not acted. During the bubble he had suggested that it was a good thing because it was helping people save for their retirement. Now, when so many investors had lost their savings in the bust, he said only that the Fed could have done nothing to help them. According to Mr. Greenspan, anything the Fed might have done would either have been ineffective or would have damaged the economy.[127] "As events evolved," explained Mr. Greenspan, "we recognized that, despite our suspicions, it was very difficult to definitively identify a bubble until after the fact—that is, when its bursting confirmed its existence."

This is a remarkable statement, and it confirms a suspicion created by many of Mr. Greenspan's statements during the 1990s that he was in fact taken in by the illusions created by false financial reports and technological dreaming that the high valuations of the bubble were in fact justified. But this is exactly what the Fed is supposed to have better judgment about.

"Moreover," Mr. Greenspan continued, "it was far from obvious that bubbles, even if identified early, could be preempted short of the central bank inducing a substantial contraction in economic activity, the very outcome we would be seeking to avoid." But, of course, the Fed didn't avoid a contraction by its chosen strategy—to do nothing—and so perhaps having tried to do something might have been useful.

In general, Mr. Greenspan's arguments are not convincing. In response to Mr. Greenspan's remarks, Stephen Cecchetti, former director of research at the Federal Reserve Bank of New York in 1997–99, wrote, "I believe that we are now paying the price for the Fed's failure in the spring of 1997 to ...place a modest brake on growth. With a slower growth forecast, the stock price bubble might have been less extreme."[128]

Mr. Cecchetti is correct, but there's much more to it than that:

1. The Fed knew of the securities market problem and added fuel to the fire. Greenspan referred in 1996 to the "irrational exuberance" of the markets; but he also repeatedly said that the economy was experiencing a new higher level of productivity increase driven by information technology. He even said that pensioners were getting better returns, which would help them in retirement—in other words, the chairman of the Fed participated in the hype that was driving the mania.
2. The Fed used monetary policy to pour fuel on the flames at the height of the bubble. In fall 1999 the Fed increased the money supply to avoid a feared downturn of the economy due to the Y2K issue; then when the Y2K crisis turned out to be an illusion, with the bubble still expanding wildly, the Fed clamped on the brakes in spring 2000, precipitating a collapse in the bubble rather than a slow winding-down.
3. The Fed accepts responsibility for the economy as a whole, and asset bubbles affect it. One in the 1920s helped throw the economy into the Great Depression. All during the 1990s there were bitter debates behind the scenes within each of the Fed banks about whether or not the Fed should take action against asset bubbles. Supporters of intervention pointed to Japan. Greenspan held out for no overt action, and prevailed. The result was a bubble and a bust and a recession.
4. All asset bubbles have as a key component a ready supply of money to finance stock purchases. The Fed was providing this. Increases in margin requirements at the proper time would have helped slow the bubble's inflation.
5. The Fed is also responsible for the nation's banks. In 1999 commercial banks were again allowed into investment banking. Immediately Citi and Chase began to work with their clients, like Enron, to disguise loans from investors via off-balance sheet financing, in order to inflate share prices. This is probably illegal. The Fed had a responsibility to know about and stop this. The Fed should have stopped banks from engaging in deception of investors with their clients. Greenspan had worked for years with Wall Street, the big banks were his clients; he was knowledgeable about the securities markets. He watched the banks take on risky credit, competing with each other to see which could better assist corporate clients to mislead investors about the financial state of their businesses. Then he watched as the banks off-loaded the risk of such loans via syndication onto pension funds and investors via their 401(k)s and other savings plans.[129] The Fed neither pricked the bubble early nor restrained banks in designing loans to help corporations mislead investors. Apparently the Fed let the banks act without restraint because the banks were profiting enormously both via the bubble and the fraud. For investors, however, it is hardly comforting to

learn that deregulation helped the banks strengthen their balance sheets by allowing them to operate unethically, take risks they should not have taken, and then pass them on to unsuspecting investors.

6. And the Fed went further in protecting the banks. For example, on April 21, 1998, Treasury Secretary Robert Rubin told the head of the Commodity Futures Trading Commission, Brooksley Born, that she should not study whether or not financial derivatives needed regulation. Fed chairman Alan Greenspan, who was also in the room, told her that she risked disrupting the capital markets. In late July, Greenspan told the House Banking Committee that Born was getting ready to pick a fight with the capital markets—saying she was contemplating punching them in the nose. Thereafter, when she persisted in wanting to study the matter, Congress passed a six-month moratorium on proposing or adopting derivatives regulation, which covered the end of Born's term.[130] Thus, the regulators made little or no effort to restrain derivative trading. During the same period the collapse of Long Term Capital Management required the Fed's direct intervention to stave off a possible meltdown of international financial markets, caused in large part by derivative trading; and the financial disaster that Enron became got its launch in part due to derivatives. Yet the Fed defends its inaction, some of its defenders even insist there is no problem that the Fed might have tacked. Alan S. Blinder, a Princeton University economist who stepped down as the Fed's vice chairman in 1996, wrote "To those who say the Fed failed to prevent this catastrophe I say, 'What catastrophe?' said Blinder, co-author of *The Fabulous Decade*, a book about the 1990s economy. "As far as I can see, the damage to the real economy and to the financial system has been somewhere between little and none."[131]

Talking Points

Boards of directors failed the shareholders they were supposed to represent. In exchange for monetary gain, flattering perks, and the feeling of inclusion in a club, directors gave up their role as checks and balances benefiting investors. Especially reprehensible was the failure of board audit committees to protect investors from accounting deceptions. Corporate attorneys who supposedly represent a company and its shareholders, not its executives, were more than willing to side with management in helping to twist the law at the expense of shareholders' interest. Finally, regulators failed to protect investors, though most corporate scandals included many actions prohibited by law.

8 Ordinary Business at the Banks

At the bank we designed financial instruments for Enron that were intended to inflate earnings, keep debt off the balance sheet, and pop the stock. The bank hedged on the other side of our business to limit our exposure to Enron by shifting the risk to other firms. The top people knew exactly what they were doing. It was ordinary business.

—An investment banker who preferred not to be identified

Investment banks play a central role in the American securities industry. They supply capital to firms and investment opportunities to the public. They are middlemen and market-makers. During the great bull market they were very active and very profitable. Their executives and partners made large sums of money for themselves. Much of what they did was proper, but some of their actions were at the heart of the scandals.

For example, without admitting wrongdoing, Merrill Lynch settled with the office of the New York attorney general and paid a substantial fine because its analysts knowingly issued misleading recommendations to investors. Apparently this was done to win the investment banking business of the companies being recommended. Investors, however, lost money on the stocks recommended. Investigators found emails written by analysts calling the stocks they themselves had recommended "junk."

Merrill Lynch also assisted Enron by doing deals that permitted Enron to boost reported sales in which it appears that no actual transactions occurred. Merrill got a fee and Enron booked the sales, but nothing except the exchange of papers took place. It appears that last-minute transactions between Enron and Merrill permitted Enron to post financial results that generated large bonuses for its executives.[132] Merrill also helped Enron set up partnerships that served to conceal the company's debt from its investors and provided very substantial fees to Enron executives. Despite the blatant conflict of interest for Enron executives, some 97 executives of Merrill invested in one of Enron's partnerships.[133]

At Citigroup, in addition to its role in scandals involving Enron, WorldCom, and other firms, the firm's leaders pursued their own interests in novel ways. At one point Chairman Sanford I. Weil asked star telecom analyst Jack Grubman to review his not-so-favorable investors' rating on ATT. Grubman complied, raising his recommendation to a buy. In part this was apparently to gain the support of the CEO of ATT, who was a member of Citigroup's board, for Weil's effort to oust John Reed as co-CEO of Citigroup, an effort that succeeded. Furthermore, following Grubman's upgrade of ATT shares, Citigroup's investment banking unit, Salomon Brothers, then got some tens of millions of dollars in investment banking fees from ATT. Months later, when ATT shares had fallen by almost half, Grubman returned to his cautious rating on the stock. Meanwhile, Weil had helped Grubman get his two children into an exclusive Manhattan nursery school, and had given the school a substantial gift from Citigroup funds.

Banks sell services to companies whose stock they also evaluate for investors. A bank is therefore in a position to gain business from companies by making favorable recommendations about their stock, even when the bank's own opinion about the shares is negative. Furthermore, banks lend money to corporations and are in a position to assist firms in hiding loans from shareholders in return for the interest and fees gained on the loans. Therefore, the banks confront a conflict of interest between their responsibilities to investors who are their customers, and their opportunity to gain fees from corporations who are also their clients. We see in the remainder of this chapter that the nation's large investment banks exploited conflicts of interest on a substantial scale—using their research analysts, on whom the public depended for leadership in evaluating corporate performance, to gain investment business by issuing falsely optimistic recommendations about the shares of client or potential client companies, and conniving with corporate clients to hide debt in order to further mislead investors.

Conniving with Corporations to Deceive Investors

It came as a stunning surprise to most investors that banks had been routinely structuring loans for client companies in a way that was intended to hide the debt from investors and regulators. Yet the top executives of the nation's largest banks acknowledged this in the summer of 2002. The CEO of one bank called such deals "Plain vanilla financing—a normal financing arrangement."[134]

The CEO of Citigroup on August 7, 2002, via a letter to its employees, stated that it would no longer provide loans to companies that refuse, or do not intend, to record the financing on their balance sheets or otherwise disclose them to investors. "In addition," said the letter, "we will only do these transactions for clients that agree to provide the complete set of transaction documents to their chief financial officer, chief legal officer, and independent auditors." This confirms by implication what Congressional committees investigating Citigroup's and other banks' involvement with Enron had already made public—that Citigroup was structuring loans to Enron (and presumably other firms) so that they would not appear as loans and were neither placed on the borrower's balance sheets nor disclosed to investors. Furthermore, it indicates how far clients had gone, and how far the bank had acquiesced, to hide these transactions from parties within the client companies—from some CFOs, some chief legal officers, and some independent auditors.[135] Citigroup lent Enron about $4.8 billion over 6 years, using derivatives to off-load all but $1.2 billion that went to investors.[136]

A series of transactions labeled "Yosemite" allowed Enron to disguise billions of dollars of debt while Citigroup was able to convert financing arrangements it made with Enron into securities sold to investors. Congressional "hearings made clear that Citigroup knew the purpose of Yosemite and had its own suspicions about Enron's financial health"—something that Congressional investigators allege makes the bank complicit in Enron's deception. One structure Citigroup created for the energy company "will allow Enron to raise funds without classifying the proceeds from this transaction as debt," according to a Citibank Global Loans Approval Memorandum dated December 21, 1998.[137]

Citigroup's activities were not limited to Enron. It "and other banks, won an assignment in May 2001 to sell an $11.8 billion WorldCom bond offering. Three California state pension funds are suing Citigroup and its fellow bond underwriters for what the funds describe as an illegal conflict of interest. The plaintiffs say in a suit filed earlier this month in a California state court that Citigroup sold bonds to investors so that WorldCom wouldn't draw on its bank credit lines. This allegedly shifted risk from Citigroup and other banks to investors. The funds also claim that in its role as lender, Citigroup should have known about WorldCom's dire financial condition and failed to warn bond buyers. "We will not stand for this breach of ethical conduct," says Jack Ehnes, chief executive of the California State Teachers' Retirement System, one of the plaintiffs.[138]

It appears Citibank was working with its clients to mislead investors about their financial condition. Were the banks accessories, or accomplices, to fraud? It appears as though the CEO of Citicorp all but admitted this in his letter to the employees quoted above. Why did he do so? We can only speculate. But there are three likely explanations.

1. The bank's activities were already so well known in the top echelons of American business that there was no reason for hiding them.

2. The bank has so much money and so many attorneys that it doesn't fear suits.
3. The bank is so well connected to regulators that it doesn't fear adverse action from public authorities.

There's no doubt that the transactions, unethical and possibly illegal, were profitable for the banks. Reports are that Citigroup and JP Morgan Chase made hundreds of millions of dollars in fees from Enron and other energy companies. The structures the banks were promoting to Enron and the energy companies relied on prepaid oil and gas contracts, in which money is paid up front for future delivery of the commodity. Those are common in the industry. But energy companies employed complex circular trades among an offshore entity, the banks and themselves, enabling them to book that cash as part of their trading operations—instead of as debt—and also keep investors in the dark.

To help sell these financing deals, Citigroup and J.P. Morgan developed pitch books about how companies could use their services. One Citigroup presentation, for instance, describes how using such an arrangement "eliminates the need for Capital Markets disclosure, keeping structure mechanics private" and says that "ratings agencies will not view the proceeds raised … as company debt." For its part, J.P. Morgan, in a July 1998 presentation, noted that such structures were "balance sheet 'friendly.'" In one February 1999 e-mail, Adam Kulick, a Citigroup vice president, told colleagues that "the client does not wish to have to explain the details of many of the assets to investors or rating agencies."[139]

A stream of documents (internal company documents from Citigroup and JP Morgan) uncovered in the Congressional investigation provided new details about the extent to which both banks knew Enron was seeking to use the transactions to mask debt as trades. "Enron loves these deals as they are able to hide funded debt from their equity analysts because they (at the very least) book it as deferred rev[enue] or (better yet) bury it in their trading liabilities," one J.P. Morgan executive said in a 1998 e-mail to colleagues.[140]

Not only Citigroup and Chase were involved. Late in December 1977, Enron made a sham energy deal with Merrill Lunch that allowed Enron to book a $60 million profit. The executives said that the energy deal, a complex set of gas and power trades, was intended to inflate Enron's profits and drive up its stock price. Enron and Merrill Lynch, they said, agreed that the deal would be canceled after Enron booked the profits, and it later was.

By allowing the company to meet its internal profit targets, the power deal unleashed the payment of millions of dollars in bonuses and restricted stock to high-ranking executives, including Kenneth L. Lay, then the chief executive, and Jeffrey K. Skilling, then Enron's president, former executives said. "This was absolutely a sham transaction, and it was an 11th hour deal," said one former Enron executive who was briefed on the deal. "We did this deal to get 1999 earnings."[141]

There is likely in the investment banks the sort of cynical calculation of gain and loss made by the accounting firms in which a fine for violation of federal securities laws is seen as a cost of doing business. For example, Citigroup paid a fine of $5 million levied by the National Association of Securities Dealers (NASD) for publicly recommending Winstar (a telecom company mentioned in Chapter 3, in conjunction with Lucent Technologies) while privately urging others to sell. Winstar has gone bankrupt. But Citigroup is reported by the NASD to have earned $24 million in fees for transactions on behalf of Winstar.[142] So Citicorp made $24 million in fees and paid a $5 million fine. The incentive to continue such business is high, so long as it isn't done so often that regulators take a harsher approach.

Thanks to Congressional hearings, investors have been given a peek into the ordinary, bread and butter activities of investment banks with their corporate clients, and it's disturbing. According to top executives of the biggest banks, responding to questions from Congress, it's standard practice for the banks to fashion loans in a way that enables their corporate customers to keep the debt off the company's balance sheet and hide it from investors. It's not illegal, the banks say, so we do it regularly. And apparently the banks just as regularly try to destroy e-mails about this side of their business, although they are required by law to retain the correspondence for a year. Some of the biggest banks are now facing penalties from the SEC and the stock exchanges for destroying e-mail messages.[143]

Greasing the CEO's Palm via IPO Allocations

During the Internet bubble, banks often allocated IPO shares to executives who would do business with the investment banking arm of the firm.[144] In the banks the practice was called "spinning"—using IPO allocations to get investment banking business.

Hot IPO shares went not just to CEOs in order for investment banks to get banking business, but to venture capitalists who could swing IPOs toward particular banks. Again, there were other investors in the startups who didn't get the IPO shares, nor did the companies benefit, but rather individuals used other people's assets to gain financial advantages for themselves.[145]

Documents obtained from three investment banks by the House Committee on Financial Services in mid-2002 showed the award of IPO shares by the banks in order to obtain investment banking business and the use of investment research done at the bank to hype companies that were investment banking clients. These records underscore banks' conflicts of interest as they pretend to provide unbiased research to investors while at the same time seeking lucrative investment banking business.

"Initial public offerings seemed to be anything but public," said a member of the House committee. "A small circle of preferred clients were given vast access by the investment banks to IPO shares and reaped large profits on the sale of these shares. What is most disturbing is that their profits were gained at the expense of the average investor whose only option was to buy the shares at the oftentimes inflated aftermarket price." He added, "when executives trade their companies' investment banking business, they use the wealth of their firms—owned by public shareholders—for their own personal gain."

For the 22 IPOs done by one of the banks, the shares of eight gained at least 173% on the first day of trading. Of 19 IPOs done by another bank, seven had first-day gains of at least 145%. Many of the executives and directors who received allocations of the IPO shares flipped them for quick profits. "As a result," wrote the House committee in its report, "small investors gaining access later in the process were more likely to be left with the losses in companies that, in many cases, never recovered."

Salomon Smith Barney, a unit of Citigroup, provided IPO shares in 21 different companies to WorldCom CEO Bernard Ebbers. "Six other WorldCom executives and directors received the opportunity to buy thousands of shares as well. Among them was Scott D. Sullivan, the chief financial officer who oversaw the company's books during the years when $7 billion in accounting misstatements were made."[146]

There's no legal obligation for an investment bank to treat customers fairly in allocations, but there would seem to be an ethical one, since such allocations are very like bribes to get investment banking business from the companies led by the executives getting the allocations. There is, however, a legal obligation placed on corporate executives who are customers of investment banks not to use the investment banking business provided by their companies as a route to their own personal riches via favors from their bankers.

Yet this is exactly what happened at First Boston and Solomon and most likely elsewhere. Corporate executives used their positions at a company to enrich themselves by giving company business to banks, which then gave IPO share allocations to the executives. The IPO shares were given not to the company's shareholders but personally to the firm's executives. This was profitable back scratching. The bank got fees, the company got loans and help in misleading investors, and the executives got IPO shares. Spinning is one of the clearest indicators that this is and has been a manipulated stock market.

Talking Points

At the heart of corporate financial scandals were the actions of investment banks. Conflict of interest played a major role. Too often investment banks knowingly issued misleading recommendations to investors regarding the shares of a company that was also their client or potential client for banking services. Furthermore, investment banks structured loans for client companies in such a way as to hide them from investors and regulators.

9 The Corruption of the Analysts

According to analysts at Salomon Smith Barney, the CEO of Conseco demanded that Salomon change critical comments it made about the company, saying, "Don't you know I spent $20 million in fees at your firm last year?!" Conseco had recently had one of the largest restatements of earnings in U.S. corporate history.[147]

Addressing the role of the investment banks in the scandals, Felix Rohatyn, formerly a banker himself, commented, "If Wall Street knows what is good for it and what is good for the country, it will very definitely clean up its act."[148] But there's no evidence at all that under its current leadership Wall Street has any concern for what is good for our country. Only enlightened self-interest (that is, the notion that it's best for a bank not to get caught at fraud) might cause the bankers to operate differently. Whether investors should place any confidence in the ability of their long-term self-interest to change bankers' behavior is addressed in the final chapters of this book.

All the major brokerage houses and investment banks have long touted their stock research as independent and objective. The reality is very different. As far back as 1995, even before the bull market really got going, the *Wall Street Journal* did an extensive examination of the practices of sell-side stock analysts and found that what was supposed to be happening in most cases simply wasn't happening. "Skirting realistic ratings," the *Journal* said, "is so commonplace that it has become an inside joke on the Street."[149]

Stock research at most of the major Wall Street firms is driven by investment banking, largely because Wall Street firms make more money from investment banking than they do from the stock research they sell and the commissions they earn on stock trades related to their analysts' recommendations. According to one Wall Street executive, Sandy Weill of Citigroup "is the guy who taught me in the mid-80's that research is a loss leader… that research has no value except, of course, to get banking fees."[150]

Having positive stock analyst coverage, however, is extremely important to publicly traded companies because it helps keep their stock prices up. Thus it has long been standard practice for companies to demand favorable coverage as a condition for giving investment banking work to an analyst's firm. It is well known that most of the year-end bonuses that analysts have received in recent years have been tied to the investment banking business they helped bring in or sustain. A longtime analyst, now an independent consultant, says it's also "not unusual for an analyst to be hired on the recommendation of an investment banking client." In 1999, for example, Merrill Lynch replaced a stock analyst after the CEO of Tyco complained in a face-to-face meeting with the CEO of Merrill Lynch that the analyst wasn't positive enough about his company. The new analyst that Merrill Lynch brought in immediately upgraded Tyco to a "buy" and responded to press reports of accounting fraud at the company by saying that the company "always opts for the most conservative way to account for everything."[151]

A Morgan Stanley analyst, Simon Flannery, was one of the first to take a close look at Qwest's financial reporting. In June 2001, he downgraded Qwest to "neutral" from "outperform," and raised questions about how the company accounted for the previous year's acquisition of local phone company US West Incorporated. He also argued that Qwest may have bolstered its operating income by changing its pension plan assumptions and capitalizing a large amount of software costs. "The company has taken a number of financial actions that could have an important bearing on the sustainability of future earnings growth," Flannery said in the report.

In response, Qwest lashed back and rebutted Morgan Stanley's findings in a press release and conference calls with investors, reporters, and other analysts. "There are no accounting issues or improprieties in Qwest's financial reporting... innuendoes on our integrity are not going to be tolerated," Chairman Joe Nacchio said in a conference call. Nacchio called the Morgan Stanley report "hogwash," but said "the integrity issue is really what burns my britches."[152]

A year later Robin Szeliga, who served as Qwest's CFO from April 2001 until July 2002, testified before the House Subcommittee on Oversight and Investigations about how former executives at Qwest quelled dissent and misled investors with inaccurate financial reports. She said that then-CEO Joseph Nacchio was upset when a Morgan Stanley analyst accused the company of inflating its revenue projections after merging with US West. When company executives met to plot a strategy, Szeliga took notes: One idea was to "quietly close" Morgan

Stanley out of the company, which meant shutting it out of banking and other business for Qwest, Szeliga testified, which was one of the ways the company reacted. Szeliga said that amid the slowing economy, Qwest faced pressure to meet Wall Street's performance expectations.[153] Nacchio "was very angry at Morgan Stanley, and he expressed it." She also said that there was "a heightened sense of pressure" as Qwest faced a sluggish economy and challenges linked to its merger with US West.

The pressures on stock analysts to toe a company's line have been intense, and the retaliation they can face if they don't is severe. For example, if analysts issued a report critical of a company, often the company would not only refuse to give it investment bank work; often it would also deny the analysts access to management for information purposes and refuse to take their questions in conference calls. In late 2000 the SEC passed a new rule, called Regulation FD (for fair disclosure), that was meant to stop this practice. Regulation FD prohibits publicly traded companies from selectively disseminating important information about their operations, for example, by giving important information to a few select analysts but not others. The rule had some effect. In spring 2002, however, analysts from Lehman Brothers and Prudential Securities testified in Congress that the old practices continued. "You may ask questions, and the company says they don't disclose that," said a Lehman Brothers analyst. "But you know full well they have disclosed it to more bullish analysts." Skeptical analysts would therefore have a hard time doing further research on the company.

Large institutional investors have also made it hard for analysts to do an honest job. If institutional investors have large holdings in a given stock, they want analysts to be cheerleaders for it; bad comments about it in the market can damage the value of their portfolios. "We've had instances," one analyst said, "where mutual funds said they wouldn't do business with us again when we turned negative." Other analysts have said the same thing about the pressures they get from mutual funds.[154]

Use It or Lose It

Once analysts had helped a company to increase its share price by making favorable recommendations, bankers were not shy about telling top executives of the firm how to run the business. "Use it or lose it," they'd tell a CEO. This meant that the CEO must either use the company's high-priced stock to make acquisitions, paying the bank substantial investment banking fees for the transactions, or watch the bank's analysts lose interest in the stock. Bankers were not hesitant to offer a list of companies for possible acquisition. The company's high stock price was partly a creation of the bank, the bank not so subtly reminded the company, and if the company didn't use it to benefit the bank (via transactions from which the bank drew a fee), then the company would lose its high stock price. Hence, use it or lose it.

May Day

It's another irony of the present state of our financial service companies that the brokerages that had invested much time and effort in building a professional status for stock analysts, including the Certified Investment Analyst curriculum, should in the past few years so corrupt the profession by having analysts issue dishonest recommendations that its reputation is now badly tarnished.

Why did the brokerage houses do this? In explanation, many observers point to a supposed change in the economics of investment research. Until 1975 the New York Stock Exchange regulated commissions for stock sales, setting them at what appear today to be high levels. Research flourished and firms tried to compete for brokerage business on the basis of the quality of their research.

Then on May 1, 1975, under pressure from the anti-trust elements of the Justice Department, the Securities and Exchange Commission ordered an end to the fixed commissions for stock trades. "May Day" (as the date became known in Wall Street lore) led to competitive pricing and the rise of discount brokers, which in some ways were good for investors. Lower commissions, moreover, led to increased trading volume, which offset some of the decrease in prices that brokers experienced. However, brokerage houses and banks insisted that stock research was increasingly hard to pay for, arguing that in the past it had been supported by the higher, fixed commissions.

In response to deregulation of commissions, many brokers merged (in order to spread costs over a larger customer base). Some diversified into different kinds of money management. But many also hooked up with investment banks, which found that stock analysts could help them gain investment banking clients and were therefore glad to subsidize research work. This, some observers believe, is one of the key things that led to the corruption of what many stock analysts do—the change in the economics of stock research, which led to its subservience to investment banking.

May Day may be part of the picture, but certainly it is not all of it. For example, in 1983 stock analysts were still issuing as many sell recommendations as buy recommendations. So eight years after May Day and the supposed change in the economics of research, analysts had not yet been corrupted into shills for investment banking. Furthermore, even today, there are some well-regarded stock research firms (e.g., Sanford C. Bernstein) that don't have investment banking operations but are nevertheless financially viable. So it would seem that research can still pay for itself. At the banks, however, revenue from banking, trading, and research is commingled and not reported separately. Hence it's impossible for outsiders to know what's profitable and what's not;

what's growing and what's not.[155] Moreover, the argument that stock research can't pay for itself and so has to be tied to investment banking if it is to survive generally fails to note that research has been made more expensive by being attached to investment banking. For example, some analysts are today paid vastly higher sums (even adjusting for the upward trend of compensation in America generally) than they were 25 years ago.

The argument that the deregulation of commissions forced banks to tie research to investment banking is hard to see as anything more than a rationalization for a step that was taken for other reasons. In fact, bankers corrupted the analysts' function in order to gain investment banking business, and they persuaded some key analysts to join in the charade by paying them well for it.

Maybe 20 Percent Are Honest

The character of the work that stock analysts do has changed over the years. There is anecdotal evidence for this change, but there is also some quantitative evidence. Stock analysts recommend to investors whether they should buy or sell certain stocks. That is perhaps the most fundamental thing they do. Thus in 1983, 24.5% of all stock analyst recommendations were "buy" recommendations; 26.8% were "sells." (The rest were "holds," or some version of that.) By the end of the 1980s, however, buys outnumbered sells 4 to 1; by the early 1990s, buys outnumbered sells 8 to 1; by the mid-1990s, it was about 30 to 1; and it kept going up.[156]

This change wasn't a direct reflection of the performance of the stock market. In 1983, for example, when 26.8% of all stock analyst recommendations were "sells," the stock market was way up (the S&P 500 had a total return of 22.6%). In the late 1980s and early 1990s the stock market had some good years as well as a few bad years. But the percentage of stock analyst recommendations to buy kept going up, while the percentage of recommendations to sell kept going down. Data for 1998 through 2001 gives an even better sense of the dynamic behind this ratio (see Exhibit 9–1). During those four years, the percentage of sell recommendations was less than one percent. Add to that the next level up in analyst recommendations (often designated "underperform" or "underweight"), and it's still around 1%. Meanwhile, the market, which went up in 1998 and 1999, went way down in 2000 and 2001. It's important to recognize, however, that even when the stock market as a whole goes up, there are always a lot of individual stocks whose prices go down (so-called "declining" issues). And during these four years, about half of all stocks traded on the New York Stock Exchange actually went down.[157]

The data we are looking at here gives only a rough picture of everything that was going on, but in a year when the stock market as a whole goes up, it would be reasonable for at least 26.8% of all stock analyst recommendations to be sell or "underperform" recommendations. (That was the situation in 1983.) In recent years, less than 1% of analyst recommendations were sell or "underperform" recommendations, and that was the case even when the stock market was going down! Clearly the change in the nature of the work that stock analysts do has been systemic.

Exhibit 9–1 Comparison of Total Stock Market Returns, Percentage of Individual Stocks with Price Declines, and Percentage of Analyst Recommendations That Were "Sell" Recommendations: 1998–2001

	1998	1999	2000	2001
Total return on the S&P 500	29%	21%	–9%	–12%
New York Stock Exchange				
Advances	1,850	1,432	2,337	2,370
Declines	2,360	2,727	1,623	1,569
Unchanged	75	47	39	34
Total issues	4,285	4,206	3,999	3,973
% declines	55%	65%	41%	39%
% of all analyst recommendations that were "sell" recommendations	< 1%	< 1%	< 1%	< 1%
% of all analyst recommendations that were "sell" or "underperform" recommendations	< 1%	< 1%	< 1%	1.4%

Note. The total market capitalization of stocks traded on the New York Stock Exchange represents the large majority of the market capitalization of all stocks traded in the United States.

Source. Wall Street Journal, *January 4, 1999, and January 2, 2002; Global Financial Data; Thomson First Call.*

Even in the most extreme cases, the unreality that pervades stock recommendations remains. An academic study looked at analyst reports on 25 of the largest companies that filed for bankruptcy in the United States from 1998 to 2000. In the year preceding their formal bankruptcy filings, a quarter of the companies were given ratings like "attractive" or "strong buy"; only 2% were rated "sell."[158] What's behind this? In 1998, Richard Strong, the chairman of a mutual fund company with $32 billion in assets, assessed sell-side analysts by saying, "Maybe 20% are intellectually honest."

Thomas Brown worked as a Wall Street analyst for 15 years, and in most of those years he was a top-rated analyst on the Institutional Investor All-America Research Team. When asked in 1998 about the alleged conflict between stock research and investment banking, he said: "Conflict? There's no conflict. That's been settled. The investment bankers won."[159] For seven years Brown worked at Donaldson Lufkin & Jenrette, one of the major brokerage houses on Wall Street. He developed a reputation for considerable honesty in the reports he wrote. Reflecting on his experience at DLJ, he says: "I don't know, frankly, how some of these analysts live with themselves. I couldn't get up in the morning and look in the mirror and know that I just caused somebody to lose 50 percent of their retirement money because I exaggerated and I lied. And that's exactly what I saw at DLJ."[160]

What's Said Isn't What's Done

When the television program *60 Minutes* broadcast a story in early 2001 about the problems with stock analysts, Merrill Lynch, the largest brokerage firm in the United States, sent *60 Minutes* an e-mail stating that its analysts "make independent recommendations based upon their best judgment."[161] Information that was subsequently made public, however, showed that in 1999, 2000, and 2001 Merrill Lynch analysts were publicly recommending to ordinary investors the stocks of companies that they privately regarded as worthless. They recommended to investors a company whose "fundamentals" they privately said were "horrible." They placed on their list of "top ten" technology stocks a stock they privately said "really [has] no floor." Other companies that they publicly recommended they privately referred to as "a powder keg," "a dog," "a piece of crap," and "a piece of shit." One analyst at Merrill Lynch said in an e-mail to a colleague that there was nothing interesting about a company she was recommending to retail investors "except banking fees." Another analyst said bluntly to a colleague, "The whole idea that we are independent from banking is a big lie."[162]

One of the star analysts of the bull market was Mary Meeker of Morgan Stanley. She sent *60 Minutes* a statement saying, "We maintain a strict separation of the [investment] banking and research functions within the firm. Our research is objective and has a long-term focus." An internal memo obtained from Morgan Stanley, however, instructed analysts very plainly: "We do not make negative or controversial comments about our clients."[163] With Meeker's help, Morgan Stanley obtained lucrative investment banking work from a variety of Internet companies such as Priceline, Amazon, Yahoo, FreeMarkets, and Drugstore. After Morgan Stanley took them public, Meeker strongly recommended all these firms to investors, and as the stock prices of all of them fell 85% or more, she continued to recommend them.

Actual and Potential Clients

Academic studies periodically attempt to document the effect that investment banking ties have on stock analyst reports. If a Wall Street firm has done investment banking work for a company, its stock analysts will evidently be more positive about the company than the stock analysts of firms that don't have formal investment banking ties to the company. These studies, however, really don't reveal much. Undoubtedly there is some additional bias that results from investment banking ties. For an investment bank, however, almost every company is a potential client. Every investment bank wants to get future business from a company. So stock analysts are inclined to be positive—or at least not negative—about every company they cover.[164] The fact that fewer than 1% of all stock analyst recommendations in recent years have been sell recommendations makes this very plain.

It's a similar story with the debates about whether analysts, in their written reports or in their comments on television programs, provide adequate disclosure of any ties their investment banking firm may have to a company being discussed. (The debates concern the kind of disclosure there should be, where it should be, whether it's OK for it to be in small type at the end of the report, and so on.) Again, this is largely beside the point. Almost every company is a potential client.

Thomas Brown, after many years of experience on Wall Street, says that analysts "literally are cheerleaders because even if…the company you're working on is not a client of the firm, every company's a potential client, so the investment banking group wants you to be wildly bullish about everybody."[165] There are obvious reasons why research analysts do this. In recent years, star analysts—like Jack Grubman, Henry Blodget, and Mary Meeker—were making $10 to $20 million a year. Analysts in the next "tier" had earnings in the $750,000 to $1 million range. So-called junior analysts still learning the trade often made $500,000 to $750,000. Even lower-level people sometimes made enormous sums.[166] This kind of money wasn't being paid because the analysts were doing superb analysis for investors. The money was being paid because the analysts were helping to bring in investment banking business, a key component of which involved their promoting the stocks of investment banking clients under the guise of independent research.

But there was more to the rule of analysts in supporting the investment bankers in a firm than cheerleading. For example, in the mid-1990s a large Midwestern medical products company was going to do a financing to raise money. One day the CEO received a phone call from the financial analyst of a major investment bank who followed his company and issued reports to investors about it, including recommendations to buy or sell the company's stock. The CEO knew the analyst personally from meetings at which the company's financial reports were discussed with analysts.

"You're going to do a financing?" the analyst asked the CEO.

"Yes."

"We'd like to do it for you."

"Who's we?" the CEO asked.

"Our firm."

"What happened to the Chinese wall between investment banking and financial analysis?"

"Oh, it's still there," the analyst replied.

The CEO understood the message—that if his company didn't give the analyst's bank the financing and the fees that went with it, the analyst would downgrade the CEO's company in his reports, and the analyst and his company would not admit that this was what they were doing.

During this time the pay of the analyst involved rose more than 30 times as he began to get a cut of the fees for the investment banking business he helped bring to his bank.

The Language of Recommendations

In recent years parts of the insurance industry in the United States have had to agree to use "plain English" in some of their insurance contracts. The "plain English" movement, however, has barely touched the securities industry.

Typically, "strong buy" has been the rating analysts use to mean they think the investor should buy the stock. A "buy" sometimes meant buy, but it often meant that the investor shouldn't buy but should just hold what they had. Terms like "accumulate" had a fairly negative meaning. "Market perform" meant that the stock wasn't worth owning. "Hold" and "neutral" meant investors should sell. Terms like "underperform," "underweight," and "avoid" meant that investors should sell as fast as possible. And the plain English word "sell," with rare exceptions, simply wasn't used.

But even these meanings often weren't accurate. E-mails that the Attorney General of New York obtained from Merrill Lynch showed that Merrill Lynch sometimes gave its very highest rating (the equivalent of "strong buy") to stocks that analysts privately thought "could go very low" or that they flatly regarded as "a piece of junk." The same sort of thing went on at other brokerage houses as well. E-mails that the SEC obtained from Donaldson Lufkin & Jenrette showed that an analyst was recommending a "buy" on a stock that his firm's investment bank had just taken public but that the analyst privately regarded as "a piece of junk" and "an embarrassment."[167]

The justifications brokerage houses have given for their "ratings" language generally rely on a variety of evasions. They say the analyst reports indicated what their ratings meant, that the many levels of ratings were meant to give investors a nuanced view of a stock's prospects, that the research was meant primarily for institutional clients, and that the ratings would "help sophisticated investors weigh their portfolios based on sectors."

Much of the audience for these stock ratings, however, consisted of ordinary investors—"retail" investors—who didn't understand the game that was being played and would make investment decisions based on what the analysts were recommending. In the bull market of the 1990s, moreover, analysts often became media stars because of the frothiness of the market and would proclaim their "buy" and "strong buy" recommendations not only in the conventional form of written research reports but also on television and online Internet sites.

Efforts at Reform

Various rules have been put in place that were supposed to control the conflicts of interest stock analysts face. Some are mandatory (securities laws that can impose criminal or civil liability on analysts if they are found to have deceived investors in significant ways); some are voluntary. For a variety of reasons, the rules have generally been ineffective.

For example, the New York Stock Exchange has for years had rules against companies' giving information selectively to different analysts. Its manual recommended that companies observe an "open door" policy in their relations with security analysts, and it also said that "a company should not give information to one inquirer that it would not give to another." It was well known, however, that these rules were disregarded. In late 2000, therefore, the SEC passed a new rule—called Regulation FD—that formally prohibited this selective disclosure of information. The rule had some effect. In spring 2002, however, analysts from Lehman Brothers and Prudential Securities testified in Congress that the rule was being flouted.

In mid-2001, after the bursting of the Internet bubble, Congressional hearings put pressure on Wall Street firms to reduce or eliminate the conflicts of interest that compromised the work stock analysts did. In response, the Securities Industry Association (SIA) announced a set of "best practices" guidelines. Wall Street analysts, the industry association said, shouldn't report to the investment banking side of the business; analysts' pay shouldn't be tied directly to investment-banking deals; and so on. Fourteen major Wall Street firms agreed to follow the guidelines. A Republican congressman said, however, that in his view the guidelines were inadequate because they were simply voluntary. Indeed, most of the Wall Street firms that agreed to follow the guidelines announced that their analysts already adhered to virtually all of them. A spokesperson for Goldman Sachs said: "We're not implementing any new policies." A spokesperson for Salomon Smith Barney said: "Nothing is going to change with us; everything is going to be status quo."[168]

In the next 12 months, as the stock market continued to slide, the percentage of all stock analyst recommendations that were outright "sell" recommendations was—according to Thomson/First Call—never higher than one half of 1%; the percentage of all stock analyst recommendations that were either a "sell" or the next highest ranking ("underperform") was never higher than 2.7%. Various analysts continued to recommend the stocks of Enron, WorldCom, and other companies until very shortly before they filed for bankruptcy. Various analysts continued to recommend the stocks of Tyco and other companies even with increasing revelations of dishonesty in their operations. In May 2002 Salomon Smith Barney voluntarily announced new rules, some of them very concrete, to prevent its investment bankers from influencing its stock analysts. These rules, they said, were meant to "ensure the value and integrity of our research product." Within a month, the rules had been violated.[169]

In May 2002 the SEC approved several new rules meant to reduce the conflicts of interest between analysts and investment bankers. One of the rules would require brokerage houses to report—both to investors and to regulatory authorities—the percentage distribution of analyst recommendations in the categories "buy," "hold," and "sell." The director of investment research at online research firm Multex.com commented: "The clarity everyone has been waiting for is coming."[170]

When the rule went into effect on September 9, however, the clarity wasn't there. Brokerage houses summarized the percentage distribution of their buy, hold, and sell recommendations, but only in a convoluted way, and most of them still didn't apply these words plainly to individual companies. The first page of most reports on individual companies continued to use terms like "underweight" and "underperform" that everyone on the Street knew were designed to confuse investors. (A Lehman Brothers spokesperson acknowledged that the definition of "underweight" at the back of its reports was a "mouthful."[171]) Morgan Stanley said in extremely small type at the back of its reports that the terms "equal weight" and "underweight" corresponded roughly to neutral and sell recommendations but weren't the equivalent of those words. Rather, they represented (Morgan said) "recommended relative weightings" per definitions they provided in another section—definitions that, like those at Lehman, would undoubtedly be confusing to many people.

Independent Analysts

There are some stock analysts who take seriously their responsibility to provide sound investment advice. In recent years, however, going down that path has been a risky business. The following are stories of what happened to three analysts, at three different brokerage houses, who did so.

Daniel Scotto

Daniel Scotto, an analyst with 30 years of experience on Wall Street, was in recent years a bond analyst for the French securities firm BNP Paribas. In August 2001, two weeks after Jeffrey Skilling suddenly quit as CEO of Enron, Scotto lowered his rating on Enron's securities from "buy" to "neutral." He said that Enron's securities "should be sold at all costs and sold now." In a later conference call with investors, Scotto said that Enron "wasn't a company with hard assets. It's built on paper and highly leveraged." His comments, of course, proved to be prescient.

Enron, however, was one of BNP Paribas' investment banking clients. A few days after he had lowered his rating on Enron, Scotto was demoted and was told by one of his superiors, "We don't think it was a good recommendation or a reasonable one." Scotto was put on "family leave," at full pay, for 120 days. He said he checked in frequently but was told he wasn't needed back at work and to take time to "cool off." Then on December 5 he received a termination letter. The letter said that, due to a lack of documentation "justifying your continued absence from work, as well as the indeterminate nature of your extended leave, BNP Paribas is left with no choice but to terminate your employment." When a *Wall Street Journal* reporter asked BNP Paribas about the reasons for Scotto's departure, a spokesperson said that the move "was completely unrelated to any research he wrote on any company, including Enron."[172]

Mike Mayo

For years Mike Mayo had been a top-rated, highly respected American banking analyst (the number one regional banking analyst according to *Institutional Investor*). In late 1994, when bank stocks were doing poorly, Mayo felt the sector had turned a corner and issued a slew of buy recommendations. Other analysts were puzzled by the call. Over the next few years, however, banking stocks posted a return of 254%.

In mid-1999, however, things looked different to Mayo. He believed that "the merger boom was slowing; efficiencies created by deals were already factored into both earnings and stock prices; many banks were covering up bottom-line weaknesses with outstretched gains from venture capital, underwriting, and trading; and there was growing evidence of an increase in problem loans." Armed with a 1,000-page report on 47 U.S. banks, he stood up at a gathering of brokers at Credit Suisse First Boston, his employer, and told them, "Sell bank stocks."

The backlash was intense. Company sales reps, rival bank analysts, portfolio managers, and bank executives turned against Mayo. The chief legal counsel at a major regional bank demanded a retraction of his call. Several bank CEOs said outright, or strongly insinuated, that they planned to end all underwriting and trading business with Credit Suisse First Boston. As things turned out, Mayo's call again proved right. Earnings at a number of banks declined, and their stock prices fell. Other analysts later lowered their recommendations as well. In the fall of 2000, however, a few days after Credit Suisse announced plans to acquire Donaldson Lufkin & Jenrette, Mayo was fired. A company spokesperson said that the merger with DLJ "gave us the opportunity to bring on board one of the best financial services teams on the Street." Beyond that, the company wouldn't say anything. (Bank-related mergers and acquisitions work, however, was one of the most lucrative parts of CSFB's and DLJ's investment banking business.)

Fortune magazine interviewed more than a dozen of Mayo's former colleagues, as well as investment bankers, research directors at competing brokerage houses, and bank executives, and the sense that most of them had was that Mayo was fired simply because he was controversial, because he upset the status quo. At Credit Suisse First Boston he had been one of the top four analysts in terms of generating commissions from institutional clients. People valued his insight. Even some people who had sometimes been targets of Mayo's criticism were surprised to find that he was out of work. The CEO of one of the five largest banks in the country said, "The son of a bitch knows more about research than anyone I know."[173]

Kenneth Boss

In the first half of 2002 major Wall Street firms were facing increasing criticism, including legal action, regarding the ways in which sell-side analysts had deceived investors in recent years. Merrill Lynch e-mails revealed that analysts there previously had a practice of recommending to investors stocks that the Merrill Lynch analysts privately regarded as worthless. Merrill Lynch agreed to pay a $100 million fine and change the way its analysts did business. (Some observers on Wall Street, however, said that the $100 million fine amounted only to a slap on the wrist.)

In this context the chief executive of Salomon Smith Barney, Michael Carpenter, announced in May 2002 new rules to "ensure the value and integrity of our research product." To prevent investment bankers from influencing research reports improperly, the firm restricted communications between analysts and bankers. Beginning on June 3, for example, the firm said that any fact checking of draft research reports by Salomon's investment banking division would be limited to the first research written about an initial public offering. In addition, the rules said that any draft research sent to investment banking for fact checking "must omit the rating and target price as well as the investment thesis and valuation analysis sections."

In June, Kenneth Boss, a Salomon stock analyst, was working on a report analyzing three office furniture companies. While working on the report, he shared with his supervisor his doubts about the sector. He felt that their stocks, at least in the near term, wouldn't be good choices for investors. The economic environment for them, he felt, was weak, and their share prices had risen in recent months. Boss said his supervisor appeared to become very anxious. Boss sat within earshot of his supervisor, and he said that his supervisor called the investment bankers in the office furniture sector to discuss the report. His supervisor used his cell phone for the calls, and he told Boss to limit any conversations with investment banking people to cell phones because of the recent release of extremely incriminating e-mails at Merrill Lynch.

Boss assigned the office furniture companies a neutral, high-risk rating. Boss's supervisor told him to put the report on Salomon's network so it could be reviewed by the investment bankers. Boss objected, noting the firm's new rules about this. Nonetheless, one of Salomon's investment bankers from the office furniture group "soon went to the research department and reviewed the report on Mr. Boss's laptop." Salomon had recently underwritten bonds of two of the companies that Boss was advising investors to be cautious about, and Boss said that the investment banker who read his report became "quite agitated." He demanded that Boss revise the report to be more upbeat. Boss refused.

A few days later, on June 27, he was fired. His supervisor told him that the reason was that he hadn't completed the report on time. The deadline for the report, however, had been July 1. A Salomon spokesperson later said, "There was no pressure from investment bankers on Mr. Boss' report. He was terminated for performance reasons." In his 2001 performance review, however, Boss received, on a scale of one to ten, all tens and was given a bonus of $100,000. In reflecting on what happened at Salomon, Boss said: "They came out with new rules and it didn't make any difference, did it?"[174]

Praise (or Rebuke) for Pay

Stock research in the major Wall Street firms has clearly been corrupted by its ties to investment banking. But an even more pernicious kind of stock research has gone on in recent years. This is "praise for pay" research. It probably hasn't been widespread, but it has had a fairly sound footing. For example, the Aberdeen Group has done both stock and market research for high-tech firms. Some of its stock research reports have been genuine. Others, however, have been paid for by clients. For example, in 2001 Aberdeen published a very positive report about a fiber-optics startup named Onetta. (Onetta, Aberdeen said, had a "commitment to high performance" and an "intelligent product roadmap" and "worked to build highly satisfied customer relationships.") Aberdeen didn't mention in the report, however, that Onetta had paid Aberdeen $8,000 to have it written.

Aberdeen not only acknowledged writing favorable reports for hire; it also defended the practice. It didn't disclose to investors, however, what it was doing. On the contrary, boilerplate language that appeared at the end of many of the reports cited the "comprehensive analytical framework" that Aberdeen provided. (Only in one section of its website did it say that some of its research "may be sponsored" by certain suppliers.)

Aberdeen has had some major clients. One of them is Intel, the computer chip maker. But Intel hasn't paid Aberdeen for praise. In spring 2002 it paid Aberdeen to write a report that was critical of one of its chief rivals, Advanced Micro Devices.

One thing that Aberdeen can definitely boast is that this kind of thing "works." Aberdeen research and analysts have been cited frequently in the business press, including the *Wall Street Journal.* When asked about this type of work, Aberdeen's CEO said he didn't see any problem with it. "What's the conflict?" he said. "I don't understand."[175]

Stealth Marketing

In recent years a number of industries have increasingly relied on "stealth marketing," for example, arranging for "product placement" in movies; having the plots of sitcoms or books designed around brands of makeup or jewelry; having celebrities appear on talk shows to praise certain prescription drugs without disclosing that they have been paid by the drug companies to do so. Marketing, it is observed, is most effective when you don't know that it's marketing.[176] That is how a lot of stock research has functioned in recent years. Unfortunately, much of it has worked, to the detriment of investors.

A Successful Investment Analyst Tells What Happened to His Profession

Source: Federal Document Clearing House Congressional Testimony
Tuesday, July 31, 2001
COMMITTEE: HOUSE FINANCIAL SERVICES
SUBCOMMITTEE: CAPITAL MARKETS, INSURANCE AND GOVERNMENT-SPONSORED ENTERPRISES
HEADLINE: QUALITY OF WALL STREET RESEARCH

My name is Ronald Glantz. I was in the investment business for 32 years before retiring last year. I began my career on Wall Street as an equity research analyst. Money managers polled by Institutional Investor magazine selected me as the top analyst in my field for seven consecutive years. I then became Director of Research, Chief Investment Officer, Director of Economics and Financial Markets, and a member of the Management Board of Paine Webber, one of *the* largest brokerage firms in the United States. I ended my career as a Managing Director of Tiger Management, one of the largest hedge funds in the world. This has given me a good perspective on how the role of analysts has changed over the last three decades.

When I began in the business, the top-rated equity research firm was named Laird. Within five years it failed. So did most of the other top-rated firms. What happened? When I began, the average commission was over 40 cents a share. A few years later, commissions paid by institutions such as banks, pension funds, and mutual funds became negotiated, almost immediately falling to less than 6 cents a share. The only way for research firms to survive was to merge with someone that could spread research costs over a larger base, usually brokerage firms whose main clients were individual investors. Retail commissions had remained fixed, and retail brokerage firms discovered that good research helped them gain retail clients and stockbrokers. By the end of the 1970s, the largest number of top analysts were at Paine Webber, which had bought the top-rated research firm, and Merrill Lynch, which hired talent from failing research firms.

Companies pressure analysts to recommend their stock, since a higher price means:

- Fewer shares have to be issued when raising new funds or acquiring another company.
- They are less vulnerable to being taken over.
- Executives make more money when they cash in their options.
- Shareholders are pleased.

It is easy to reward favored analysts. They are given more access to management, "helped" in making earnings estimates, and invited to resorts for "briefings." And, most important, their firm receives lucrative investment banking business.

Companies penalize analysts who aren't sufficiently enthusiastic. Let me give you a personal example. When I was a brokerage firm analyst, I downgraded a stock. The company's chief financial officer called my firm's president to say that unless I recommended his stock, he would cease doing investment banking business with my firm and would order the bank that managed his company's pension fund to stop doing business with my firm. I have seen top analysts removed from company mailing lists, their telephone calls left unreturned, and even physically barred from company presentations. Once I was doing a reference check on an analyst I was considering hiring. A CFO told me that the analyst was disliked so much that he was deliberately given misleading information.

In 1980, top analysts made just over $100,000 a year. Today, top analysts make up to $20 million a year. How is this possible, considering that institutional commissions have fallen even further and brokerage firms now discount retail commissions to avoid losing customers to such firms as Schwab and e-Trade? What happened is that brokerage firms discovered that highly rated research helped them gain investment banking clients. Soon the largest number of top analysts were at investment banking Goliaths such as Morgan Stanley and Goldman Sachs. They could pay considerably more, because investment banking transactions were much more lucrative than trading stocks. The institutional commission on trading $300 million worth of stock was only $300,000, of which less than $25,000 would go to the research department. This barely paid for printing and mailing research reports on that company. However, underwriting a similar dollar value of a new issue would bring in at least $10 million, and bankers thought nothing of giving a million-dollar fee to the analyst responsible for the business. A merger or acquisition could bring in even more. Soon firms were including anticipated investment banking fees in the contracts they offered analysts. The huge fees earned by investment banking gives them the ability to influence and, in some cases, even control the equity research department. As we all know, whoever "pays the piper" names the tune.

Analysts used to view retail customers and investment managers as their clients. My first boss told me, "Widows and orphans depend upon you to give good advice." Now the job of analysts is to bring in investment banking clients, not provide good investment advice. This began in the mid-1980s. The prostitution of security analysts was completed during the high-tech mania of the last few years. For example, in 1997 a major investment banking firm offered to triple my pay. They had no interest in the quality of my recommendations. I was shown a list with 15 names and asked, "How quickly can you issue buy recommendations on these potential clients?"

Let me pause here to assure you—most analysts still want to give good advice. Not only is it the right thing to do, it helps their reputation, which brings in investment banking business.... Nevertheless, the pressures are enormous.

When I was Director of Research, analyst compensation was based upon the performance of his or her recommendations, omissions generated, and ratings by institutional clients and the retail system. Today, name analysts are given guaranteed contracts, whether or not their recommendations are any good. Every year the *Wall Street Journal* lists the analysts who have provided the best investment advice. These analysts are rarely the best paid in their field. Why is that? Investment banking. It is an open secret that "strong buy" now means "buy," "buy" means "hold," "hold" means that the company isn't an investment banking client, and "sell" means that the company is no longer an investment banking client. Less than 1% of all recommendations are "sell." Some analysts call their best clients and tell them that their real opinion differs from their published opinion, even though this is illegal. But what about the individual investor? No one told my 86-year-old widowed aunt that the Internet stocks she was buying in 1999 had no hope of ever earning any money, that the analyst recommending the purchase was being paid by investment banking. Investment banking now dominates equity research:

- Bankers often suggest and are usually asked to approve hiring analysts from other brokerage firms.
- Investment banking provides the bulk of proven analysts' pay packages.
- Some analysts report directly to investment banking.

Analysts routinely send reports to the companies and to bankers for comment before they are issued. Three years ago, Tiger was able to hire the top-rated analyst in his field. He had consistently been negative on one company, a major source of investment banking fees because of its many acquisitions. Then his firm hired an investment banking team from another brokerage firm. As reported in the *Wall Street Journal*, the analyst was fired so that a "more compliant" analyst could be hired, one who would recommend potential investing banking clients.

Disillusioned, the analyst moved over to money management, where the quality of recommendations was still more important than the quality of relationships with potential buyers of investment banking services.

To give one of many personal examples, 4 years ago, I came up with some extremely negative information on a company, including bribery, defective products, accounting irregularities, and serious pollution problems. I called the three most visible analysts recommending the stock, one of them the top-rated analyst in his field, and gave them my evidence. Everyone continued to recommend the stock. Why? This company was an investment banking client.

The genie has been let out of the bottle. As long as investment banking is the most profitable part of the firm, then investment bankers will find a way to pay analysts who bring in business.

Money managers can hire their own analysts. But my elderly aunt will never know whether the advice she is receiving is unbiased or not. That's not only bad for the average investor, it undermines one of the primary reasons for having a stock market—the efficient allocation of investment dollars.

My proposals can only address part of the problem. At the least:

1. Brokerage firms should list in large type on the first page of all buy recommendations any investment banking business they have had with the company over the last three years and any equity ownership by the analyst, members of his or her immediate family, or the firm.
2. No buy recommendation should be permitted if the analyst, members of his or her immediate family, or the brokerage firm purchased stock or options for their own account in the month preceding the report, nor should they be permitted to sell stock until three days after a sell recommendation is issued.
3. Any shares purchased of a new issue by the analyst, members of his or her immediate family, or a money management arm of a brokerage firm should be held for a minimum of one year.

Thank you.

Talking Points

The reports of financial analysts are important to investors, who ordinarily lack the time and expertise to pour over financial reports of companies. For several decades investment banks had built up the reputation and professionalism of analysts. But in recent years investment banking fees grew so substantially, and investment banks so hungry for them, that analysts' reports were prostituted to gaining investment banking business: banks gave favorable reports to companies to get their banking business.

Thirty years ago a substantial number of analysts' reports urged investors to sell poorly performing stocks. Today a sell recommendation is a rarity. Investment banks doing business with companies recommended their stocks even as the financial performance of the companies collapsed. The result is that the analyst function has been perverted and investors are no longer able to place confidence in it.

IV Why It Happened

"Corrupt corporate executives are no better than common thieves."

—Attorney General John Ashcroft at press conference on day of the arrest of the former CFO and controller of WorldCom.
August 1, 2002

Comparing and contrasting the motivation and incentives above gives rise to the Great Chicken and Egg debate—did these CEOs corrupt the system, or did it corrupt them? Did the incentives the system provided corrupt otherwise ethical CEOs, or did unethical CEOs corrupt the system?

10 The Temptation to Steal

The New Very Rich: CEOs

A recent story in *New York Magazine* relates how the board of the Whitney Museum in New York was reviewing a list of "20 or so CEOs" who could be invited to give a multimillion dollar contribution and become a member of the board. The board decided to try to get Tyco CEO Dennis Kozlowski, who "commanded a salary package so outrageous that it stood out even in such exuberant times." On the Whitney board was Goldman Sachs vice chair Robert Hurst, whose firm was said to have made over $100 million in fees from Tyco. Kozlowski accepted the invitation to join the board and promised a $5 million gift. Later, Kozlowski was arrested but remains on the board, and Tyco, under new leadership, was discussing whether or not the gift was to be honored in full.[177]

A team of reporters from *Financial Times* assessed what CEOs made via some of the scandals. Some 25 executives walked away with a total of $3.3 billion in compensation from a group of seven companies that went bankrupt, and the executives made all the money in 3 years. None have yet been indicted; none of the money has been returned to shareholders. The companies are Enron, Global Crossing, WorldCom, Exodus, McLeodUSA, Metromedia Fiber Network, and XO Communications.[178]

The opportunity to do so well is mainly for CEOs, and without CEO's approval, tacit or explicit, other executives could not take advantage of the opportunities created by stock options. But some CEOs have given their approval so that other executives could make it aboard the gravy train. For example, in 1998 WorldCom's CFO Scott Sullivan was the highest paid CFO in the United States, making tens of millions of dollars. In 2002 he was arrested for fraud.

How CEOs Get Rich

With such an opportunity to get rich, the incentive to do it by whatever means is enormous. The elements of the incentive to steal have been identified in earlier chapters; they are: the means—stock options (Chapter 5); a high payoff (Chapter 5); available accomplices—accountants, banks, and attorneys (Chapters 6 and 7); and a low risk of being punished by boards or regulators (this chapter).

The opportunity for the CEO is obtaining stock options from his company's board, getting the share price up, and cashing in the options. If the share price goes up and he cashes in options, then he's rich.

It hasn't been quite as easy as shooting fish in a barrel, but it has not been much more difficult than that to get the firm's share price up, for at least a while. During the 1990s the economic environment was favorable—low inflation, a growing economy, a bull market; but still earnings had to show a steady and predictable increase. In each instance the executives took credit for the rise in their companies' share price. It doesn't appear that boards asked whether or not the increases would be sustained over a longer period.

These facts created large loopholes in the incentive effects of options. CEOs ended up being paid for improvements in the share price of firms that they did not cause and that were not sustained. In effect, the option mechanisms rewarded CEOs when they had little to do with share price increases and when those increases were ephemeral.

The great bull market of the 1990s caused CEO pay packages to balloon with increasingly valuable options. Yet corporate executives did little to cause the increase of share prices. The market rallied in large part because of major changes in the world situation—the end of the Cold War (which greatly reduced political risk in the world economy) and the emergence of China as a major producer of manufactured goods (which helped keep inflation low in America). A related major contribution to the bull market was the long-term decline in interest rates by which the Fed reacted to lower inflation and the shift from a federal budget deficit to a surplus. The price/earnings multiples on stocks rose dramatically, reflecting lower interest rates, and stock prices rose correspondingly.

This result was appropriate. What was not appropriate was that corporate CEOs benefited enormously from it. Had options been indexed to the market, this benefit wouldn't have occurred, and the great incentive to CEOs to mislead investors about company performance in order to cash in on short-term stock options wouldn't have existed.

CEOs had been blessed, largely on their own doing through their influence on the boards of directors of their companies, with pay packages stressing short-term stock options, at the very time that circumstances in the economy as a whole were turning hugely favorable to a bull market. CEOs were in the right place at the right time with a means to profit from something with which they had nothing to do. They were in the classic place of people who happened to be standing in the street holding buckets when it began to rain dollars.

Even in this greatly favorable environment, some CEOs were so incompetent that they couldn't make money the old-fashioned way, by earning it. So they resorted to deceiving investors about what was really happening in the company, with financials that appeared far better than they are, and share prices rose accordingly. If other companies are doing the same, then so much the better—then the market as a whole is rising, success is widespread, and with little suspicion, it's easier to nudge the company's shares upward.

If the share price rises substantially, the CEO cashes out options for a substantial fortune. Perhaps he takes only some of his option grant, and then he can point to how little he took from investors. The former CEO of Global Crossing, who denies knowledge of widespread fraud in the firm, has hired an attorney to tell reporters that his client was not greedy but in fact very modest. It seems he cashed out only one-third or so of the options the company's board had granted him before the company went bankrupt. That those options constituted a large fortune, and that the total number of options granted to him was far beyond anything justified by his contribution to the firm, is not mentioned.

Perhaps even with imaginative accounting, the company's share price stagnates. Then the CEO agrees to leave the company in return for walkaway money that is in itself a small fortune. Once he's rich, by whatever means, it doesn't matter whether he or she continues to run the company. Perhaps he retires or gives up his position to a rival. With enough money, attorneys can be hired, arrangements made to live abroad, and usually he gets away with his wealth. Even if, in the worst outcome, he's prosecuted and goes to jail for a while and pays a fine, ordinarily he's still very rich.

If he stays on, at some point the game is up, investors get suspicious, both revenues and earnings have been overstated, or expenses hidden and the company is forced to restate its financials. The stock price crashes. The CEO leaves under a cloud. There are investor suits against the company and against him; the SEC investigates. If he is very unlucky he may be forced to disgorge his gains and even spend some time in jail. But the probability of this is very, very low. Most likely his attorney makes a settlement with the government and he retains most of his fortune.

In America, very few securities law violators have gone to jail. From 1992 to 2001 SEC attorneys referred 609 cases to the Justice Department for possible criminal prosecution and 87 executives went to jail. America has 17,000 publicly traded companies, and the period from 1992 to 2001 includes the largest set of corporate fraud scandals in our history, so these are almost insignificant numbers. CEOs know that the probability of going to jail for cheating investors is very, very low.[179] So for anyone who makes it to a CEO's position, the temptation is take the money and run—and they do.

Cashing in Early

Recent years have provided numerous examples of CEOs cashing in large amounts of stock before the company's share price crashed. This opportunism was what one writer has called the "not-so-secret dirty secret of the crash." Even as investors were losing much of their money, top officials were becoming wealthy via the company. "They got rich because they were able to take advantage of the bubble to cash in hundreds of millions of dollars' worth of stock—stock that was usually handed to them via risk-free options—at vastly inflated prices. When the bubble burst, their shareholders were left holding the bag."[180]

Taking Golden Parachutes or Walkaway Money

If you can reach the rank of CEO, the chances of not getting rich are low, no matter how badly the company performs. How come a CEO gets so much money when the company does badly? How come people are paid huge sums not for performance but for failure? Many Americans ask this continually and find it very difficult to believe that it is really happening. We accept the notion that people who do extraordinary things, including leading large firms successfully, should get extraordinary rewards, but that a person who has failed can also get extraordinary rewards puzzles and angers us.

Here are a few examples:

- Jill Barad, CEO of Mattel, Inc. The company missed its sales targets by $500 million in 1998; she resigned in February 2000 and received approximately $50 million from the company.
- Stephen Hilbert, CEO of Conseco, Inc. He resigned in April 2000 with the company's stock down 90% and received approximately $50 million from the company.
- Dirk Jaeger, CEO of Procter & Gamble. During his 17 months at the top, the stock fell 50% in value and he received about $10 million in walkaway money.
- John W. Snow, appointed Secretary of the Treasury of the United States in December 2002, "was paid more than $50 million in salary, bonus, and stock in his nearly 12 years as chairman of the CSX Corporation, the railroad company. During that period, the company's profits fell, and its stock rose a bit more than half as much as that of the average big company."[181]
- Bernard J. Ebbers. Founded, led, and then resigned from WorldCom before its bankruptcy and received walkaway money from the company of

$1.5 million per year for life. The company has since indicated that it might try to revise Ebbers's severance package.[182]

That these payments are often provided for by the severance provisions of the CEO's employment contracts or are intended to buy out the contract's remaining years explains nothing. It only raises the question of how such an employment contract came to be. How and why did the board approve?

That the CEO was expected to be a success or was induced by the contract to take the position is no explanation either, for the payments remain excessive for this purpose. The point is that these agreements and payments removed the risk of failure from the CEO and left the company holding an empty bag for which it paid dearly. This wasn't pay for performance, clearly it was pay for nonperformance.

Getting Paid for Failure

There are three ways CEOs have been getting paid not only for nonperformance but even for actual failure:

- By being allowed to cash in options when the share price is high, although the share price then falls dramatically, in effect being paid for short-run improvement in the share price when long-term performance is poor.
- By being given golden parachutes when the company has performed badly.
- By being allowed to cash in options before the company goes bankrupt.

Getting paid for failure has a striking element, one so ironic as to appear almost a parody of the notion of paying CEOs for performance on behalf of investors. When a company gets into trouble and its stock fails dramatically, or it goes bankrupt, its CEO or former CEO who made himself rich may be challenged by investors as to his right to the big payouts. To this challenge, CEOs have often defended themselves by insisting that they really believed the companies would be successful but they were merely wrong about the product market.

"I made the money honestly," such a CEO insists, "because I was mistaken. I didn't know the company would fail." This is a critical argument because, if the CEOs *had* expected the company would fail, it would have been fraud to entice investors to invest while top executives were cashing out. So we have the novel spectacle of wealthy CEOs insisting they're entitled to their large compensation packages not because they were right about the business, but because they were wrong. After all, it's not illegal to be wrong.

It's tempting to say that people who were wrong about such a major thing were dumb, but these executives weren't at all dumb. They got investors to buy into companies at high share prices while they themselves were cashing out. The perverse career path to riches for many CEOs is clear: build a company, entice investors, cash out, and watch the company collapse. Failure is thus made into a path to riches. What a wonderful economic environment this has been for CEO's—both success and failure are paths to fortunes.

The Ignorant CEO

"The nation, it's I," said Louis XIV, meaning that France was his to do with as he liked. Today's CEOs have their own version of Louis' famous aphorism: "The company, it's me!"

This is the imperial CEO, the executive who dominates his board of directors, the other executives of the company, the auditors, and the bankers, and gets very rich in the process. We'll return to the topic of the imperial CEO and what might be done about him or her in Chapter 11. But here we want to deal with one of the most unusual aspects of his character. When scandals are discovered in the imperial CEO's company, he often insists he knew nothing about what was going on!

CEOs at Tyco, Enron, WorldCom, and Global Crossing, to name but a few firms, insist, usually through their attorneys, that they didn't know about massive frauds occurring at their companies. This is surprising since the frauds were usually conducted at the heart of the companies' financial activities and often benefited the CEOs directly. Yet CEOs say they didn't know about these things, even though they were being paid very well by shareholders to oversee the companies. Since they didn't know, they say, they are not guilty of securities fraud. They suggest their underlings, who were more directly associated with the fraudulent acts, might be guilty.

Peter Tafeen is a former deal-maker for Homestore.com and a central figure in investigations of accounting irregularities at AOL Time Warner. In his defense, Tafeen's attorney said that "Mr. Tafeen was a businessman, not an accountant, and not responsible for Homestore's financial reports."[183]

It's common for senior executives of corporations charged with accounting fraud to say that they're not accountants and they didn't know enough about accounting to recognize fraud. Instead, they say, they delegate that sort of thing to other people. So common has the "I'm not an accountant" refrain become that a search on Lexus-Nexus for the phrase, "not an accountant," came up with hundreds of references. Many CEOs are not accountants. But how much should a CEO know about accounting, especially when he or she is the leader of a publicly traded corporation? This is a key question. The amount of accounting that business executives need to know in order to avoid being implicated in most accounting fraud isn't all that much. And many of the clues are things that savvy businesspeople with little background in accounting would know instinctively aren't right. From the *New York Times,* it's evident that Tafeen understood quite well what was going on. Colleagues of his have testified that he deliberately "circumvented the rules" that the SEC had set up regarding revenue recognition. He also told a trade publication: "I don't believe in balance."[184]

A larger problem is the asymmetry of credit and blame in corporations. When a company's stock price goes up, the CEO argues that he or she is responsible for it, and that justifies a very large pay package for them. But if the company's stock price tanks and all sorts of irregularities in accounting and business practices are revealed, the CEO argues that he or she's not responsible for that; such matters are delegated to other people. This is the argument made, for example, by Kenneth Lay, CEO of Enron, but Lay is obviously a smart man, and early in his career he worked as an officer in the Pentagon helping to improve the Navy's accounting systems. In consequence, he must have understood the accounting at Enron, its objectives and methods (SPE's for example), if not its details. Walter Forbes said something very similar when all sorts of accounting fraud at Cendant was revealed, but colleagues of Forbes said that the man had a mind for detail. Gary Winnick, chairman of Global Crossing, had insisted that he was not aware of the company's problems while he was selling his shares and while investors were bidding up the price of his company. But a memo from the company's president to Winnick in June 2000 told Winnick that the company was going to collapse.[185] These examples indicate that the businesspeople who run companies keep on top of their financial situation and the prospects for the firm, and it's only after they've cashed out and the companies have seen their share price collapse that they suddenly suggest they were ignorant of the most important information about the companies they led.

Finally, some key elements of recent accounting fraud entangled more than one company, for example, the swapping of capacity among companies, which each company then booked as revenue, although no true economic transactions had taken place. In one such case Global Crossing and Qwest Communications worked together to create swaps that allowed both companies to exaggerate their financial results.[186] Complex deals were often sealed between two or more companies for the purpose of inflating the share price of each company. The deals directly benefited the top executives of the companies involved; and the conclusion is inescapable that the CEOs knew about them. The whole structure of the frauds was marvelously clever, not the clumsy efforts of a few executives to cover up shortfalls in sales or attain forecasted results—which the press often suggests, and which prosecutions of middle-level executives, at WorldCom, for example, imply. In fact, much more sophisticated deception was being conducted.

But even if investors accept CEOs' assertions that they were ignorant of fraudulent practices, it matters little. A CEO on whose watch a massive fraud occurred is guilty of perpetrating fraud upon his or her investors, whether or not he can be proven to have had direct knowledge of the fraud. If he had direct knowledge, then he's guilty of defrauding his shareholders by way of the fraudulent actions. If he didn't have direct knowledge, then he's guilty of defrauding his shareholders by receiving compensation for doing the job of CEO when he wasn't really doing it—he was negligent or illegally "blind" (not seeing material matters because he chose not to see them). Legally, he was in violation of a fiduciary's duty of care, which we'll examine in detail in Chapter 13. It hardly matters which form the fraud took—direct or indirect—the CEO was guilty of it. Our courts may make distinctions—having direct knowledge may be illegal and having no direct knowledge held to be exculpatory—but both are fraud against investors and both should be illegal.

So Strong a Temptation

In the United States in the last few years, the rewards of being a top corporate executive with lots of options and high-flying stock have grown so high that executives with the opportunity seem to feel it's worth it to abandon ethics, perhaps even to go to jail, because ordinarily they can keep a large part of the fortunes they've amassed. Against this opportunity, what's the risk of some time in jail or embarrassment?

It's embarrassing to be handcuffed and taken to arraignment by prosecutors, but the risk of this happening is not large. It's distasteful to go to jail, but it's not likely to happen, and if it does, it's not likely to last very long. It's upsetting to have to give back some money, but ordinarily a lot remains. Once out of jail, a person can hire public relations experts, give some money to charity, and wait confidently for the American public to very quickly forget about the offense. Meanwhile, the money's been made. So if someone can become a CEO in a publicly traded company, he has a road to riches. Under current law an executive or former executive charged with accounting fraud by the Justice Department is free to keep and spend his personal holdings until the Justice Department wins a criminal case against him, or the SEC a civil case. It's as if a bank robber caught with a bag of cash he stole from the bank was permitted to keep and spend it, including on attorneys, until he's convicted. In fact, today, it's as if the nation's securities industry were a big bank from which robbers steal and keep and spend the money until finally convicted, should that ever happen. There are some statutes that permit the government to seize funds allegedly obtained illegally, and sometimes they are used in cases involving securities fraud. But it is not yet usual. Ultimately, it would be far more just for the government to seize whatever funds they can find of those who have been involved in corporate fraud, and after convictions, redistribute them to the shareholders of the company. But that isn't usually what happens now.

The Crucial Importance of Leadership

Leadership matters. In the events discussed in this book, it matters a lot. Had many CEOs of large companies made different choices in the past two decades about their roles in American society, then the financial scandals and the exploitation of shareholders, which are the topic of this book, would not have happened.

Everyone in corporate America in recent years has talked about good leadership, but there has been precious little of it. In fact, when it comes to explaining the securities crisis, the general opinion in corporate and academic America is that systems and markets matter much more than leadership. Corporate executives are said to be driven to misbehavior by systems within their companies and by markets external to their firms. The excuse for misleading investors is that executives were unaware of what was happening in their companies because of the complexity of modern business and the administrative and technical systems by which it runs. The explanation for fraud is that the market made executives do it.

For example, CEO compensation is argued to be market based, and therefore, it is concluded, there is no reason to question its ethical or moral appropriateness. But the defense is deficient in two ways: first, it does not follow that because the market generates a result, it is not questionable in ethical or moral terms; and second, the market, which is supposed to generate today's executive pay packages, is strongly rigged by executives in their own favor (see Chapter 5).

Discussing the scandals with a reporter, a prominent academic said: "It is important to recognize that this doesn't come about as a result of crooks. This comes about as a result of honest people being subjected to forces that they don't understand. The forces are very strong, and this evolves over a period of time. You end up with highly moral, honest people doing dishonest things. It wasn't as if the Mafia had taken over corporate America. We are too quick to say—and the media feed this—that if a bad thing happens it's because a bad person did it, and that person had evil intentions. It is much more likely that there were some bad systems in place." He added, "The design of enormous stock-option packages had a disastrous effect on corporate ethics."[187]

In this view, the CEOs of Enron (Kenneth Lay), Tyco (Dennis Kozlowski), and WorldCom (Bernard Ebbers) are "highly moral, honest people" who were victimized by bad systems that had developed around them. They were forced to accept huge compensation packages that undermined their ethics.

Following this logic, it appears that top executives were compelled to become very wealthy by forces beyond their control. What a fortunate fate! Investors must wish to become the victims of such marvelous external and irresistible forces, because their own experience has been rather less favorable. Strong evidence requires rejection of the notion that top executives who got rich are the victims of external forces. Instead, this book sees the current situation in which CEOs got rich but investors didn't as arising not from market forces, but from the pursuit of personal interest by people in a position to affect the market—affect it by co-opting boards of directors, auditors, and regulators, and by intentionally misleading investors. The framework of analysis in this book takes leadership very seriously and holds people in leadership positions accountable for what they did for themselves and didn't do for others.

CEOs in large American companies have the power to bend others to their will; they have incentives to make different choices; they have the opportunity to make their choices and they have the choice as to how to use their power, choices, and opportunities.

CEOs are influenced by a variety of factors, including their boards, regulators, the law, the expectations of their boards of directors, customers, investors, and society at large. They are central to the direction of our economy and our economic culture—to the way Americans do business.

My research for this book has convinced me that the behavior of many top executives of our large, publicly owned firms were a key cause of the crisis of confidence we have experienced in our securities markets. Their behavior is not the only cause, but it is one of the most significant causes. Other factors that were supposed to act as checks and balances were instead manipulated by top executives.

This book has described in previous chapters how this happened and its consequences for investors. In the following chapters we will explore what can be done about it. At all times we will focus on CEOs as the key factor in our story, convinced that unless the ethics of many top executives are improved, and their power limited, there can be no truly successful reform of American securities markets.

This is a different focus than is common for an inquiry into a stock market boom and bust. It's not first and foremost a story about securities firms and analysts, because their role, important as it was, remained primarily supportive. Nor is this primarily a story about corporations, because companies don't do things, people do. A corporation is a fictional person in law; it acts only through its human agents, and the most important of its agents by far is its CEO. Furthermore, our story is not first and foremost an economic analysis, though it's grounded at every step in economics, because what happened in our equity markets was the result of the objectives and actions of top corporate executives. Finally, it's not first and foremost a story about markets, because what happened in the markets was a response to the information, often misleading, given them by top executives of companies.

In summary, the first half of our book has demonstrated that investors' losses originated in the actions of top corporate leadership; and the second half of our book will apply a leadership framework to the question of what should be done about it.

The Courage to Speak Out

President William J. McDonough of the New York Fed had the courage to tell CEOs in a speech, "CEOs and their boards should simply reach the conclusion that executive pay is excessive and adjust it to more reasonable and justifiable levels." He also said that the huge increase in CEO pay in recent years was "terribly bad social policy and perhaps even bad morals."[188] Several days later the Conference Board, a business study group, issued a report under the name of several business and investor leaders urging major changes in the way top executives are compensated in American firms.[189] It was the president of the New York Fed and a few business leaders who had the courage to openly tell CEOs to shape up. They said what everyone except a few CEOs and the compensation consultants know—executive pay has become a scandal itself and requires reform. But it's regrettable that other voices seem to have been reluctant to say this—the top university presidents, the leading politicians, the church leaders.

Just a few years ago, the CEO's of large companies were America's most admired people. Today they vie with used car salespersons for the people most mistrusted in America.

Talking Points

Our legal system allows executives to make very large sums via deceptive and fraudulent means and then punishes them, if at all, with a slap on the wrist. Therefore, the incentives for fraud are immense. The temptation must be eliminated if there is to be any different behavior in executive suites. Yet a small fine and a few months in prison (if that) are a small price to pay for making and keeping a fortune. That this small price is generally all there is to fear from the law today is the single most important factor in causing the current scandals and the losses suffered by investors. In effect, today's very high compensation via standard stock options for CEOs provides an overwhelming incentive to steal.

11 The Ethics of the Gutter

The former CEO of a Fortune 500 company had just built himself an ocean-side summer home and was playing tennis at a nearby club in the summer of 2002. When one of his opponents asked him during a break about corporate ethics, he replied, laughing, "Corporate ethics? There aren't any. It's an oxymoron."

Do What's Right: Why Ethics Are Very Important

In Chapter 8 we asked how is it that regulators and boards of directors failed in their oversight of corporate financial reporting. In this chapter we ask how is it that self-restraint and personal ethics failed to do what other checks and balances didn't.

Key observers have stressed that individual ethics are the financial system's ultimate line of defense. For example, although Warren Buffett is one of the most strident critics of the way corporate executives in America have been treating investors, he doesn't advocate strong new regulations to compel greater honesty in executive offices; he sees the solution as much more basic.

"To clean up their act on these fronts," Buffett wrote, "CEOs don't need 'independent' directors, oversight committees, or auditors absolutely free of conflicts of interest. They simply need to do what's right." Then to reinforce the point, Buffett cited the words of the Fed's chairman. "As Alan Greenspan forcefully declared last week," Buffett wrote, "the attitudes and actions of CEOs are what determine corporate conduct."[190]

Doing what's right, and adhering to the attitudes that cause powerful business executives to do what's right, are what we mean by ethics. As Buffett and Greenspan suggest, ethical attitudes are at the core of proper conduct of a company, and proper conduct is itself the key to investor confidence.

This is not a new notion. Adam Smith, one of the first people to understand the economic potential of free enterprise, insisted that freedom of action and economic power must be accompanied by moral restraint. Adam Smith's first major work was not his well-known *Wealth of Nations*, but a book on ethics titled *Theory of Moral Sentiments*. As an ethicist he understood that the mechanism of the "invisible hand"—his term for the workings of the market—could be effective only if self-interest were restrained by conscience. With remarkable prescience, Smith warned that corporations (in his day called joint-stock companies) could slip the restraints of human conscience.

This is a significant problem for us today, and it is recognized as such within the corporations themselves. In recent years more and more corporations have been establishing a code of ethics for their employees. Did this mean that ethics were becoming more deeply ingrained in our firms? Certainly not with respect to the treatment of investors, as we've seen in preceding chapters. In fact, the printed codes of ethical conduct of such firms as Enron and WorldCom are now for sale as ironic mementos of the current scandals.

Regardless of how much they may currently be ignored or violated, ethics are the foundation upon which a successful business can be established, and the framework upon which the securities market can be successfully conducted. Without ethical behavior in our corporations we can't trust each other, and we must rely on supervision and oversight alone. Clever and unethical people can usually escape detection, and they can make the cost of oversight so high that the whole enterprise becomes pointless.

What has happened to American ethics, and how? If ethical standards have declined, they are presumably a causal factor in today's scandals and investors' losses; if they've not declined, the incentive to ignore them may have gotten much stronger. This is the explanation Alan Greenspan gave to a Congressional committee early in 2002 for the scandals. "The incentives created [that is, stock options] overcame the good judgment of too many corporate managers," Greenspan said. "It is not that humans have become any more greedy than in generations past. It is that the avenues to express greed had grown so enormously."[191]

There have always been people in business whose ethics are not high, and we've had repeated incidents of financial fraud in our history. But whatever the causes—whether there's been a decline in ethics or an increase in the temptation to steal, or both—never before have we had fraud on today's scale. Our economy is larger today, and there are many more investors in the securities markets both in absolute numbers and as a proportion of the population, so that securities markets today support not primarily the wealth of a few, but instead the savings and pension—actual and prospective—of the many. Today's scandals have a much more serious impact on people's lives than ever before.

What Are Ethics?

We might think, since there is so much discussion of business ethics in today's America, and since both the nation's president and the chairman of the Fed refer to ethics as the primary line of defense for investors against corporate chicanery, that there would have been much written and debated about business ethics. This is not the case. A major book on ethics, compiled from the writings of many commentators, has only a small section on business.[192] The section is labeled, showing its very limited focus, "contract ethics."

What do we mean by the term "ethics"? Business ethics are, we are told, "Responsible actions and positive…impact of corporate activity on people, institutions, the environment and the fabric of community."[193] The last item in this list gives away its focus—ethics are about the impact of business on the environment and the community. These are important issues, and until recently, the matters that were of most concern to progressive commentators, but they have little to do with the question as to what ethics requires in dealings between corporate executives and their investors. This is an arena in which basic values such as honesty and basic human qualities such as greed are dominant. We are a stage below social concerns such as the environment and the welfare of our communities—we are in the realm of the Ten Commandments (sacred to Christian, Jew, and Muslim alike): "Thou shalt not steal; thou shalt not bear false witness; thou shalt not covet…"

Ethics requires us to make normative judgments about what is morally right and wrong. It is based on underlying moral standards. Its key question is: Does a decision violate any moral standards? Moral standards are supposed to override self-interest. These are standards about how we deal fairly with each other. "Ethics is what my feelings tell me is right and wrong. But it's not a fixed standard, so it's difficult."[194]

Law is the lowest common denominator of ethics; it's what the whole people can agree on via their representatives in Congress. It's about the level of trust necessary to permit the simplest transactions. It's insufficient to provide the level of trust requisite to running modern capital markets. Seeking to restore investor confidence in the capital markets via law alone is a dead end.

The heart of business ethics is the recognition that what's allowable in accounting and the law isn't necessarily what's right. The courage not to do something unethical just because it may be allowable and/or beneficial to oneself is what it means to be ethical. If we confine ethics to what is legal and leave it to Congress and the courts to define what that is, we'll end up with a system that is driven by rules but not morality—very much the system we have now.

Writing in 1987, Robert S. Bachelder observed that Wall Streeters saw the securities markets as a game; if you break the rules, you pay a penalty and then go back to the game.[195] Ethics used to constrain us in how far our behavior would go, Bachelder insisted. But no longer. "Will our financial temples have to fall on our heads... before we are brought back to our senses?" he asked at the end of his article.[196]

Today we know the answer to his question—it is "yes."

The Failure of Ethics Programs in Companies

It seems that in today's America, the more ethics and integrity are mentioned by a company or its executives, the less likely they are to pay attention to them. Enron's corporate stationery contained, at the bottom of the page, the words: "Respect. Integrity.[197] Communication. Excellence." Sloganeering seems to have replaced commitment in the realm of corporate ethics.

Above we mentioned that more and more companies have established codes of ethics and training programs about ethical behavior for their employees, and we said that this effort apparently exerted little restraint on their top executives in the recent scandals. Why was this programmatic approach to ethics so unsuccessful?

Here's one explanation. To a Congressional committee, a Qwest employee described a "Code of Business Conduct" that ordinary employees like her were trained in and certified for every year. Among other things, the code warned of the dangers of insider trading. The employee held onto her company stock partly because company executives insisted that it would do well and partly because she was prohibited by the regulations of the investment plan from selling a lot of what she had. Meanwhile, top executives were selling large amounts of stock as the company headed toward financial collapse. The company's formal ethics program had no meaning for top executives.[198]

Four common mistakes are made by executives promoting ethics in their companies:

1. Believing that having corporate compliance programs means higher ethical standards in the company. Business ethics about such things as employment discrimination began to be emphasized by legislation starting in the early 1990s. In 1991, the concept of culpability was introduced in new laws. When sentencing companies convicted of federal offenses, judges were instructed to take into consideration whether the firms had effective

compliance programs, had provided full cooperation during investigations, and expressed clear acceptance of responsibility.[199]

Around the same time, companies started to express greater interest in social responsibility. Compliance programs and emphasis on social ethics started to gain popularity in corporations. However, these efforts didn't mean that a company's ethical standards had improved. The new initiatives seemed often to be mere reactions to the "leniency factor" should a company face charges in court.

2. Believing that an increased involvement in charitable activities in the community demonstrates an increased commitment to ethical behavior. Although constructive in themselves, community activities do not necessarily express an underlying ethical standard. Too often they are merely an instrumental way to build community support, attract talent, even do soft marketing, among other things.

3. Confusing company culture with individual ethics. Companies that have books of ethical behavior sometimes believe that a corporate culture paying lip service to ethics translates into ethical actions by individuals. It does not necessarily do so. For example, Enron and WorldCom both have had a comprehensive code of ethics in place for a while.[200] The provisions of these two corporate codes were not observed by key individuals in the companies.

4. Failing to recognize the limits of an ethical code imposed from above. A large, publicly owned corporation is a multinational society that has its own ethics, derived in part from the practices of its industry, of the nationalities that dominate it, and of its leaders. Morality is therefore implicit in its culture. But if the leadership of the company tries to be more explicit about corporate ethics, then it runs into the same problems that our schools do: that we have multiple cultures, and people shy away from involving morality, and therefore ethics with business. So there are limitations to what can be done in corporate ethics just as there are in the schools.

Despite the difficulties listed above, companies headed by moral leaders can enforce ethical behavior by employees. But the failure of moral leaders to set standards for others in their companies hasn't been today's problem. The crux of today's scandals is immorality at the top of the companies, where no one else in the firm can do anything about it. This is exactly where top executives have too much power—they have the power to induce others to fraudulent behavior and to prevent detection for long periods of time.

It's not at all uncommon for lower-level people in business firms to be instructed to falsify financial records, or to see others doing it. But what can they do about it? In some instances the action is isolated, and if a person complains to a superior about someone else's behavior, the matter may be corrected. But often, it's at the instigation of the superior that the fraud is being done. Then a person who complains to top management, who becomes a whistle-blower, quickly finds himself or herself accused of some trumped-up violation and transferred or discharged.

CEOs, other top executives, and the directors of firms make up the leadership that sets the values of a firm. This is where the problem has been in the recent scandals—right at the top. With the example of greed and corruption at the top of the firms, whatever the formal statements of moral rectitude, it would not seem there could be a healthy set of values in the firm as a whole. Yet despite malfeasance at the top, millions of working Americans continued to do their jobs ethically. This is the most remarkable aspect of these years, and it may give us hope that if the top of our firms again find the right path, then there can be a better America.

The Decline of American Ethics and How it Happened

A young man was hired in Latin America as a representative of Citibank and was assigned to Argentina, where he spent 3 years. He continually ran into dishonest business practices. When he objected to them, his Argentine friends told him, "Don't be so proud. We know how business is done in New York. It's the same." But he protested that it wasn't the same at all, and that American standards were far higher.

Then he was assigned to an investment bank in New York City, and was soon structuring derivatives for the Enron account. He discovered violations of GAAP as egregious as anything he'd experienced in Buenos Aires. He saw GAAP completely disregarded to produce pro forma earnings, and the results fed to the investing public. He found deception and sharp practices rampant. He found that the Argentines had been right. We now had on Wall Street the ethics of the most corrupt business and political regimes in Latin America—the ethics of the financial gutter.

American business ethics have changed dramatically in recent years. We had big problems before the Great Depression of the 1930s; then lots of new regulation and a certain cleansing of the whole system during that period improved things greatly. But in the last two decades we've slipped badly, as the story above suggests, to levels not much better than those of some of the most corrupt societies on the globe. During the stock market boom of the late 1990s, ethical concerns in America ceased to exert much if any limitations on the rush to riches. How did this happen?

When a means becomes an end, there is no result of the means that its supporter doesn't endorse. If a product market ends in starvation for many, that's tolerable—because it's what a market does. If a capital market ends in destitution for many (their pensions are lost), that's tolerable, because it's what a market does. If a legal process ends in execution of an innocent person, that's tolerable, because it was with due process of law. If a legal process permits defrauders to go free, that's fine, because it's what due process of law does. Letting a means justify any end is as bad as letting an end justify any means. Only a moral compass quite separate from a particular process can provide a foundation to judge means and ends.

Another major contributor to the decline of ethics in America is that many Americans have opted for detailed rules rather than general ethical principles for guiding and judging behavior. In effect, we've tried to substitute law for ethics. We're a multicultural society in which generally accepted ethical standards are sometimes difficult to identify. We don't agree about what is right and wrong, so we look to a political process that makes laws to give us direction. But law isn't morality—it's only rules, made by imperfect political processes and by an imperfect court system. With law as our standard of ethics, we've become a nation of sharp, clever dealers rather than a nation of honest people who can trust one another.

What and how did this happen in the securities markets? The answer is a story about increasing financial incentives that cause people to abandon ethics for their own interests and to take refuge in legal technicalities; and about a society and its schools and families that haven't been able to effectively counter this powerful trend.

The change has been gradual, and it's difficult to find a signpost. But one is provided by the moment, about 15 years ago, when the nation's leading business schools went from stressing how to make money by certain methods—especially via efficiency in production and by identifying and satisfying consumer needs—to stressing making money by virtually any means possible, especially by smart dealing and getting advantages over your competitors. Strategy, for example, became a matter not of developing and introducing new products and services, but of creating barriers to stop competitors and exploit positions of quasi-monopoly.

As taught in business schools, strategy was repositioned to be about monopoly ("barriers to entry") and profit, not about efficiency and resource allocation. The elements of economics that studied monopolistic behavior were dusted off and brought into the field of business strategy as prescriptions for how companies should be managed. In this way they influenced a generation of business school students, corporate planners, top executives of firms, and strategy consultants and regulated to the background as a sort of nostalgic curiosity of the more traditional approach of out-competing the competitor.

Our business schools began to teach people to think in terms not of right and wrong but of public relations. The message was no longer to do what's right and be sure people know you're doing that, but to do what benefits your company or yourself and put the best possible face on it, including employing dishonesty when that helps.

The American economic system that we prize so highly came to be seen as one with imperfections that were subject to exploitation for an executive's personal wealth. It's supposed to be a competitive system, but clever executives could build barriers to competition. It's supposed to be a regulated system, but political processes can be corrupted so that regulators look the other way. It's supposed to be a system of checks and balances, but a clever executive can cancel them out—he can check the balances and balance the checkers. It's supposed to be a transparent system, but a clever executive can fool people by concealing key facts. An executive is supposed to be the agent of investors, but he can make himself rich, no matter what happens to them.

Such behavior was certainly unethical, maybe even illegal, but so what—a clever executive could take the money and run. He could hire lawyers to defend him (in America they're even required to defend you without regard to the truth, whatever you've done) and there are places to stash the money so that an executive and his family can live well whatever investors and the courts try to do. Making money was always a basic objective, but how it was done used to matter—this was the core of ethics. Ethics governs not just what you shouldn't do, but what you should do. There are right ways to be successful, as well as wrong ways.

In part, ethics came to be seen as purely instrumental, a way to gain an economic advantage rather than as a moral imperative in itself. The argument was, and is, that good ethics are good business. It's a direct analogue to the argument that good employee relations are good business. Often, both are true. But what happens when an executive sees a clear opportunity to profit by unethical behavior—are good ethics good business only in certain circumstances?

This question is of course the key test of the rule, and here ethics as an instrumentality fails. After all, the executive's ethics were only skin deep—he was being ethical for the business advantage it brought him. So we understand if he abandons good ethics for financial advantage.

Nor is this result undercut by pointing to long-term rather than short-term gain from being ethical. Some would argue that unethical behavior provides financial advantage in the short run, but not the long. This may be the case. Years of research didn't establish that ethical behavior is good for a company in the long term; there were no conclusive correlations. But now there are. It can hardly be denied after what happened at Enron and WorldCom that unethical behavior by executives can destroy a company.

But what about situations in which the long term is of no concern?—for example, a CEO seeing the opportunity to raise his company's stock price in the short run so he can cash out options and leave the company. Here there's an enormous incentive for unethical behavior in the short run, and no long run (he's left the firm and it's gone bankrupt). In effect, a person who adopts ethical standards only when they appear to be good for business is a person who has become amoral and behaves amorally. We saw in Chapter 3 that accounting firms came to see fines paid as a result of fraud charges as a cost of doing business, and also as good advertisements to potential clients who were seeking flexible audits.

The "Push the Limits" Environment

In the midst of the stock market boom of the 1990s it was common to hear statements such as "Today money is made by the business that will push the limits the furthest—in accounting: to book the most sales and hide the most expenses in order to report the highest profit; and in financial disclosure: to reveal as little as possible about debts and the company's business model." Thus it was that investors were fooled into believing companies were much larger and more profitable than they actually were; misled about the amount of debt companies had, and confused about how they made money, if they did. As we've seen in the previous chapters, this is exactly how top executives in many companies made their fortunes—by using creative accounting or outright fraud to exaggerate sales and profits, and by revealing as little to investors as possible about the real financial situation of the firm and the way it made, or didn't make, money.

The "push the limits" environment reveals much about what had happened to ethics in American business. Its very emergence indicates a deterioration in ethics. In other words, executives, accountants, bankers, and consultants all used this term, "push the limits," for what they saw as a new approach—one in which ethics were much less a concern than before.

Since the whole notion of "push the limits" is to go as far as possible without ending up in jail—that, after all, is what "the limits" are—ethics, other than the most technical concerns about legality, are essentially tossed out the window. This is strongly suggestive of a very substantial decline in business ethics. It's important to further distinguish law and ethics. Interestingly, in securities law, the two come closer together than in most other areas of American law because the legal principle of fiduciary responsibility closely resembles the ethical requirement of fair treatment.

So where lies the important difference between ethics and law? The answer is that the American business system is too large and complex, and the American legal system is too cumbersome for our system of commerce, and especially our system of financial investment, to be supported and sustained by law alone.

In part the effort to sustain business by law alone occurs because "law" itself is a rather abstract concept. When we refer to an executive obeying the securities (or any other) laws, what do we mean? At first glance, it seems self-evident. We expect the executive to comply with the provisions of the laws, which were enacted to protect investors. But the laws are complex, and their application is spotty. If we apply a concept of ethics to interpreting the laws, then their meaning becomes much clearer. But if we don't, then the laws are all very technical and full of loopholes—what the laws are isn't clear at all.

Today's attorneys step in and offer the following conception of the law: "The law is whatever the courts say it is after full litigation." This means that a business executive doesn't read and follow what he believes to be the provisions of the law, using if you will a standard of ethical behavior, but he relies only on the clearly stated rules applied by a court after full consideration of the technicalities of the law, all possible defenses, any ambiguities, any mitigating circumstances, and so on. It is the law stretched to the breaking point—or it is the law at the breaking point—and it has nothing to do with ethics and everything to do with bureaucratic rule-making and the vagaries of enforcement.

Another version of this approach to defining the law can be put this way: "The law prohibits only what someone has gone to jail for—anything else, that is, anything one can get away with, is okay." There haven't been many prosecutions of executives for securities fraud in recent decades, so there isn't a lot of guidance for executives about what is really prohibited.

In a "push the limits" atmosphere, many things that ethics would otherwise prohibit become possibly legal. There is a misconception of law that things are clearly either legal or illegal. This is an error. Many things are possibly legal, depending on the outcome of litigation about them. In the "push the limits" environment, people develop expertise in identifying things that may be legal. That's its whole point. An executive looks around at his predecessors or his peers in his own or other firms and he sees this type of creative accounting here, and that type of rich option package there, both pushing the limits, and no one is holding back, and he thinks, "I can do it too." And now the executive is pushing the limits to get as much as he can for himself, and the investor is left in the lurch. And in a nutshell, this is what has happened in the current scandals.

The law is not a sufficient protection for the investor. Investors must be able to trust corporate executives and financial professionals (including accountants, banks, and attorneys) beyond the limited ability of the system of justice to identify and punish violators of the law. There must be more than legal restraints, just as Warren Buffett and Alan Greenspan, and of course, many others, recognize. There must be fair dealing between executive and investor. This is the core of why ethics are so important—they are more than the observance of the law, and without them the financial system cannot function properly. Alan Greenspan referred to the "attitudes" of CEOs, and ethics is very much a matter of attitude.

In the 1970s Reg Jones was CEO of General Electric and one of America's most influential business leaders. He was the tireless proponent of the attitude that the company belonged to the investors and that the CEO was the steward of their property. In the 1980s this attitude came to be seen as old-fashioned and insufficiently aggressive. By the late 1990s it had largely been replaced with the attitude that the company is the CEO's (hence the notion of the imperial CEO) and that the CEO could and should do with it whatever he or she liked, so long as he or she didn't do something that got him or the company caught. This was yet another instance of the shift in attitude from ethics to push the limits.

Reg Jones had sponsored the attitude that investors are well-intentioned people who'll be with a company for the long term. By the late 1990s the attitude was far more common that investors are greedy fools suitable for fleecing.

Hamstringing Ethics in America

In U.S. society there are five basic impediments to ethical behavior:

1. Human nature, including greed and dishonesty and the hypocrisy and fear that tries to disguise these things. This applies, of course, to any human society. We know about this aspect of our nature, and it's the function of ethics to restrain our self-serving behavior within socially acceptable limits. By the mid-1990s in America ethics had so far been subordinated to self-seeking that Americans joked about and partly accepted the aphorism that "greed is good."
2. A polyglot society in which there are no common norms of ethical and social behavior. It's sometimes pointed out that ethics are driven by a moral code. Since we lack an agreed-upon moral code, how can we have generally accepted ethical standards? Some answer that there are universal moral principles from which can be derived universal ethical standards. But this is too facile. That Americans differ very much in their approach to ethical issues is evident to someone who has conducted discussions about ethical behavior with many groups of American business school students and executives, as I have. No matter what the ethical dilemma, Americans approach it differently. They reflect differences not in self-interest—because these are defined as discussions of ethics—but in the attitudes with which they've been brought up. Different religions, different sects, different ethnic groups, and different nationalities have divergent standards of fair treatment. Americans increasingly come from all over the world, and even those born here are from many different backgrounds. Each of us is sure of the ethics with which we were brought up, and many of us have very different ethical standards. To get a group of Americans to agree on the proper ethical approach to a business situation often requires lengthy discussions until a new sort of synthetic attitude emerges out of the mixture of many different ingredients. Most companies and most schools don't make an effort to have such discussions.

   Multiculturalism is a more significant barrier to a generally agreed-upon ethics, even in the business world, than many people recognize. In our society, people are often uncomfortable with the notion that ethics requires a moral or religious foundation. They are convinced that there is available a nonmoral or nonreligiously based ethics. But the attempts to formulate one have been largely unavailing.

   The problem of multiculturalism as a barrier to a consensus on ethics is nowhere better evidenced than in the efforts that have been made to craft a universal set of ethics. In what is perhaps the most significant example, Louis Finkelstein, chancellor of the Jewish Theological Seminary in New York, in 1940 convened a conference of scholars from various religions and disciplines to attempt to device a universal code of ethics. Its ambition went further than to create a business or economic code, so perhaps its task was more difficult than business ethics alone. The conference met several times over several years only to end in failure. The major fault lines in the conference were among advocates of various religious traditions and humanists.[201]

3. A large and varied society in which there is no sense of community and obligation, so that those outside the family or religious, social, or ethnic group are fair game for sharp dealing and exploitation.
4. A certain myopia even in the social responsibility community. Americans seem to be overlooking basic personal behavior such as honesty as a matter of ethics, and instead focusing on social matters such as the environment, pornography, and so on. For example, "socially responsible" mutual funds have almost completely missed the collapse of social responsibility implicit in these corporate financial scandals. One "socially responsible" fund invested in Adelphia because Adelphia didn't carry "adult entertainment" on its cable systems. Another "socially responsible" fund invested in Enron in early 2001 because it determined that Enron had improved its environmental practices. The possibility that a firm has defrauded investors of their life savings doesn't appear on the radar of most of these funds.[202]
5. American ethics are confused and made ineffective by our society's widespread adoption of relativism: the conviction that anyone's culturally (or religiously or philosophically) based ethics are likely to be wrong for others. Because we hold ethical issues to be personal, there appears to be no basis for a corporate leader to make ethical judgments for the firm as a whole. Hence, as the CEO of a company said to a class of business school students during the corporate financial crises: "In a contest between the moral and the legal, the legal should always win out, because there are different moralities." Pressed by questions from students about this position, he added, "Ethics means abiding by the law, nothing more."

Many Americans accept the view that law can substitute for ethics and believe that it offers a way out of the dilemma of finding ethical standards in a relativistic society; that is, a way to make judgments in a society in which people prefer not to be judgmental.

But what does defining ethics as law and nothing more mean?

First, law is created by a legislative process that is itself part of a political process. Hence, to adopt law as the standard of ethics is to adopt a political solution to a moral challenge. This is not likely to be a good outcome.

Second, legislation in this country is badly tainted by a political process that is widely recognized to be corrupted by money and private influence. Since the law is itself made by a process that is deeply flawed ethically, the result is that our ethics are made by an unethical process. This irony bodes badly for our ethical standard.

Third, the law is changed frequently, so that there will be little ethical continuity. Ethics that change often are not ethics at all, but rather a form of expediency.

Fourth, law is complex, not direct, and must be continually interpreted. It is sometimes defined in America as what the legislatures enact and the courts decide it means after full litigation. This makes our ethics the result of a process of litigation that is a contest often resolved by technicalities. This also bodes poorly for ethics.

Fifth, the law is silent on many significant ethical issues, so that unless we want to invite lawmakers into more and more intimate involvement with all aspects of business, the law leaves us uncovered in many situations.

In consequence, the law isn't a satisfactory basis for ethics and will not resolve the problem of providing sufficient trust in the ethics of executives and financial professionals to give investors confidence in our equity markets.

The attitude of American society—acceptance and admiration of the rich, whatever the source of their money—plays a major role in the place of ethics in American business. We don't really care how people make money as long as they have a lot of it, so many people have few scruples about how they get it. Money in America buys acceptance, enjoyment, and security. Ethics, therefore, has a large obstacle to overcome to act as a significant barrier to personal enrichment by certain means. The existence of this obstacle is complicated in America because we are, and have been since early in our colonial beginnings, a nation of new people, one in which wealth is respected regardless of how it has been acquired, and in only one generation all wealth is made respectable—children who have inherited money are not asked to explain its origin, even one generation back.

A story goes that two people jointly owned and ran a store. One day only one of them was at the counter, and a customer gave him a twenty-dollar bill. "I gave him change for a ten," said the partner who was working that day. "Now the question is, do I tell my partner?" This story, like many others, illustrates the popular attitudes advocates of ethics must overcome to restrain people's efforts to get rich.

The Role of the Business Schools

Investors want to be sure that if they return to the stock market, their money won't be stolen from them. Tougher laws against corporate fraud that are rigorously enforced would help greatly. But it's difficult to rely on law alone in what is, after all, a huge economy. Investors need to be able to trust the men and women who run the companies in which they place their money. One possible source of ethical influence on future CEOs is the nation's business schools.

The role business schools play is important because it is to train leaders. The alumni of Harvard Business School alone hold about 20% of the top three executive positions of Fortune 500 companies. But it's easy to overestimate the influence of business schools on their students, and to blame the schools for problems that they had little opportunity to prevent. So we need to assess what they've done and are doing, and in a later chapter turn to what they can do.

The major business schools now tend to accept students not directly upon graduation from college, but only after the applicants have had several years of business experience. The result is that students come to the schools not at 21 or 22 years of age, but at 26, on average, after 3 or 4 years on the job. The young people who enter the nation's business schools are generally of high moral character and ethical standards. They are adults who, by the time they reach the schools, believe their ethics to be strongly fixed and see no need to challenge their own attitudes or spend precious time on the subject of ethics. They often view ethics as a personal matter and wonder what role a business school has in it. Many don't realize that in the business world their ethics will be strongly challenged—that they may lose promotions or jobs for resisting unethical or illegal instructions by their superiors. They don't realize that in school they could learn how to handle such situations, and the lesson might be more valuable to them than more classes in marketing or finance. They believe they know how to behave ethically and don't have much to learn about it.

But experience in a classroom suggests otherwise. For example, a simple case discussion in classes at some of the nation's top schools recently revealed how much can be gained from teaching about ethics. The case describes the chair of the board of a company—one of the unusual companies in which the chair is not the company's CEO—who one evening receives a call from a corporate vice president. The vice president says, "I think I've got to tell you that our company has been booking fictitious revenues and imaginary costs." After a discussion the conversation ends. The students are asked, "As chair of the company, what would you do?"

Inevitably some students propose trying to talk to the CEO without revealing the conversation with the vice president. They are trying to protect the person, even though the conversation with the CEO then loses much of its point. Others want to try to avoid the whole matter by questioning whether or not the vice president is lying; what is his or her motivation for the call; asking the vice president to go to the CEO (which he or she has probably already done or knows will not be fruitful) or even ignoring the call altogether. Some students propose that the chair call his or her attorney and wait to see what happens, having already protected himself or herself as well as is legally possible. Still others suggest dealing immediately and directly with the matter by a meeting between the CEO, the vice president, and the chair is also mentioned. These are very different approaches to what is both an ethical and a business problem. So there is evidently much to be fruitfully discussed about business ethics in our schools.

But this conclusion is not generally accepted. In the most prestigious business schools, many students arrive from jobs at investment banks and consulting firms, and are already thoroughly imbued with the arrogance of the investment community. They say, "I don't have anything to learn here, but I need my ticket punched." That is, they've already learned about marketing and finance and operations on the job, they think, and have come to the school merely to get a diploma, which is like a ticket for a higher job in the future. Unfortunately, their superiors at the banks and consulting firms from which they come have encouraged them in this attitude.

Many students see themselves in a race with each other for CEO positions and the enormous payoffs that are offered. Their idea is to work 15 or 20 years, get rich, and then go sailing. There are a limited number of opportunities to be CEO and only the top schools provide a likely ticket to such a career. Such students feel their responsibility is to themselves and it means filling their own bank account. The schools do not advertise this common attitude because it reflects poorly on them and their faculties, but they are well aware of it.

Furthermore, companies often have special career paths for MBA graduates. Labeled fast tracks, the paths allow a person to advance very quickly in managerial ranks with promotions based on the company's financial performance. Fast tracks contribute to the mentality that it is desirable to get results fast and dirty. With an attitude that I already know it all and am only here to get a diploma, and with the fast track looming as the goal, the last thing new students want is a course in ethics. Here's the comment of a young man taken from a conversation with me on a radio talk show.

> I go to a top business school and I'm about to take the Professional Responsibility course. To be honest, I consider it as a waste spending thousands of dollars to learn moral ethics. What I mean to say is, do I go to a business school to learn ethics, or how to conduct a business? I mean I get my moral values from the society and my upbringing, not in a business school.

Here's another student's comment:

> I just want to make a few points about ethics. I just graduated from business school, and I've got to tell you, I really wouldn't pay a dime to take an ethics course. I think it's a very good topic and it's important for a lot of people, but I wouldn't have paid a dime for it because I feel I'm an ethical guy. I want to learn about equity valuation, corporate finance, financial accounting. I don't want to pay for something like ethics.

There are exceptions—some students who are very uncomfortable with what they perceive as the amorality of the banks and consulting firms, and who look for some reassurance that what they learned about fair dealing at home and in their churches is relevant. These students take electives that deal with ethical issues. But these are courses for the already convinced and have little impact on the majority who are marching to the drums of ambition and amorality.

These students quickly find that the business world does not encourage their interests in ethics. A recent graduate of Harvard Business School described her job-hunting experience this way:

> When I was exploring a career in business ethics in companies, I was told that it's better for me seek a position with profit and loss responsibility in those com-

panies and demonstrate that I could deliver good financial performance. Then, when I'd shown that ability, I might be able to move into an ethics role with good credentials. If I didn't take this career path, I was told, people wouldn't respect or listen to me. I took this advice to mean that financial performance is always number one and ethics comes second.

In fall 2002, in the midst of considerable publicity about ethical failings at major corporations, some polls of prospective MBA students reported majority support for more ethics courses in business schools. But it seems likely that this reflects no more than what prospective students think is the response desired by the poll takers. Furthermore, most of respondents are likely to be still in college and looking for admission to other schools than the nation's few top business schools (which provide less than 10% of the nation's MBA degrees). In the major schools, which train a very disproportionately large proportion of future top executives of large firms, student attitudes toward courses in ethics are not likely to have grown more positive.

For all these reasons—the already strongly developed ethics (or lack thereof) of incoming students, the unfavorable attitudes of students toward ethics courses, and the lack of practical reinforcement from corporations for students who care about ethics—business schools have been unable to make much of a difference in the attitude of American executives toward ethics. Still, the schools have been making an attempt and ethics are not absent in MBA curricula. For instance, Harvard Business School has a compulsory, nongraded two-week course called Leadership, Values, and Decision Making for incoming business students to take before the required first-year curriculum begins. A second-year elective course, The Moral Leader, is also available. At Wharton Business School students are required to take a graded six-week course called Ethics and Responsibility. Other schools offer optional ethics courses. Stanford Business School has a second-year elective course, Ethics and Global Business. At MIT's Sloan School of management, an elective course, Literature, Ethics, and Authority, is also offered to students.

Talking Points

All that's needed to clean up American companies, some major investors have said, is for CEOs to do the right thing. This suggests that ethics must play a crucial role in real reform. But not much is being done to improve ethics in America, including in American business.

Many large corporations have established formal ethical programs for employees. But instead of focusing on ethical behavior in the executive suite, where it is most important, most run ethical programs for middle-level managers. In effect, they don't go where the sinners are. Furthermore, in the middle management programs, managers aren't instructed how to deal with corruption when they see it emanating from the top offices of the firm.

Ethical standards in our society seem to rise and fall in a long cycle. Standards fell to a low immediately after the Civil War, recovered a bit, then fell again in the 1920s. They rose after World War II, then began a long decline to their present level.

The current low level of ethics in the American investment business is associated with the "push the limits" environment in financial reporting.

Ethical standards are complicated by the cultural diversity of America and by the feeling of many people that ethics are very private matters that cannot be usefully addressed in business schools.

V Reforms to Help Investors

In 2001, Enron retiree Jan Farmer watched her $700,000 401(k) retirement plan evaporate with the collapse of Enron's stock, leaving her with just $20,000 for her retirement and about $500 a month net in Social Security survivors benefits. Farmer, a single mother, spent 16 years in the natural gas industry starting with Florida Gas Transmission, which later became a part of Enron. She worked at the training center, where people were trained to handle natural gas safely. She built up her life savings, all in Enron stock, over 16 years with what had been the seventh largest company in the United States, a company touted by the press and Wall Street analysts as the future of American business. "I was proud to invest in Enron stock," Farmer told a Senate committee in December 2001. "We were a loyal and hardworking group of employees. We lived, ate, slept, and breathed Enron because we were owners of the company. I trusted the management of Enron with my life savings."[203] She continued in a radio interview: "And whatever will I do if I ever get sick or if anything breaks down? I don't know. I'm afraid of my electric bill now. At night, I sit home in the dark. And I use no heat during the wintertime, and I don't allow myself to use air conditioning."[204]

"Today's workers own more than $1.5 trillion in assets through their 401(k)s. Younger workers have an average of about $10,000 in their accounts, while workers near retirement hold closer to $100,000 in their 401(k)s. This is real money for real workers, and we must do all we can to help make sure it's there for them when they retire."

—President Bush, radio address, October 19, 2002[205]

12 Ties, Belts, and Shoelaces: Changing Incentives for CEOs

Ties, belts, and shoelaces

—What marshals took from WorldCom's CFO when he was arrested

A business executive was continually urging his associates to be concerned about ethics.

"Why is he so concerned with ethics?" a close friend was asked.

"Because most of his friends are in jail."

Americans are basically tolerant people, adopting a live-and-let-live attitude. Many of us think that, "as long as my own money wasn't lost in investments taken by fraud, it's of no interest to me." When fraud occurs on a small scale, that attitude may be justified. But when fraud occurs on the scale we have seen recently, then everyone is affected. The value of all investments becomes suspect, the shares of legitimate companies decline just as dramatically as do those of guilty firms; the economy tips into recession. What others have done then is shown to affect us all seriously, and we must all be interested in a solution.

We saw in Chapter 5 how some CEOs cashed out in the bull market regardless of the performance of their companies. We saw in Chapter 10 how strong the temptation was to cook the books in order to get rich. We saw also that the temptation was made up of the likelihood of reward—via share options—and the unlikelihood of penalty. To date only a few CEOs have been indicted for their recent excesses, none have been convicted, and no top executive of an accounting firm or an investment bank has been arrested or indicted, despite the central role of both in the scandals.

To reverse the temptation to steal we must lower the probability of gain and increase the probability of punishment. The two changes alter the calculus—the benefit versus cost calculation that executives make when they are tempted to defraud investors. To reduce the probable gain, we should eliminate or index options and require executives to dispose of them over time so that the value of the options is tied to long-term stock performance. But this isn't the situation today. Instead, standard (nonindexed) options continue to be issued by companies at a rate of about 2.7% of outstanding shares per year (more than twice the rate in 1991 before the bull market began)—so there is plenty of opportunity via options for executives to profit from upward movements in the price of their companies' shares, even if brief.[206] The temptation that drove the scandals remains.

Some CEOs voice anger about efforts to reform the system. "This outrage over Jack Welch [GE's former CEO] is ridiculous," Barry Diller, himself a CEO, told a reporter. "I think it's offensive to the core.... The truth is GE shareholders had the great good fortune to have Jack Welch, a unique executive, earning their equity growth for years. For those shareholders to begrudge Mr. Welch anything financially is really rotten."[207] It's hard to imagine a more defiant statement of the position of the imperial CEO. "For shareholders to begrudge Mr. Welch anything financially is really rotten." *Anything* is a broad and inclusive term, reflecting arrogance toward the owners of the firm. It reflects much thinking in corporate executive suites today.

Nor is there much punishment. Few indictments are brought, but many more are appropriate. It seems incredible, but at the end of 2002, despite all the scandals, only about 10 executives had been indicted, of whom only two were CEOs.[208] It appears from two substantial investigations that Enron's board, made up mostly of outside directors, knew about much of the fraud that went on and failed in their duties of oversight on behalf of investors. They are not likely to be prosecuted or even penalized by the SEC. Whether it's because the authorities concluded that in the presence of an imperial CEO the board couldn't perform its duties properly, or whether the Feds are simply husbanding their resources to go after other targets, is not clear. What is clear is that it remains very possible to be involved directly or indirectly in major corporate fraud at the expense of investors and walk away without prosecution.[209] To increase the likelihood of punishment, we should insist on jail time for those convicted of fraud and full disgorgement of improper gains. These things can both be done, but they haven't been done yet, and the temptation to steal from investors remains enormous.

What To Do about CEO Compensation

What policy on CEO compensation should investors favor in the aftermath of the stock option fiasco? It made sense before and still does today to link executives' interests to those of shareholders via stock ownership in the company. The problem wasn't in the compensation objectives, but in the way it was implemented.

It's a mistake to think of the short-term large option grants that have characterized CEO pay in the past decade as an initiative of boards of directors seeking to align CEO and shareholder interests. This is an after-the-fact rationalization. Short-term option grants were made at the initiative of CEOs and rubber stamped by compliant boards. In effect, boards adopted a strategy (or rationale) and CEOs proposed the means by which it was to be implemented. It shouldn't be a surprise that the scheme favored CEOs to an unreasonable extent.

This time around, boards must set the terms of the options, with CEOs having far less input. Reformed CEO pay packages should include stock grants and stock options; options should be indexed to market and industry performance and exercised only over a period of several years and then on a planned schedule.[210] Furthermore, salary and bonuses should be a larger part of the total value of the pay package, and CEOs must be given operational goals.[211] In effect, this is the sort of pay package that CEOs have applied to the people who report to them. It goes without saying that the package should include no pay (other than a base salary) that is guaranteed regardless of performance and regardless of conviction for felonies or securities fraud.

The overall objective must always be kept clearly in mind: Investors should see pay packages that motivate executives toward strong performance in building a company and the value of its stock—but not only that. The package must also provide a reason for the CEO to be honest in dealing with investors. Strong incentives without honesty got investors in the soup in the bad years just past. Instead, investors now need a bit less incentive and a whole lot more honesty on the side of executives. How can pay packages be fashioned for these equally important objectives?

Standard Options

Standard options are surprising elements of CEO pay packages in our large, publicly owned companies. They are highly vulnerable to manipulation against the interests of shareholders, in ways that will become clearer below.

But here it's important to realize that options originated several decades ago in a very different form. They were developed by venture capital and private equity funds to incentivize and reward, but also to punish, entrepreneurs who obtained capital from the funds. Option awards were coupled with shares bought by the executives—for example, buy a share and get two options. The notion was that the executive had to put up his or her own money—become an investor like other investors in the company. Then he or she had a downside; if the company went under, the executive lost money just like other investors lost theirs. But the executives were special—they were responsible for running the company—so they got options also. If the company failed, the options were valueless. If it succeeded, the executives got a substantial payoff.

When the notion of options suddenly spread to large, established companies from the venture and buyout industry in the 1980s, the downside disappeared. Executives were not required to put up real money to buy shares in order to obtain options. There was no downside, no money on the line from the executives. Options became merely a game by which large-company executives pried money out of complacent boards.

Tying options to the purchase of shares is still good policy today, but in large companies it remains very uncommon.

Indexing Options

If we can reform options so they motivate executives on investors' behalf, another much recommended reform is to index them to the performance of the industry and the economy as a whole. In this manner, executives are compensated for causing a company's shares to outperform the market, and they are not rewarded just for a bull market—nor, for that matter, and equally appropriately, are they penalized for a bear market.

However, current accounting practice permits the company not to expense regular options and requires it to expense indexed options. This is completely perverse. Regular options, which have been a disaster for investors, are treated as having no cost, while indexed options, which could be valuable to investors, are treated as a cost to them. It's hard to imagine a better example of how the provisions of the current accounting system have come to work against investor interest.

Indexed options are the better choice in theory and always preferred by academics. However, they face two major barriers. First, indexed options currently require expensing, while at-the-money options (those with exercise price and number fixed when granted) do not. Second, it's complicated to reevaluate the "cost changes" occasioned by changes in the index and expense them accordingly (and differently every month). Apparently there's just too much work involved in the current accounting system to make indexed options practical under current practice. Therefore, almost no companies use them. In order to make indexed options work, the accounting rule for indexed options should be simplified and normal options have to be expensed.

Summary of the Major Elements of Optimal Option Packages

Options should be retained in CEO pay packages, but they should

- be indexed to the performance of the share indices for the industry and the market as a whole—that is, CEOs should be paid only for outdoing their competitors and peers;
- make up a smaller part of the pay package as a whole;

- be exercised on a planned basis with the CEOs retaining ownership of the shares for a period of years;
- be taxable when the shares are sold, not when the options are exercised (this requires a change in current tax law); and
- be expensed by the company.

To structure options in this way, we have to have some changes in tax law and accounting standards, and we have to exercise vigorous security law prosecution. None of these changes are easy to get, but all are required to prevent future scandals.

A Critical Change Needed in Federal Tax Law

The federal tax law must change to permit these reforms. The tax owed by a person who exercises options should be levied only when he or she sells the shares, not when he or she exercises the options and buys the shares from the company. Current law taxes so-called "shadow gains"—the difference between the exercise price of the option and the price of the share on the day the option is exercised. That is, the tax law treats the difference between what a person paid for the shares and the value of the shares on the day they were purchased as income to be taxed, even though the shares haven't been sold by the person being taxed. This is unusual in federal tax law, and is unreasonable. The taxpayer has received no cash for the shares, and in fact has simply paid for them, and still owns them, and their value is still fluctuating, but he or she is taxed as if the shares had been sold by him or her. Unless Congress makes this necessary change in the tax law, then boards cannot expect executives to exercise options without simultaneously selling the shares, and the desired alignment of executive and investor interests cannot be made. This is a very important matter, and one almost never mentioned in proposals for reform of corporate pay packages.

Boards of Directors versus the CEO in Setting Pay Packages

It will not be easy for boards to establish pay packages that are in investors' interests. There will be resistance from CEOs, who are still receiving the old lucrative packages featuring standard options despite the current scandals and despite investor dissatisfaction. CEOs dominate American boards in ways that make it very difficult for most directors to act on shareholders' behalf against the CEO, no matter what the legal responsibility of the board is. The existence of an imperial CEO with disproportionate power is a fundamental barrier to all attempts at reforming CEO pay, a problem we address in Chapter 14. Yet were major investing institutions, the stock exchanges, and the press to support boards in limiting CEO pay, it might occur.

Expensing Options

CEOs have benefited from the fact that the costs of their option grants are not counted as expenses by their firms. Protecting the interests of investors requires that options be counted as expenses in corporate financial accounting. The issue is controversial because a great deal of money is involved. Options pay off for executives when stock prices rise. When corporate profits rise, stock prices often follow, so executives benefit directly if options aren't treated as costs and deducted from profits. Investors might also gain, at least in the short term, if corporate profits are higher than they otherwise would be.

According to Alan Greenspan, in March 2002, research by the Fed found that the average earnings growth rate of 500 of America's largest companies (the S&P 500) would have been reduced by nearly a quarter if they had reported stock options as expenses.[212] Yet today, major investors such as Warren Buffet argue strongly for expensing options. Why?

Today for tax purposes companies deduct from their accounts an item reflecting the cost of stock options. It amounts to many billions of dollars when aggregated for all companies. A company deducts on its tax return the difference between the price at which an executive bought options from the company (the strike price) and the price of the company's shares in the stock market that day. The company deducts this amount whether or not it actually pays any cash to the executive (normally it doesn't), and whether or not the executive actually sells the shares that he or she has purchased.

To be specific, an executive might exercise an option to buy 1,000 shares of stock from the company. The company issues the stock and receives a payment from the executive for the shares; the payment is the strike price times the number of shares. The company doesn't record the payment from the executive on its income statement, but it does record, as an expense, the difference between the amount of money it received from the executive for the shares and the price of the shares in the market that day. If all the executive did was hold the shares, and not sell them, this makes no difference to the company's tax accounting. If a year later the executive were to sell the shares, the sale would have no impact on the company's tax accounting.

In sum, stock options aren't an expense for financial reporting purposes but definitely are for tax purposes; corporations benefit enormously from the tax-deductibility of stock options. Senator John McCain has for years submitted bills in Congress intended to end this "double standard." People who argue that stock options aren't an expense virtually never acknowledge that they most definitely are an expense for tax purposes. In this situation, tax accounting is much closer to the proper accounting than is financial accounting companies do for investors.

To understand why, it's necessary to look at the underlying logic of accounting. The objective of financial accounting (the accounting that provides financial statements to managers and investors) is to show all the expenses that a company incurs to produce products and services; that is, to identify completely and accurately the cost of doing business. These expenses are then deducted from sales to determine the company's profitability.

Are stock options a cost of doing business? They're compensation to employees of the firm for the purpose of engaging their time, talent, and energy so the company can produce products and services to sell. This is the same purpose that any other type of compensation serves (for example, salaries and bonuses), all of which is clearly a cost of doing business. So yes, options are a cost of doing business because they are compensation to people who work for the business. Since options are a cost of doing business, should they be deducted against revenues? Yes, clearly, just like any other compensation and any other cost. The tax accounting is right about the appropriateness of expensing options, and today's financial accounting (which ignores options) is wrong (although a few companies have begun to expense options recently).

Incidentally, though tax accounting is right about the need to expense options, it may not be right about exactly *how* to do it. The way in which stock options are measured as an expense for tax purposes is very different from the way in which the Financial Accounting Standards Board recommends that they be measured—as an expense for financial reporting purposes. But this highly technical part of the controversy need not concern us further here.

From an investor's point of view it might seem preferable not to have options expensed on the financial statements because to do so lessens reported profits, and that might lower the price of a company's stock. But not to expense options is to hide the real financial situation of the firm, and that's not good for shareholders either.

For example, the logic behind not expensing stock options, if applied to other resources a company uses, leads us to a circumstance in which a company "could issue stock options to, say, a supplier of materials or energy, and not record the materials or energy consumed as an expense."[213]

There's a basic difference in financial accounting between financing events and operating events. Financing events—such as taking out a loan—don't appear on the income statement because they are not costs or revenues of operations. The intent in making the distinction between financing and operating events is to permit a manager or investor to determine whether a business is profitable and if so how much. The sale of stock to an investor is not an operating event, so it doesn't belong in an income statement. But the payment of stock to an executive or other employee of a firm is compensation and is an operating cost, so it does belong on the income statement. Accounting standards state that when a company issues stock in exchange for certain assets or services, it has to record the fair value of what it receives as an asset or expense.[214]

This rule has been followed by American companies. Again, however, toying with a measurement issue has essentially undermined the accounting principle: the FASB (under political pressure) was forced to allow the use of "intrinsic value" for measuring stock options, and the "intrinsic value" of most stock options is zero. Because most American companies don't count options as an expense, they've used options to conceal compensation expenses, thereby inflating corporate profits.

In a hearing before a Senate committee, Senator Barbara Boxer asked Jeffrey Skilling, once CEO of Enron, about this very matter. She asked whether a company can use its own equity to affect its income statement. The answer should have been no—that if a company issues equity for materials or labor, it must record them as costs. But Skilling gave a different response—a completely honest one. 'There are cases," he said, "where you can use equity to impact your income statement. And the most egregious one, or the one that is used by every corporation in the world, is executive stock options.... Essentially what you do is you issue stock options to reduce compensation expense, and therefore increase your profitability."[215]

Finally, if standard options are to be expensed, then there will be a move toward restricted stock in executive pay packages. If this happens, then there will be closer alignment between shareholders and executives, since executives will have an incentive to get long-term equity price growth and will want dividends, as do shareholders.

The CEOnistas—A Parody

It cannot be surprising that there's a push back against business and businesspeople generally in America now—a cynical conviction that they're all corrupt. The following article, a parody that was circulating on the Internet in the spring of 2002, is illustrative. Its author was not identified. I have removed all references to real individuals.

"REMAINING U.S. CEOs MAKE A BREAK FOR IT"

Band of Roving Chief Executives Spotted Miles from Mexican Border

San Antonio, Texas (Reuters). Unwilling to wait for their eventual indictment, the 10,000 remaining CEOs of public U.S. companies made a break for it yesterday, heading for the Mexican border, plundering towns and villages along the way, and writing the entire rampage off as a marketing expense. "They came into my home, made me pay for my own TV, then double-booked the revenues," said Rachel Sanchez of Las Cruces, just north of El Paso. "Right in front of my daughters."

Calling themselves the CEOnistas, the chief executives were first spotted last night along the Rio Grande River near Quemado, where they bought each of the town's 320 residents by borrowing against pension fund gains. By late this morning, the CEOnistas had arbitrarily inflated Quemado's population to 960, and declared a 200% profit for the fiscal second quarter. This morning, the outlaws bought the city of Waco, transferred its underperforming areas to a private partnership, and sent a bill to California for $4.5 billion. Law enforcement officials and disgruntled shareholders riding posse were noticeably frustrated. "First of all, they're very hard to find because they always stand behind their numbers, and the numbers keep shifting," said posse spokesman Dean Levitt. "And every time we yell 'Stop in the name of the shareholders!', they refer us to investor relations. I've been on the phone all damn morning."

"YOU'LL NEVER AUDIT ME ALIVE!"

The pursuers said they have had some success, however, by preying on a common executive weakness. "Last night we caught about 24 of them by disguising one of our female officers as a CNBC anchor," said U.S. Border Patrol spokesperson Janet Lewis. "It was like moths to a flame." Also, teams of agents have been using high-powered listening devices to scan the plains for telltale sounds of the CEOnistas. "Most of the time we just hear leaves rustling or cattle flicking their tails," said Lewis, "but occasionally we'll pick up someone saying, 'I was totally out of the loop on that.'"

While some stragglers are believed to have successfully crossed into Mexico, Cushing said the bulk of the CEOnistas have holed themselves up at the Alamo. "No, not the fort, the car rental place at the airport," she said. "They're rotating all the tires on the minivans and accounting for each change as a sale."

Talking Points

Many CEOs today pay little attention to shareholder interests, preferring instead to build personal fortunes. Ideally, they could do the latter only by doing the former, but it hasn't worked out that way.

At the core of the problem is the current method of CEO compensation that depends primarily on standard options. This system permits CEOs to enrich themselves at the expense of shareholders. There are options systems that prevent an executive from leaving investors behind while he or she becomes rich, but they're not used in corporate America. They should be. Proper, not standard, options would provide the incentive carrot to make CEOs perform for shareholders.

There must also be a stick. Executives who violate securities laws, and cause them to be violated by companies, should spend considerable time in jail and should return their gains to shareholders. Unfortunately, this happens rarely. Instead, companies are assessed fines for securities fraud. For the company to pay a fine to the government is simply to make the shareholder pay again for the fact that the executives of the firm stole from him or her (from the investor). When the executives who oversaw the fraud is permitted to retain their positions, insult is added to the multiple injuries already imposed on the shareholders. But this is what happens most of the time in America today.

13 Total Regulatory Reform

"We will do all in our power to protect and secure the savings of ordinary Americans."[216]

—Attorney General John Ashcroft

"America's scandals stem from ...insufficient checks and balances on corporate managers. Managers perform most effectively and honestly when they face the external discipline of fierce competition, shareholder power, and strong regulatory supervision."[217]

—Richard Katz, writing in the *Financial Times*

The aftermath of a financial disaster, like the aftermath of a lost war, provides an unusual opportunity for people to think about the future and what it should be like. American equity markets are enduring a crisis. It is not certain that investors will simply resume their former behavior, and market prices will recover. Instead, people may change their long-term behavior. Hence there is now a unique opportunity to shape the future of our equity markets. Do we want small investors to play the increasing role in equity markets, which they were playing until the current crash? If so, then a thorough-going reform of financial regulation is likely to be necessary.

Financial markets are among our most heavily regulated. But regulation is done badly. We need better regulation, not more regulation; smarter rules, not more of them.

A System Full of Holes

The current regulatory system has huge loopholes and often protects the wrong people. Adding more rules and bureaucracy to this structure isn't going to help much. We can't go back to before the scandals—to before fraud, and concealment of material financial information. What is needed is not just limited reform but a new start.

The SEC is the star of the nation's investment regulatory system. Since 1934 its responsibility has been to protect investors and ensure the integrity of the securities markets.

It's responsible for administering all federal securities laws, and has a staff of about 3,000 people, which is fairly small by federal agency standards. It's responsible for seeing that all publicly traded companies (of which there are at least 15,000 in the United States) provide full and accurate disclosure to the investing public of all relevant financial information. Information is contained in annual and quarterly reports, registration statements for newly offered securities, proxy statements regarding the work of boards of directors, documents regarding tender offers and proposed mergers and acquisitions, and other documents. The SEC is responsible for overseeing the development and interpretation of generally accepted accounting principles. It's responsible for monitoring the activities of the auditing profession; for establishing and maintaining fair and efficient securities markets through oversight and regulation of the various market participants (stockbrokers, stock exchanges, transfer agents, and so on); and for overseeing and regulating the whole investment management industry (for example, the financial responsibilities and sales practices of mutual funds and individual financial advisors). It has a Division of Enforcement, which is responsible for investigating and sometimes prosecuting violations of securities laws; an Office of Education and Assistance, which is responsible for answering questions and responding to complaints coming from the investing public; and an Office of Municipal Securities, which is responsible for assisting in policy matters and enforcement actions pertaining to the securities issued by states, cities, and other political subdivisions.

The key enforcement tools of the SEC are civil suits tried before administrative law judges or in the courts. The SEC can sometimes bar lower-level executives from the securities industry; it can sometimes bar high-level executives from positions in publicly traded companies; or it can impose financial penalties, some of which are large but which in recent years have been cynically treated by most securities and accounting firms as a cost of doing business. When it does bring a case, most of its complaints are settled without an admission of wrongdoing by the target company or a detailed statement of what occurred. Since the SEC lacks the power to bring criminal charges, it can't use key investigative methods such as wiretaps and broad, not narrow, searches. Criminal matters must go to the Justice Department, which can initiate actions on its own.

The SEC is only one of a large number of organizations that have regulatory authority in the nation's security markets. America has too many regulators in its securities industry, each imperfectly watching aspects of the system as a whole. Among the most important are:

Security and Exchange Commission

Department of Labor

Department of Justice

Internal Revenue Service

Federal Reserve System

Comptroller of the Currency (in the Department of the Treasury)

Congress and Congressional committees

Attorney generals of the various states

Financial Accounting Standards Board

Exchanges (New York Stock Exchange, National Association of Securities Dealers)

The agencies are a mixed bag from the investors' point of view. Some of them try to do a good job but have limited resources and lack of political support, for example, the SEC. Some do a better and fairer job than might be expected, such as the two exchanges. Some are hopelessly compromised, like the Emerging Issues Task Force of the Financial Accounting Standards Board, which is so potentially important and so compromised that it deserves a brief description. The Emerging Issues Task Force of the Financial Accounting Standards Board deals with those instances in which firms and their auditors push the limits of financial accounting standards and supports the efforts of the Board to rectify accounting standards mangled by the likes of Enron. Yet the Task Force is made up solely of representatives of the banks, accounting firms, and a few industrial corporations. There are no public members—either from government agencies, the academic world, or retired executives. The result is yet another of the conflicts of interest that now dominate the American financial services industry. The members of the Task Force are supposed to look to the general interest in the issues they confront, but their own companies have much at stake. After all, investors have learned about how American investments markets work to the advantage of the financial services firms, it would be naive to think that the members of the Task Force vote any other resolution than that favoring the interests of their employers. Again, investors are left out in the cold.[218]

Sometimes the regulators cooperate, as for example when the SEC, the NYSE, and the NASDAQ joined recently to hold six major investment banks accountable for destroying e-mail in violation of regulations and when the SEC joined with the Justice Department to seek criminal penalties for corporate fraud, sometimes including state attorneys general as well.[219] But despite some cooperation among them, no regulator watches the entire system—nowhere is the investor given thorough protection. The system was erected almost 80 years ago, and much has happened since. As it happened, ad hoc changes were made, and responsibility was divided.

For example, when the Securities and Exchange Commission was established in the 1930s, Americans didn't have pension plans. Corporate plans, which were initially defined benefit plans managed by the companies, came along in the 1940s. About 30 years later defined contribution benefit plans (401(k)s) emerged, and soon many defined benefit plans were converted to defined contribution plans and individuals were permitted to manage their own pension savings.

To protect employees' pension funds, the Department of Labor, via ERISA (the Employees Retirement Income Security Administration), was made a major regulator of pension plans. But when individuals were invited to manage their own pension savings—via individual retirement accounts (IRAs), Keogh plans, annuities, and 401(k)s—and when the total size of these plans became a major factor in the stock market, no significant revision of the regulatory system was made. If anything, the IRS regulates defined contribution plans and pays little or no attention to whether their owners are defrauded in the marketplace.

CEOs, accountants, and banks were not slow to perceive the opportunities created for them by this sieve of a regulatory system. For example, the Financial Accounting Standards Board is supposed to establish accounting regulations and keep them up to date. But when it tried to deal with such glaring conflicts of interest as the refusal of corporations to expense options, Congress intervened on behalf of the companies.

Imperiling Investors by Keeping the SEC Weak

During 2002, as corporate financial scandals dominated the headlines, there were continual reports of SEC investigations. An investor might have assumed that the agency was effectively protecting investors. But this impression, of course, would have been seriously wrong.

The SEC had been intentionally underfunded by the White House and Congress for the full decade of the bull market. It has a small staff relative to its workload, and one that is poorly compensated relative to what its employees' credentials and skills can earn elsewhere (both inside and outside the federal government). In consequence, the SEC reviews only a small part of the corporate financial information that comes to it and has high turnover that prevents staff from gaining the expertise necessary to handle its workload efficiently.

Lack of funding was evident in the SEC's limited performance. For example, in 2000, the Commission reviewed about 25% of corporate financial reports it received, and in 2001 about 16%.[220] More than 1,000 employees, or one-third of the SEC's staff, left from 1998 to 2000. More than half were lawyers. Nearly 300 positions were unfilled last year because of a dearth of qualified applicants at the relatively low levels of pay offered. The average SEC lawyer in 1999 had only 2 years of experience there. As of February 2001, 76% of financial examiners had worked for the SEC for less than three years. The SEC oversees about 12,000 publicly traded companies and gets about 12,000 annual reports, about 12,000 proxy statements, and 36,000 quarterly reports every year. The Commission is said to have about 90 accountants to review the material.[221]

The SEC has also had difficulty retaining an adequate enforcement staff. During one 2-year period in the late 1990s, the SEC's New York regional office, critical to large corporate investigations, lost more than half its 137-member enforcement staff, which "critics say hampered both the level of scrutiny the agency could bring to the markets and its ability to pursue cases."[222]

Ironically, the SEC not only protects the investor, when allowed to, but it makes money for the taxpayer. Corporations pay a fee every time they file a document with the commission, and since 1983 the SEC has raised more money than it has spent. In 2001, the SEC had a budget of $423 million and collected $2.06 billion in corporate fees that went to the federal treasury for general government purposes.

Apparently, the lack of money for a stronger SEC reflects a philosophy in Congress and the White House that it's best not to offend business with an aggressive regulatory agency. The SEC isn't needed, the argument goes, because there's already a system of checks and balances in place to protect investors in big public companies—a board of directors, auditors, corporate legal staff, and state attorneys general. When all these ceased to protect the investor during the bull market, the SEC was unable to pick up the slack, not by accident but by design.

For example, in 1995, Senator Phil Gramm, who was then chairman of the Senate Securities Subcommittee, proposed to slash the SEC's budget by 20%, and to terminate its Office of Investor Education and Assistance, which handles inquiries and complaints from investors, and which generates about 18% of SEC investigations.[223] Gramm failed in his effort, but the SEC got the message that it had little effective support from the Senate for its task of protecting investors. During the Enron collapse, the White House proposed to cut the SEC budget, and helped to prevent an appropriation of funds to the SEC to raise salaries in the agency. In general, the SEC hasn't done a good job, not because it's incompetent, but because it was frustrated by lack of resources and political support.

In 1999, when the SEC proposed a rule preventing accounting firms from doing consulting for firms they audit, which is a conflict of interest that contributed to corporate financial fraud, the Congress threatened to cut the SEC budget if the rule were adopted. Threatening budget cuts that would cripple an agency is a classic means by which Congress dictates policy to agencies, while maintaining for the public that the agency is free to pursue its mission without political interference. The SEC was subjected to this type of Congress policy dictation in key circumstances during the bubble; it was dissuaded from requiring that options be expensed, and from prohibiting accounting firms from doing both audits and consulting for the same clients. As we've seen in previous chapters, investors were the big losers from Congress's intervention.

Similar efforts to weaken investor protection continue. For example, there's a distinction under SEC regulations between financial advisors, who are fiduciaries and who must disclose to clients conflicts of interest, and broker dealers, who are agents of their employers and need not disclose conflicts of interest. Today as brokerages (like financial advisors) offer advice to investors along with trades and asset-based fees, they want their brokers to be exempt from the regulations covering investment advisors. The SEC proposes to exempt them but hasn't yet done so.[224] This wouldn't be a good thing for investors.

Strengthening Investor Protection via a Consolidated Agency

During the great bull market, when investors were being defrauded en masse, the complex body of law and regulation that in America applies to the investment industry neither prevented nor punished most of the illegal activity. In large part this is because the American financial regulatory system is a complex puzzle of which almost no one can make sense. It's no surprise, therefore, that when something goes wrong—like the greatest financial rip-off of investors (to use the colorful and accurate expression of a former director of the SEC) in our history. Each agency blames the other—the SEC blames Congress for not giving it the resources to do a better job; the FASB blames Congress for not letting it regulate corporate accounting more rigorously; the Fed says that what happens in the stock market isn't its responsibility (though the investment banks that it regulates were at the heart of the frauds) and it's powerless anyway; Congress blames the White House and the SEC for insufficient regulatory zeal, and so on.

To a degree, all are right. The system is complex and expensive, and it doesn't work—or at best it works only in limited situations and slowly and uncertainly then. The last thing our regulatory system currently needs is what it's getting—more detailed regulations from Congress and the White House. Although there's an argument for each proposed change, they simply complicate and confuse the overall system and imply that investors will be better protected when that's unlikely.

Nothing in the new legislation or the proposed new regulations of the SEC would have prevented most of the fraud now being uncovered. The incentives to

CEOs to defraud investors remain enormous; the conflicts of interest that drove accounting firms and banks into complicity with CEOs in misleading investors remain largely unchanged; the likelihood of punishment of wrongdoers remains low.

The most important thing Congress and the President could be doing for investors is putting all these laws and agencies together in a sensible way so investors could be protected as a whole, not just in a few isolated situations. A good place to start is to create a new agency with the SEC as its core that combines most current public and private agencies of regulation. Its charter should give it overall responsibility to protect investors and to look at the whole picture.

The objective of reforming the regulatory system is to protect investors from deceit and fraud, not to criminalize bad outcomes. The core of the American system of free enterprise is to permit people to follow their ideas in the marketplace. Some ideas will be good, some bad; some will work, some will not; some will succeed, some will fail. Some investors will pick only winners, some only losers; many will get some right and some wrong. We cannot put firms in such a position that every failure becomes a criminal activity, or we will destroy the system we are trying to improve. It's not evidence of malfeasance that a business initiative failed; what is malfeasance is misrepresentation, deception, and fraud. The responsibility of regulators is to know the difference, and of Congress and the courts not to mistake one for the other.

Letting Investors Leave the Market

Small investors have played a larger role in America's stock markets in recent years. They were given their pension savings to manage and they were invited into the equity markets by professionals who assured them that over the long haul—which is what people investing their pension money are concerned about—stocks would provide a better return than other forms of savings.

Initially, all seemed to go well, and more and more small investors were lured into the market. Then the market collapsed, imposing very substantial losses on many small investors, effectively wiping many out. They lost at the hands of more sophisticated market participants, and now they've realized through month after month of national publicity that much of what they lost was taken from them by fraud. Some have left what little remains of their investments in the market, but they are no longer active investors; no new money is going in. Others have pulled out entirely and now sit on the sidelines.

Small investors can be brought back, but they need not be. If they are to be brought back, there must be far-reaching reforms to protect them from disaster. An alternative is to leave them out of the market permanently and change the role of the market in our economic system. Lest this seem an extreme and unlikely alternative, we should reflect that it is exactly what is happening now—by default, that is, without plan or thought of consequences but as the direct result of the operation of a poorly regulated market in which fraud and exploitation put small investors at a critical disadvantage.

Without small investors—who actually are investors for the most part, in for the long term, not traders and speculators—we'd have very different performance from our stock markets. We would not have long bull markets with periods of the bear, but rather markets that fluctuate wildly around a stagnant trend line. The markets would resemble a zero-sum game at the Las Vegas tables. No one will make money in the long term except the houses (the investment banks and brokerages) and a few especially lucky professionals.

This is what American equity markets will be without small investors. And that's likely to be what happens, because small investors don't belong in the type of market we have today—that is, they belong only in a market that in the long term is a bull market—with an upward trend in share prices. After all, if the long-term trend isn't up, investors (though not speculators) do better to stay out of the market.

Keeping Investors in the Market

There are two major reasons why Americans may want to have small investors in our equity markets. One is to provide investors with a source of funds for retirement and for the college education of their children. The second reason is to add political support to our system of investor-owned private corporations. It has been argued over the past decades that the increasing proportion of Americans who own corporate stocks provide a bulwark of support for our capitalist system.

But whatever the reason that America may want them in its equity markets, small investors are very disillusioned and will not return unless much changes. If we want them back, we'll have to provide an infrastructure in our markets that over time will ensure them a decent return and minimize their risk of being again exploited by fraud and deception.

There is much confusion about what small investors desire in terms of market reform, and for a very good reason. When Americans consider reforms in the stock markets, they hear the voice of large institutional investors coming through loud and clear, and the voice of small investors coming through softly, if at all. And the two groups want different things.

Large institutional investors (pension funds, mutual funds, and hedge funds) are sophisticated investors with large reserves of capital. They're angry about the fraud that has cost them so much in losses in recent years, but they're confident of their ability to manage money successfully if they're given the truth. For example, McKinsey and Company's Global Investor Opinion Survey, undertaken in the spring of 2002, found that for large institutional investors (the more than 200 fund managers responding to the survey were collectively responsible for assets valued at some 2 trillion in U.S. dollars—the total amount under management by their funds was some $9 trillion) the single most important factor for good investment decisions was accurate accounting disclosure by firms. More than 70% of respondents gave this answer; the nearest other factor got less than 45% support.

The response to this survey represents the confidence of professional money managers that if they are given honest financial information by firms, they can successfully allocate the capital they manage to earn with a good return for their clients. Because this is the position of professional money managers, many commentators assume that honest financial reporting and transparency in disclosure will be sufficient to reform our security markets, and to cause capital to return to them. This is true, but only for institutional investors.

The situation is very different for small investors—and their needs are different. They have neither time nor expertise to manage their savings with confidence in a market being driven by large institutions—and it's ridiculous to them too. Instead, they must rely on financial professionals to guide them through the maze of conflicting claims and promises that are our equity markets. Ironically, the primary threats to the financial welfare of small investors are the predatory actions of professional financial firms and the self-serving behavior of top corporate executives.

Overuse and Abuse—the Gnomes of Norwalk

Much of the damage done to investors by the overuse and abuse of stock options could have been prevented if the SEC had taken action early in the 1990s. The Financial Accounting Standards Board ("the gnomes of Norwalk") proposed an accounting rule that would have required firms to expense options. This was the proper action, and had it been taken, the temptation for executives to mislead investors in order to inflate share prices (so that they could cash in options) would have been much reduced. The FASB's proposal to require expensing of options was in fact one of the few critical junctures in the entire history of stock market bubbles and we went down the wrong path.

The Clinton administration had just taken power. Arthur Levitt had just become chairman of the SEC, and there he found the FASB proposal. What happened thereafter has been described in detail by Levitt in several forums. The center of the story is that in June 1993, the FASB voted unanimously for a rule that would make companies put a fair value on their stock option grants and record that number as an expense on the financial statements they made to investors.

Then, Levitt tells us:

> Corporate lobbyists, outraged by the FASB's perfidy, persuaded Congress to hold hearings.... Even the Clinton administration opposed the rule. Senator Joe Lieberman...led the charge. He introduced legislation to bar the SEC from enforcing the rule.... At a December 1994 meeting with FASB members in Norwalk, I urged them to retreat. I warned that if they adopted the new standard, the SEC would not enforce it. The FASB soon backed down.

Levitt has said that he considers this his biggest mistake as SEC chairman. He has also said that he believes that if he'd not intervened against it, the FASB would have stuck to its guns and forced the expensing of options.[225]

The story then, in capsule, is that the private sector regulatory body, the FASB, intended to issue a proper rule about accounting for options, and would have done so had not the American business community pressured Congress to pressure the SEC to oppose it, and the SEC then pressured the FASB to back down. Thus it was that the business community and the federal government (both legislative and executive branches) worked together to create the conditions for what Levitt later called "the rip-off" of the American investor.

When we turn below to the government's role in rectifying today's mess and reforming the financial markets for the future, it's important to remember that the government did much to create the mess in the first place. It was the government that turned corporate executives and their accountants and banks loose with investors' money.

Each type of financial professional (analysts, attorneys, auditors, bankers, brokers, chief executive officers, chief financial officers, mutual fund managers, venture capitalists—all the members of the financial value chain) took part in the practices that defrauded investors. But the reform legislation enacted by Congress in the summer of 2002 addressed the practices of only three of the players—auditors, CEOs, and analysts. Mutual fund managers, venture capitalists, brokers, investment bankers, attorneys, and the politicians themselves were largely left untouched. It was a very incomplete reform and insufficient to reassure small investors that the markets are not still unfairly stacked against them.

In consequence, the regulation that small investors require is not more disclosure but more reliable protection from exploitation by market professionals and corporate executives. They need the sort of protection the SEC was originally intended to provide, but which has become ineffective as markets have changed over the years and regulators have increased in number but narrowed in focus and responsibility. The best place to start is with a complete reform of our regulatory system—a system that is supposed to protect the small investor but that does a lousy job of it.

There are so many alternative approaches to revising the regulatory system as a whole that it would not be useful to detail one here. The proper way to start is with a Presidential blue ribbon or Congressional commission whose assignment is to review and revise the nation's security regulation apparatus in order to protect investors so that what happened to them in the past decade does not happen again.

Talking Points

America's current regulatory system is a largely dysfunctional system that has huge loopholes and that often protects the wrong people. Adding more rules and bureaucracy to this structure isn't going to help much. America has too many regulators, each watching imperfectly aspects of the securities industry. Despite the number of regulators and some cooperation among them, no regulator watches the entire system—nowhere is the investor given thorough protection. The system was erected almost 80 years ago and much has happened since—and as it happened, ad hoc changes were made, and responsibility was divided.

In sum, the American financial regulatory system is so complex that almost no one can make sense of it. It's no surprise, therefore, that when something goes wrong, like the greatest financial victimization of investors in our history, each agency blames the other—the SEC blames Congress for not giving it the resources to do a better job; the FASB blames Congress for not letting it regulate corporate accounting more rigorously; the Fed says that what happens in the stock market isn't its responsibility (though the investment banks that it regulates were at the heart of the frauds), and it's powerless anyway; the Congress blames the White House and the SEC for insufficient regulatory zeal, and so on.

To a degree, all are right. The system is complex, expensive, and it doesn't work—or at best it works only slowly and uncertainly in limited situations. The most important thing Congress and the President could be doing for investors is to put all these laws and agencies together in a sensible way so investors will be protected generally, not just in a few isolated situations.

14 Restraining the Imperial CEO

"The finger of blame is pointing at dishonest executives and lax accountants. The wider balance of power between corporations, shareholders, and government is not even on the agenda.... The snag is that neither the President nor Congress shows any interest in tackling such a contentious issue."[226]

Previous chapters have shown that the functions of the board of directors, the chief financial officer, and the chief human resources officer have each been corrupted in American business by today's imperial CEO. Can effective reforms be made with the imperial CEO still in place, or are the board and top executives certain to be corrupted again by CEOs at the first opportunity?

American CEOs Have Too Much Power for the Safety of American Investors

As we saw in previous chapters, a huge fissure developed in large, publicly held American companies between the interests of CEOs and the interests of shareholders. CEOs have found a way to enormously increase their own wealth by a variety of means in a period in which shareholders have been losing their shirts. Surprising as it may sound when the matter is put directly, the core of the problem faced by investors today, as revealed by the corporate scandals, is that investors must be better protected from CEOs.

Academic analysts first recognized the problem thanks to the work of Berle and Means in 1932, who wrote about the separation of ownership and control in the large, modern corporation. Later, academics thought the problem had been resolved by stock options, which supposedly created an identity of interest between executive and shareowner. Now, belatedly, academics have recognized that the issue is not resolved and have returned to it, asking such questions as how do suppliers of capital control managers and how do investors try to get their money back if they've been defrauded?[227]

Earlier chapters suggest that CEOs clearly believe the purpose of investor-owned business in America is to make CEOs rich. Investors don't see it quite that way. For investors, it's all right if CEOs do well financially so long as the investor does also. But the purpose of investor-owned business is to advance the interests of investors and of the American consumer. If these things are done well, a CEO might get rich; if they are not done well, the CEO should not get rich nonetheless. But this is, of course, what has been happening.

CEOs have so much power and so many financial resources to make their desires come true that in recent years they have corrupted many of the checks and balances—corporate boards, accountants, and banks among them—that were intended to restrain them. Boards were corrupted by fees and perks, accountants by consulting fees, and investment banks by large transaction fees. Boards became blind, deaf, and dumb; accountants became partners in deceiving investors; and banks became co-conspirators in deception.

The most obvious impediment to outside directors exercising their power is that the acknowledged and formal leader in most U.S. boardrooms is the CEO, whose power is greater primarily because of his knowledge of and expertise in company matters. Although directors feel they receive adequate information, their time, knowledge, and interpretive ability are no match for those of a full-time and long-service CEO, and since the CEO determines what information directors receive, it's no exaggeration to say that, in most instances, directors understand the company through the CEO's eyes. In addition, the CEO controls the agenda, the meeting process, and he or she still plays a key role in the selection of new outside directors.[228] So great is the power of American CEOs that not even the best-intentioned board of directors nor the most alert government regulators can effectively oversee a strong CEO. Only sometimes are frauds discovered after the fact, and in even fewer cases are they rectified.

When a CEO is effective and ethical, our system works well by concentrating enormous power in his or her hands. But when a CEO is ineffective or unethical, or both, our system invites disaster for investors. It's surprising that American investors accept the danger to their financial interests that is inherent in the too-powerful CEO, because under American law investors own the company and the CEO is their agent. Yet American investors routinely rest too much power—for their own good—upon their agents.

American CEOs are very jealous of the power they possess. Probably the surest way for a director to get dumped off an American board is not to oppose the

CEO on a matter of corporate policy or strategy, but to propose some limitation to the CEO's power in the firm, for example, that the CEO should no longer be chair of the board of directors. CEOs have told me that those CEOs who are not chair of their boards are often embarrassed to admit it to other CEOs. The fact that good corporate governance begins with an outside director as chair of the board has little or no influence on the attitude of American CEOs to their own power. They want to keep all they have and to acquire more if possible. They have little tolerance for those among their number who might have a different opinion or accept a different outcome. So strongly is the notion of the CEO as dominant in a corporation accepted in America and so strongly do CEOs insist upon it, that in this chapter we'll be at pains to try to establish that there really is an alternative.

Proposals to Strengthen Corporate Boards

In the aftermath of the recent scandals, many proposals have been advanced to straighten corporate boards and better oversee top executives. The reforms could be achieved by any of a number of devices, including actions by the stock exchanges, which set standards for companies whose shares are traded on the exchanges; actions by legislation or government regulatory bodies such as the SEC; and actions by boards themselves and/or shareholder votes.

Among the most important reforms are the following:

- That a majority of the members of boards be truly independent outsiders.
- That all members of the executive compensation and audit committees of a board be truly independent outside directors.
- That boards should prohibit accounting practices and transactions that put a company at high risk of being in noncompliance with accounting principles or that misrepresent the company's financial position.
- That boards prohibit conflicts of interest transactions by senior company executives.
- That boards bar company loans to directors and senior executives. (These are some of the recommendations of the Senate subcommittee that investigated Enron's board and reported in early July 2002).

These are proposals with great merit, and if adopted they might lessen the risk of the kind of scandals corporate America has seen recently.[229]

Another set of recommendations would change boards into smaller, almost full-time supervisory units. They are:

- That the CEO not be chairperson of a board.
- That boards have only five or so members.
- That all members of boards be outside and truly independent directors.

- That the board operates as a whole, with no committees.
- That boards meet frequently, at least once a month.
- That directors serve on no more than three boards so that they can devote sufficient time to each board on which they serve.
- That there be more advisory boards, and fewer advisers as directors; and that members should be expert in the business and in protecting investors, not simply those with connections to government or academia or foundations.
- That board memberships be full time.[230]

These recommendations are for a different sort of board, but one that might be far more effective than today's larger and less attentive boards.

A further recommendation is to publish the votes of directors of publicly held companies. This would put pressure on directors to vote as they think proper, not to simply go along with proposals that they could not defend in public.[231] This might help to overcome the "group-think" that takes over in many corporate boardrooms and that allows management proposals to be rubber-stamped by the board with little discussion or debate. Publishing votes, however, would also encourage grandstanding and offer competitors insights into a company's decision making, which could be damaging. And in an independent and well-functioning board, the matter that receives a unanimous vote is often not the original proposal put forward by management (other than in routine matters) but the product of an active dialogue that produces consensus. The important point is to make sure that the board is effective in the preliminary discussion so that its votes are not a rubber stamp but rather the collective views of the entire board. The basic point is that many of these proposals, meritorious in themselves, do not really reach the heart of the matter, which is whether a board is fully active on behalf of shareholders and closely oversees management. Boards must be flexible to fit the very different circumstances of different companies. Hence, it's unlikely that enough rules can be put in place to have a perfect board.

It is possible to have boards made up of outsiders that are still subservient to top management; it is possible to have small boards that are still subservient; and it is possible to have published votes that still represent only management's views. In fact, it is not only possible, but it is likely if the CEO still controls all information going to the board and still retains practical control of who is on the board.

Increased Shareholder Activism

An additional approach to better oversight of corporate boards is to encourage greater activism by shareholders. In practice this means greater activism by large institutional investors because small individual shareholders cannot accomplish much.

Trustees managing pension money have an obligation under federal pension law (ERISA) to administer plan assets for the "exclusive benefit of plan participants." But often asset managers have conflicts of interest, including relying on companies for contracts to manage corporate pension plans. So it is uncommon for fund managers to act against corporate executives by being aggressive shareholders in other firms. This is a conflict of interest as blatant as that of accounting firms relying on the same clients for both auditing and consulting contracts.

In 1994 the United States Department of Labor issued statements the purpose of which was "to send a clear signal that we want corporations to become more active monitors of long-term corporate performance." The Department continued, "Plans may engage in activities to influence the management of companies … when they would be likely to enhance the value of shares." It spoke of "a regulatory seal of approval" for such activism, and lest there was any possible misunderstanding of its intent, it added, "We are trying to encourage corporations to be activist owners" of shares via their pension plans.

Among the issues that pension plans were encouraged to consider by the Department of Labor in their role as activist shareholders were:

- Independence and expertise of candidates for the Board of Directors
- Sufficient information for the board to monitor management
- The mergers and acquisitions policy of a company
- Extent of debt and capitalization
- Nature of long-term business plans
- Appropriateness of executive compensation
- Investment in training to develop the workforce
- Workplace practice
- Measures of corporate performance

The Department's guidance came just as the bull market was taking off, and it was largely ignored. But in the aftermath of the decline of the markets and publicity about the scandals, the way corporations are governed has become of interest to a few large-scale investors.

There are many types of institutional investors, and if active, they could make an important difference in how corporations are governed. For example, the list of institutional investors includes:

- Banks
- Insurers
- Brokers/traders
- Pension funds
- Venture capitalists
- Mutual funds

- Private equity funds
- Investment managers

In 2000 institutional investors owned 48.3% of the value of the American stock markets, and individuals 41.5% (the majority of the remainder, 7%, was owned by foreign holders). Of the institutions, mutual funds owned 18% of the market, corporate pension funds 13.2%, state and local government retirement funds 10.9%, and life insurance companies 5.1%.

A poll by a major consulting company asked the following question of large institutional investors headquartered in North America: How important is corporate governance versus financial issues in investment decisions? Fifty-seven percent replied that governance was as or more important than financial issues. Asked whether they were willing to pay a premium for a well-governed company—defined as having a board on which a majority of members were independent of management—76% of institutional investors in North America replied yes.[232]

But it seems that even though the quality of corporate governance is important to them, most institutional investors do not want to be actively involved in affecting the governance of firms in which they invest.[233] This may seem a contradiction, but it is not. It's not at all unusual for human beings, and human institutions, to recognize that something is important to them, but to hesitate to do anything directly about it. If they can, they'll flee from the problem rather than confront it. Leading mutual funds, for example, evidence no interest in intervening in corporate governance; they won't vote on issues in annual meetings. They prefer to rely on the old approach—sell if dissatisfied.

In consequence, when most public firms turned to increasingly misleading financial reporting, the large institutions ignored it and continued to invest as before. Much of the bull market was built on misrepresentation—yet the institutions treated it as if it had been an act of God that couldn't have been avoided or foreseen. They didn't play an active role—they merely bought into a rising tide and held on during an ebbing tide—in their investors' loss. And there's little evidence that, except for some of the large public employee pension plans run by our states, large institutional investors will act any differently in the future.

Thus we have a variety of proposals for strengthening boards and for increasing the oversight of governance provided by large investors. But can we expect that these proposals, if adopted, will actually succeed in the face of the American paradigm of the imperial CEO?

America's Imperial CEOs

What is the American paradigm of corporate leadership—the so-called imperial CEO, or, as Alan Greenspan terms it, the dominant CEO? It's the model of one preeminent leader who embodies all the authority and all the responsibility of the corporation for its day-to-day activities—that is, there is single-point accountability to the board of directors and shareholders for the success or failure of the company.

It is the concept of the boss; of the general or ship captain. The CEO is not an unlimited authority, for it's constrained by law and corporate bylaws, but it is a dominant power in the corporation. The imperial CEO is an autocrat. CEOs may have different personal styles, including being more or less a delegator, more or less charming, more or less effective, but always an autocrat. There may be a velvet glove on the iron hand, but the autocrat's iron hand is always there.

Today, American companies have a leadership structure that emphasizes the CEO as a boss and a single point of accountability for investors in the company. All other executives owe their positions to the CEO and report to him or her and receive directions, budgets, and so on, from the CEO. Moreover, most CEOs chair the boards of directors of their firms and as a practical matter control who is on the board and his or her compensation. This is a boss system—a system that depends on a single individual to make the more important decisions for the firm. It's not a system of joint responsibility, or of shared leadership.

Americans seem to be comfortable with this system not only in business but in the executive branch of our governments (federal, state, and local), in unions, in not-for-profit organizations, in sports, and in the military.

In a large company the CEO controls vast resources. He or she has many jobs at his or her disposal; large sums of money to pay compensation or consulting fees; large staffs to gather and analyze information so that he or she can dominate a discussion in a board of directors meeting; access to professional talent such as attorneys or publicists; and access to political figures via campaign funds, jobs, or other favors. It is a very substantial arsenal that can be used to dominate not only the people in a company but also its board.

Smaller companies don't have imperial CEOs. Board members are more likely to be on the same level as the CEO, since the resources at the CEO's command in a small company are not sufficient to imperial pretensions. Furthermore, rarely is the CEO so skilled politically as in a large organization; rarely is he or she charismatic, as is often the case in a large company.

The strength of the single leader system is that it provides unity of command, clearness of purpose, clear assignment of responsibility, ease of communication, and so on. But these advantages are gained only when the leader is exceptional. That is, when you have a genius, the single leader is the best system. But when the leader is not so outstanding, or when his talents and concentration fade, then inevitably ruin follows. When a company lacks a genius, lacks the ability to change leadership when the leader begins to fade, or has a leader who is out for himself or herself rather than the shareholders, then the imperial CEO becomes a danger.

How Imperial CEOs Control their Boards

Ordinarily a CEO controls who is on a board (through relationships with a majority of the board), what board members are paid, how long they serve, and what perks they receive from the company. It's a poor excuse for a CEO who, armed with all this power and influence, fails to dominate his or her company's board of directors.

There are three main devices by which CEOs control boards:

The CEO chairs the board. First, it's common practice in America for a CEO to act as the chairman of the company's board of directors, and for other company executives to serve as board members. The CEO ordinarily has a very substantial, if not decisive, role in the selection of board members and in determining their perks and compensation, which is true of either inside directors (company executives) or outside directors. In consequence, where there is a strong CEO, as in most companies, the CEO dominates the board as well as the management of the company.

The CEO is the source of information and initiatives. Second, the board, especially its outside directors who do not know the company intimately on a day-to-day basis, should rely on company executives for information and suggestions as to what needs to be done in the company. For example, when the Audit Committee of the board chooses an auditing firm, it usually does so based on a recommendation from the management team (especially the CFO). A harsh or uncooperative auditing firm is unlikely to receive the CFO's or CEO's recommendation. So the choice of auditor is made by the Audit Committee of the board, which has no inside directions in its membership, but which depends on the CFO of the company for information and recommendations upon which to make its selection, and the CFO serves at the will of the CEO. It cannot be surprising if an auditor is more loyal to management than to the Audit Committee. Moreover, the auditor prepares financial statements using data provided by management, which serves except in very unusual circumstances at the pleasure of the CEO.

A similar process occurs with respect to executive compensation, including that of the CEO. The Compensation Committee of the board, usually comprised of outside directors only, depends upon the chief human resources or personnel officer of the firm for information upon which decisions about executive compensation are made; and upon the CFO for information and recommendations about stock option plans. Both the HR officer and the CFO are agents of the CEO. The Compensation Committee can hire its own consultant, and should do so, but this often invites a conflict with the management of the company, which a board generally prefers to avoid. The result is that compensation, like auditing, while ostensibly in the control of the outside members of the board of directors, is subject to control or dominant influence by management and the CEO.

A recent example of the way CEOs help themselves when they chair compliant boards is Michael Eisner at Disney. According to news reports, the Disney board has permitted itself to apply a remarkably liberal profit test for Eisner's performance, including adding back into profit seven sorts of expense deductions to arrive at an "adjusted net income." These include charges arising from layoffs, from closing a business, and so on.[234] It is unclear whether Eisner used any unethical influence to obtain the generous performance test for his compensation. But this example serves as a warning sign that so much power is concentrated in the hands of a CEO in many American firms that there is no effective protection when a greedy or incompetent leader is present. With these hidden issues, a serious risk of the current push for reforms is that they will not be as effective as one would hope.

Exploiting the dual and conflicting roles of the board. Third, a board of directors has two functions that can come into conflict with one another. Its overall responsibility is single—to create value for shareholders—but to do this it should do two different things: it should support the executive team and it should oversee their behavior. This problem is similar to the conflict faculty members in a university face with respect to their students—they should facilitate the student's learning while also evaluating their progress. To some people, there seems no conflict between the two—either on corporate boards or in the classroom—and perhaps for strong-minded outside directors and instructors there is none.

But for many people, including most CEOs and students, there is a potential conflict. To a supporter, the CEO or the student provides information about his or her problems, failures, and so on, in order that the supporter can help him or her make progress; but to the evaluator, the CEO or student wants to provide only evidence of success. An outside director trying to support a CEO in a difficult business situation says to him or her, "You're doing a great job, keep at it," and offers his or her advice. It's difficult then at a board meeting to say to the CEO, "You failed in that endeavor and your compensation is going to be lower as a result." The CEO is likely to respond, "But you suggested that course of action," or "You supported me in that course of action." The outside director's answer should be, "Yes, but it failed and you alone are responsible for the failure. And it's my job to objectively evaluate whether you succeeded or failed." The CEO could be forgiven if he or she responds, "You suggested this course of action, you participated in our discussions about it, you supported me in it, and now you step back and say, 'It's failed and it's all your fault'—that's not ethical." Does the outside director then reply, "Perhaps it's not, but it's my job"?

In general, the American system of having dominant CEOs means that boards of directors are unable to serve effectively as an oversight mechanism on behalf of shareholders. Our system is designed for success—to provide single-point accountability, clear direction, decisive leadership, clear chains of command, and so on. With an effective CEO, the firm's executives and the board of directors support the direction laid down by the CEO and the firm prospers. But if the CEO is ineffective or corrupt, then the system breaks down. Too much power is in the hands of the CEO for the board to operate effectively as an oversight mechanism, except in few and very extreme situations.

The Danger of Ineffective Reforms

"The era of the dominant CEO died a quick and painful death, and it will be a long time before it comes back," says Charles Elson, governance expert at the

University of Delaware.[235] Is the matter really resolved, as Elson says? If so, what is the resolution, simply a more vigilant board?

Many American boards of directors, responding to scandals at some companies, are trying to assert themselves more vigorously, promising more energetic and objective valuation of corporate management. And many observers are proposing reforms to make boards more independent and stronger. This is all to the good. But what if it isn't sufficient? What reform proposals and increased board activism have in common is the conviction that reforms within the current structure will be sufficient to restore public confidence.

What if this is not the case? Then they are likely to be followed by ham-handed legislation at the federal and state levels, and the unintended adverse consequences of legislation may be severe. And there are strong reasons to fear that sufficient changes cannot be made within the existing framework of corporate leadership and governance in America. Furthermore, there's a missing piece in proposed reforms: corporate leadership structure. About all that is said of CEOs is that they should be more ethical, and be subject to closer supervision by their boards. But the first is likely to be insufficient and the second to set off a power struggle between the CEO and the board.

Finally, and most importantly, if boards reach for greater powers, and reforms that strengthen them are enacted but CEOs retain most of their powers, then again it's likely that debilitating power struggles will ensue in American corporations. The newly assertive board will come into direct conflict with the CEO who is trying to preserve his or her power. The fact is that American CEOs now dominate their boards, and if they are to retain the power they now take for granted, it will be very difficult for them to allow outside directors the greater access to management and greater input to decisions about accounting, auditing, and executive compensation for which investors are clamoring. Contests for power are likely to happen out of view of investors, breaking out occasionally into the business media, but they'll be nonetheless damaging for being generally concealed.

Power Struggle: What Will Happen with Governance Reforms if the Imperial CEO Retains His or Her Power

Alternatives to the Imperial CEO

"After considerable soul-searching and many Congressional hearings, the current CEO-dominant paradigm, with all its faults, will likely continue to be viewed as the most viable form of governance for today's world."

—Alan Greenspan, remarks prepared for delivery at Stern School of Business, NYU[236]

Greenspan tells us just the opposite of the notion that the dominant CEO has disappeared. But he goes further to tell us that it's the most viable form of corporate governance. To this, chairman of the International Corporate Governance Network, Alastair Ross Goobey, replies that it is "nonsense on stilts."[237]

What's a reader to make of this?

We have seen that the imperial CEO is the paradigm of corporate leadership in large American companies; and we've seen that the power concentrated in the CEO has allowed many to corrupt their companies to enrich themselves at the expense of their shareholders. In consequence, many reforms have been proposed to strengthen corporate boards, but if more aggressive boards meet powerful CEOs, the likelihood is for power struggles that will both frustrate the boards and damage the companies involved. Hence, if boards are to be more effective in protecting shareholder interests, they must confront less powerful CEOs. Can this be achieved? Are there alternatives to the imperial CEO?

Effective leadership is of utmost importance in the success of any firm. But while leadership is crucial, it does not follow that the form of leadership has to be an imperial CEO. Leadership might instead be shared successfully among a group of top executives in either a collegial or a consensus fashion. There are alternatives to the American paradigm of corporate leadership in northern Europe and in Japan. The Northern European paradigm is significant—especially the German model because of the large size and complexity of the Germany economy, rather like our own—because of the similarity in cultures of northern Europe and America. The German system relies on a more collegial form of corporate leadership.

Structurally, a German company possesses a dual board, supervisory and management. The supervisory board includes both inside and outside directors. The management board is made up of executives of the corporation only. But the management board has status under law, and some members of the management board, especially the personnel executive, have statutory responsibilities under German law that are independent of the CEO's authority. Behaviorally, German managers are also more likely to consult with their colleagues and to work with them as a team than are American managers. Since Germany has numerous global business organizations that successfully compete with American firms, there would seem to be some effectiveness in the German model.

In keeping with their greater reliance on group management and responsibility, German firms have objected to the 2002 American legislation that requires CEOs to certify their companies' financial reports. (It applies to foreign firms whose shares are listed on American stock exchanges.) German firms insist that such responsibility lies with the entire management board, not just with individual members.[238]

The Japanese system of consensus management is currently in a certain amount of disrepute due to the difficulties of the Japanese economy, but it has been a very effective system for a number of years and remains so in some global competitors operating from Japan. Behaviorally, rather than structurally, the Japanese system is rather different from our own. It is a system in which much leadership is exercised from the bottom up—comprehensive consultations take place within a management team before decisions are made. It has been asserted that a Japanese firm takes longer to reach a decision but much less time to implement it than does an American counterpart. The consensus system so dilutes individual responsibility for a decision that when something goes wrong, it is not uncommon for an executive, sometimes the chief executive, to resign to accept the responsibility symbolically, since rarely does he or she have the actual responsibility of the decision.

Because of their greater diffusion of responsibility among executives and managers, both the German and the Japanese leadership paradigms permit a board of the American type (partly executives and partly outsiders) to reach further into the corporation's decision and control processes. It is possible for an outside director to deal directly with executives without raising the concern of a CEO. In America it's not unusual for a CEO to control tightly who in the company's management talks with an outside director, and what information is given. This is a severe constraint on the oversight function of outsiders on a board in the United States, and it is less common abroad where executives other than the CEO have more independent status in the organization.

Since American CEOs are generally of a controlling personality, it would be difficult to implement the Japanese style of consensus decision making in our companies. But establishing a management board in which all members by law participate in the management of the company on nearly equal terms, as in the German system, might usefully provide more effective checks and balances on the CEO than we now have. In effect, the American CEO would be stripped of certain power in order to facilitate better oversight of the firm. Many students of corporate performance in different countries would argue that American firms might be more successful in business with a system other than the current imperial-CEO paradigm.

A reform of the leadership model in the American corporation is not likely to be a panacea for today's problems. A series of questions associated with a new form of management will likely arise. But such a change does have merit in providing an effective corporate governance capability that America badly needs today without creating a dysfunctional power struggle between the board and management that is likely to occur if our boards now seek more power at the expense of our CEOs.

America's Leadership Paradigm Is Upside Down

American corporations have our leadership model upside down. We presume that single-point accountability and decisiveness are greatly needed at the top, and less so below. But this is wrong. Single-point accountability and decisiveness in action are needed at the lower levels of leadership, not the higher. In fact, military training often expressly recognizes this, understanding that leadership qualities are more important at lower levels of authority, where contact with the enemy is immediate, than at higher levels where there is greater distance from the action.

Applied to World War II, our current notion of the dominant CEO would have replaced Eisenhower, the careful leader of a coalition, with Patton, the aggressive commander of an army group; and would have put the slow, cautious Eisenhower in command of Patton's troops. The result of this switch would have been disaster, and most people who have studied World War II would recognize that. But again, America's ordinary model of corporate leadership is exactly the opposite of what we did to win the war. In contrast to our ordinary way of thinking, the fact is that at the top of a company there is time and distance, which permit collegial leadership. Group accountability is possible and even best.

We Don't Have to Have Imperial CEOs

What follows may be considered Corporate Organization 101, which is familiar to everyone who has attended a major business school in the past 20 years, but which has not made its way yet into the public consciousness, via either the media or political discussion.

There is no compelling reason why the CEO of a company should be a dominant figure, an imperial CEO. There are compelling reasons why this should not be so: it drives too many decisions to the top that should be made lower in the organization and closer to the customer, it causes lengthy delays in decisions and actions while initiatives make their slow way through a corporate chain of command (a bureaucracy) to the top for review and determination.

There is often a good reason why the CEO should be charismatic—because charisma helps to provide effective human leadership. This is important for building good morale in a company and for closing top-level sales, both important functions of a CEO. (Charismatic doesn't mean a celebrity; it's not a role but a characteristic of the individual's appeal to others.) Decisive, fast action at operational levels (in production facilities and in dealing with customers, both for sales and service) is a critical element of success in modern business. Mature reflection and careful shifts of strategic direction, as well as oversight of the outcome of lower-level decision making, are important at the top levels.

- It follows that collegial decision making is dangerous at operational levels, where quick decisiveness and single-minded direction are crucial.
- It follows that collegial decision making is appropriate at top corporate levels.
- It follows that except in unusual circumstances, in particular in a crisis or turnaround situation, the dominant-CEO paradigm is an error—it's an error as a prescription, and it's an error as a description of fact.

The truth is, it's where we had a dominant CEO that we got the scandals: the management of earnings, the falsification of sales and expenses, the hiding of debt via creative accounting and off-balance sheet special purpose entities, the loans from the corporation to top executives and their families, and so on. It is much more difficult, though not impossible, to have such violations of shareholder and employee interest where there is a shared responsibility at the top of the corporation rather than an imperial CEO. If it's objected that providing such oversight is the role of the board of directors, then that simply turns the discussion to the failure of boards to perform their oversight role effectively, and the reasons for the failure—a key one of which goes right back to the existence of an imperial CEO.

Reining in the CEO

It's the responsibility of the board of directors to restrain the greed of the CEO, and it can't be done in large companies with today's too-powerful CEO, even if most of the reforms proposed are enacted. Even if it remains American practice that the CEO should have all power over the organization, he or she should not have it over its governance. If a board wants to effectively oversee a CEO, what should be done? These are the key steps:

1. The CEO should not be chair of the board of directors; that position should be assigned to an outside director. A blue-ribbon commission empaneled by the Conference Board recommended a separation of CEO and chairman in companies (Conference Board, Commission on Public Trust and Private Enterprise, January 9, 2003), provoking observers to comment that both Enron and WorldCom previously had such a separation. But this was somewhat disingenuous, since in both cases the chairman of the board was the former CEO of the company and the CEO his hand-picked successor. In fact, in only about 3% of publicly held American firms is the Chairman someone who was not previously the CEO nor the current CEO.
2. The board should select both the CFO and the chief human resources officer (CHRO), with the involvement of the CEO, and should review their performance periodically.
3. The CFO and the CHRO should both have certain key responsibilities for which they report to the board as well as to the CEO.
4. A management board should be established that is chaired by the CEO and whose members are the top executives of the company, and that is reviewed periodically by the board of directors.

These steps give the board of directors both far greater power in selecting the leadership of the company and reviewing its performance, and far greater direct access to information about the firm independent of the CEO's direct control.

That is, these steps take from the CEO both complete power over the other executives in the firm and complete control over information that reaches the board from the firm. Currently, virtually all information going to board of directors in most large companies is effectively screened or censored by the CEO; these reforms will permit the CFO and the CHRO to get information to the board without having to become whistle-blowers on the CEO.

A great problem is that in the current situation, with a majority of the directors of large companies themselves CEOs or former CEOs, a club-like atmosphere exists in which proposed reforms are not likely to lead to the psychological independence necessary to effective governance. Only a change in the attitude of directors toward the behavior which has been going on at investors' expense can make that change. We must ask that business leaders become intolerant of the crooks in their midst.

Initial efforts to restrain strong CEOs have not been promising. Boards have begun to cut back the severance packages of retired or resigned CEOs, especially those under investigation for fraud. Some boards are said to be getting less generous with pay packages.[239] But salary and perks are not the key to the imperial CEO, power is. Excessive pay is but a reflection of the dominant position that most CEOs have in their firms. Unless the disproportionate power of the dominant CEO is addressed, it will soon provide him or her a way to again push compensation up dramatically and again afford the independence from checks and balances that enables investors to be defrauded.

Talking Points

Many useful suggestions for change in the operation and structure of American corporate boards of directors have been made recently. But will they work in the face of the power of the American imperial CEO?

There are numerous important reasons why most boards are dominated by the CEOs of companies. There's a distinct likelihood that if boards attempt to assert considerably more power, as reformers desire, then they'll set off debilitating power struggles with the CEOs. In this case, the company and investors will lose.

There are alternatives to the imperial CEO. Companies can be managed on a more collegial basis, in which not so much power is concentrated in the hands of a single person. But if collegial management is too much of a change for most American firms, it's still possible to establish a balance of power between a CEO and a board in a large public company. The CEO must not be chair of the board, and the board must have access to key executives—in particular, the chief financial officer, who controls the company's financial reports, and the chief human resources officer, who controls the compensation of executives, independently of the CEO. Access to the CFO will help ensure that the financial accounts of the company are honest; access to the chief human resources officer will help to ensure that the pay package of the CEO is reasonable and related to actual performance on behalf of the shareholders.

VI *The Market's Role in a Solution*

"My husband went bankrupt and left me with four children to raise. It was very difficult. Then my parents died and I got a small inheritance. I hadn't worked regularly before, just for my husband's company, so I had no Social Security. I went to a major mutual fund company, one I'd heard good things about, and asked them how to invest the money. I explained my situation and how this money was going to be all I had for retirement. From what the representative responded, I was sure he understood what my situation was. He put me into a variable annuity that was to pay me in 20 years to support me then. He advised me what mutual fund to invest the annuity in. He said it was good because it had been going up rapidly. I bought it and it started down. Now I have about 20% of what I put in, and no way to pay for my retirement. The children are struggling through college, but I have nothing at all."

—A middle-aged New England woman

15 Let the Market Choose

Limitations of the Market

The market is a powerful mechanism that does some things very well, but not everything. It is often argued that the securities market should select honest, principled firms and reward them with high share prices, and conversely penalize with low valuations firms with dishonest accounting and limited reporting. But this is naive. Dishonesty provides a firm with an apparent (though not real) advantage in performance, and as long as the dishonesty doesn't call attention to itself, and as long as there are professionals who profit from accepting the numbers uncritically (accountants, analysts, bankers, and brokers who, if challenged, will say, "Oh, but accounting's not an exact science"), then dishonest reporting will have the advantage. But can markets be better utilized to restrain conflicts of interest and financial dishonesty? A commentator in the business press put the limitations of the SEC's reliance on disclosure very well: "Disclosure is a good thing. But as an investor safeguard it's outdated and naive, and about as effective as rubbing two sticks together to start a fire. The average investor doesn't always know where to find these disclosures. Besides, reports…contain enough mumbo jumbo to drive even professional traders to the Tylenol bottles. How effective is disclosure if investors can't process the information and, when aggrieved, have no clear recourse? What the SEC has done, in effect, is build a confessional, but it hasn't stopped the sin."[240]

Markets work most effectively in a proper context—where there's accurate information readily available, a reliable enforcement mechanism for contracts, honesty in dealings, and where buyers have a choice in what to purchase. A limitation of American financial markets during the great bubbles was that in their structure, and their governance, American companies were all very similar. Almost every company had an imperial CEO (Greenspan prefers the alternate term "dominant CEO"), and the same formal objective—to maximize wealth of shareholders of the company. Most companies didn't work that way—they were instead maximizing the personal wealth of executives—but the investor couldn't see it clearly because options weren't expensed and many perks (especially large loans and living expenses) weren't disclosed. So the market offered no clear choice among firms being run for the benefit of executives, and those that left investors some wealth as well.

It would be great if the market had different approaches from which to choose—if it were to avoid imposing a standard approach, (a template) on companies, whether by regulation or by the subtle pressures of ideological conformity. The herd instinct is very strong in financial markets, but it does much damage—sending the market reeling between extremes of high and low valuation and causing all companies and investors to try to do the same things at the same time. Investment bankers and analysts have preferred a particular type of corporate governance, and expressed their preference so strongly that almost every company adopted it (otherwise, investment capital and analysts' recommendations were very difficult to get). They wanted a dominant CEO with lots of options (supposed to align executives' and investors' interests) and a mission to maximize shareholder wealth. It sounded great to investors, but it didn't work out well. It turned out to be wealth maximization for CEOs and bankers.

Investors might be well advised to take another direction this time, seeking real choices as to corporate governance and corporate mission. Some companies might retain an imperial CEO; others might use a management board, with greater independence for the CFO and CPO. Some companies might take a direct route to shareholder-wealth building by stressing it as the company's mission without qualification; others might approach shareholder wealth-building indirectly via a primary commitment to customers, suppliers, employees, and communities (the stakeholder approach). If there were a variety of approaches, then the market could evaluate how the different companies with different approaches perform, and the market could value each accordingly.

Freeing the Market from Ideological Constraints

What may be termed the market solution for the securities market is to add risk valuations for different qualities of corporate governance, and then let investors select what companies in which to invest. A market can only make choices where there are different approaches available. If we have real alternatives from which the market can choose, we must also require proper financial disclosures so that there is information upon which to base market choices. Hence, to make a market solution work, investors must have alternatives among which to choose.

It would be appropriate to let companies' boards define both their own approach to governance and a mission—the way trustees do for a not-for-profit institution. Corporate missions would then vary and the market could decide what works best. Ideology would no longer be the criterion for corporate governance (as it is today, each company has an imperial CEO and shareholder primacy because everyone else does), but performance as judged by financial results would be. This is a real market solution.

What might some different approaches be? The most thoroughgoing change in corporate governance would include a weakened CEO, a much more powerful board and board leadership, more collective leadership, a management board with which the board of directors would deal, and a stakeholder orientation to shareholder value creation rather than shareholder primacy. Such a model might well work better for increasing shareholder wealth than the current model, and it would certainly be less vulnerable to misrepresentation designed to defraud investors. But it would be inappropriate to impose such a model on every company by regulation—its performance is not yet demonstrated sufficiently for that. The shareholder primacy model looks like a direct route to wealth for shareholders because it appears to commit corporate executives to the single-minded purpose of benefiting shareholders. It's direct, but direct isn't always best.

The stakeholder model is indirect but may be as or more effective—increasing shareholder value via helping customers and suppliers, employees and communities, and the investment markets might reward such a model if it were shown to be profitable. Markets should have this opportunity, rather than being rigidly attached to an ideology, shareholder primacy, which has just led investors into disaster.

Trusting the Imperial CEO Again

One alternative is to simply try the dominant CEO and direct shareholder primacy model again, with a new set of incentives for CEOs. This is what the proposals for indexed and expensed options amount to, at the most basic level. Will this solution work? Will indexed options tie CEOs' and shareholders' interests together securely (so that CEOs can't use them to their own benefit without shareholders benefiting as well), and will expensed options give shareholders the information they need to avoid being exploited by executives? Certainly both will be an improvement, but it's not so certain that the result will be positive and that other possible solutions should be rejected without trial.

The notion that the primary purpose of each corporation is the maximization of shareholder wealth may have a more subtle and important flaw, one that has contributed greatly to the decline in ethical standards so lamented by President Bush and Chairman Greenspan (among others). The *singular* focus of the shareholder primacy model on increasing wealth tends to undermine ethical standards by suggesting that no other consideration is as important to a company than making money.

Hard as it will be for many business executives and investors to accept, it may be that the shareholder primacy model of corporate governance will not maximize shareholder wealth—because it is impractical in execution (we cannot successfully tie the financial incentives of executives and shareholders together, executives will always have an incentive to make gains for themselves at shareholders' expense) and because it is inappropriate and self-defeating in ethical terms (it invites executives to act unethically, and shareholders are as likely to be the victims as customers and employees). The possibility that the shareholder primacy model of corporate governance is fatally flawed reinforces the argument that the market should be permitted to decide among alternative forms of governance.

Finding a Market Solution in the Not-for-Profit World

There is an alternative that involves a much more dramatic reform. It requires that the power of the CEO be reduced, and that of a board enhanced. Then it goes further to modify the legal tie of corporate boards to the shareholder's interests alone by borrowing an idea from not-for-profit organizations. The board of trustees of a not-for-profit is responsible not to shareholders but to the mission of the organization, and it holds the same power with respect to a CEO as does a for-profit corporate board. The board of directors of a for-profit corporation could be made responsible to the mission of the corporation rather than to shareholders. Creating value for investors would be a part of the mission, but the board, and its agent the CEO, would now be responsible to a broader set of constituencies.

Mission statements are much more important documents in a not-for-profit organization than in a for-profit company. In a not-for-profit they are the basic purpose of the organization, which it has a legal duty to pursue. In a for-profit firm a mission statement is ordinarily a rather vapid collection of homilies that have no legal standing and little influence on how the firm is managed. But corporations are familiar with mission statements, and it would not be an insurmountable leap to turn them into strongly meaningful documents for which top executives and board members have a serious accountability.

Mission statements generally serve several functions for an organization (see Oster, *Strategic Management of Nonprofit Organizations*, Chapter 2): the primary one is to set forth the basic objectives of the organization for which its executives and leaders have a legal responsibility; but the mission statement also sets out the limits of the organization's activities, motivates its adherents, and provides a basis for evaluation of the organization. A mission for a for-profit company would serve the same purposes and would include more than creating wealth for investors. It would identify the products and services offered by the company and the customers it seeks, thereby providing focus for the organization. It could also separate primary and secondary responsibilities among several components. A mission statement can form a boundary to limit strategic controversies within a company when there are many competing directions in which it could move forward.

For example, a telecom company's mission might be to provide convenient, quality long-distance phone service to home users while generating profits for shareholders. Three constituencies the mission statement will affect are home long-distance phone users, shareholders, and employees. With that in mind, investors can then evaluate the company's performance based on criteria other than profits. These are a variety of indicators not captured entirely in net income, such as customer satisfaction, penetration rate, retention rate, and so on. Though more qualitative, these qualities are not as misleading as when questionable accounting is used, yet still very important to build a sound, sustainable business. For employees, the motivation is to generate good return for shareholders and provide customers with good phone service. Management would no longer be compelled to focus purely on quarterly earning when customer satisfaction is equally important and is also evaluated by investors. This is what is now tried in the Balanced Scorecard approach to measuring corporate performance.

The decision whether or not companies should adopt such an approach might be decided by the market, based on how it values the shares of the companies involved. If companies with such missions beat shareholder-primacy companies in the marketplace, then investors will recognize that companies can take care of stakeholders without sacrificing shareholder value, and will value such firms highly. Maybe it will work, maybe it won't. It would be worthwhile to test it in the market.

Relying on the Market to Reform the Securities Industry

It may seem a radical response to the current scandals to rely strongly on the investing public for a solution—because most American business executives prefer markets structured to their own benefit—but such a market-based approach has much to recommend it. Investors would be confronted with real choices about corporate governance and the quality of financial reporting. Companies would chose different modes of governance along a wide spectrum of possibilities—some with imperial CEOs and some with management boards, for example; and some with a direct mission of shareholder primacy and others with an indirect mission of stakeholder responsibility—and investors would choose among them.

Finally, it's not difficult for companies to design financial reports that disclose information completely and accurately to investors.[241] It's a matter of having the will to do so—after more than a decade in which the objective of top corporate executives has been to conceal rather than disclose crucial financial information in order to benefit themselves personally. Still, proper reporting and disclosure isn't difficult, so the markets should be able to choose between companies that provide honest and clear financial information and those that don't, while revitalized regulatory agencies ferret out companies that directly defraud investors.

Comments of Fed Chairman Alan Greenspan on the Corporate Financial Scandals

Below are important comments by Fed Chairman Alan Greenspan on the corporate scandals. His comments are worthy of special attention because they are comprehensive and carefully thought out, and supported by the excellent research capacity of the Fed. Furthermore, the Fed is the key regulator of the banking system, which, as we've seen in earlier chapters, was deeply implicated in the major corporate irregularities. It's interesting, therefore, that Greenspan discusses the scandals as if the banks were not involved.

In this Senate testimony, Greenspan defines accounting fraud as theft; he sees it as a threat to the effective functioning of our economy. He says that effective capital markets require transparency and honesty. These points are well made.

But ironically, Greenspan supports a market solution and yet opposes a change in the system of the imperial CEO, which has exploited the markets in ways he finds disturbing. He goes so far as to define failures in corporate governance as failures of the CEO; that is, he blames the CEO for the lack of an effective oversight system that would limit CEOs' own actions. This is rather like blaming a thief for the lack of effective police protection for the bank he robs.

Given his commitment to the current system (dominant CEO and all), how does Greenspan propose to cause securities markets to operate better? He doesn't tell us, but because he sees the root of the scandals in dishonesty of some corporate leaders, presumably he seeks a way to establish higher ethical standards among CEOs.

Following Chairman Greenspan's comments, we will turn in the next chapter to how ethics might be improved in American companies and especially among their executives.

Greenspan on Corporate Governance

Testimony of Chairman Alan Greenspan; the Federal Reserve Board's semiannual monetary policy report to the Congress before the Committee on Banking, Housing, and Urban Affairs, U.S. Senate, July 16, 2002.

The recent impressive advances in productivity suggest that to date any impairment of efficiency of U.S. corporations overall has been small. Efficiency is of course a key measure of corporate governance. Nonetheless, the danger that breakdowns in governance could at some point significantly erode business efficiency remains worrisome. Well-functioning markets require accurate information to allocate capital and other resources, and market participants must have confidence that our predominately voluntary system of exchange is transparent and fair. Although business transactions are governed by laws and contracts, if even a modest fraction of those transactions had to be adjudicated, our courts would be swamped into immobility. Thus, our market system depends critically on trust—trust in the word of our colleagues and trust in the word of those with whom we do business. Falsification and fraud are highly destructive to free-market capitalism and, more broadly, to the underpinnings of our society.

In recent years, shareholders and potential investors would have been protected from widespread misinformation if any one of the many bulwarks safeguarding appropriate corporate evaluation had held. In too many cases, none did. Lawyers, internal and external auditors, corporate boards, Wall Street security analysts, rating agencies, and large institutional holders of stock all failed for one reason or another to detect and blow the whistle on those who breached the level of trust essential to well-functioning markets.

Why did corporate governance checks and balances that served us reasonably well in the past break down? At root was the rapid enlargement of stock market capitalization in the latter part of the 1990s that arguably engendered an outsized increase in opportunities for avarice. An infectious greed seemed to grip much of our business community. Our historical guardians of financial information were overwhelmed. Too many corporate executives sought ways to "harvest" some of those stock market gains. As a result, the highly desirable spread of shareholding and options among business managers perversely created incentives to artificially inflate reported earnings in order to keep stock prices high and rising. This outcome suggests that the options were poorly structured, and, consequently, they failed to properly align the long-term interests of shareholders and managers, the paradigm so essential for effective corporate governance. The incentives they created overcame the good judgment of too many corporate managers. It is not that humans have become any more greedy than in generations past. It is that the avenues to express greed had grown so enormously.

Perhaps the recent breakdown of protective barriers resulted from a once-in-a-generation frenzy of speculation that is now over. With profitable opportunities for malfeasance markedly diminished, far fewer questionable practices are likely to be initiated in the immediate future. To be sure, previously undiscovered misdeeds will no doubt continue to surface in the weeks ahead as chastened CEOs restate earnings. But even if the worst is over, history cautions us that memories fade. Thus, it is incumbent upon us to apply the lessons of this recent period to inhibit any recurrence in the future. A major focus of reform of corporate governance, of course, should be an improved functioning of our economy. A related, but separate, issue is that shareholders must perceive that corporate governance is properly structured so that financial gains are fairly negotiated between existing shareholders and corporate officeholders. Shareholding is now predominately for investment, not corporate control. Our vast and highly liquid financial markets enable large institutional shareholders to sell their shares when they perceive inadequacies of corporate governance, rather than fix them. This has placed de facto control in the hands of the chief executive officer. Shareholders routinely authorize slates of directors recommended by the CEO. Generally, problems need to become quite large before CEOs are dislodged by dissenting shareholders or hostile takeovers.

Manifestations of lax corporate governance, in my judgment, are largely a symptom of a failed CEO. Having independent directors, whose votes are not controlled by the CEO, is essential, of course, for any effective board of directors. However, we need to be careful that in the process we do not create a competing set of directors and conflicting sources of power that are likely to impair a corporation's effectiveness. The functioning of any business requires a central point of authority.

In the end, a CEO must be afforded full authority to implement corporate strategies, but also must bear the responsibility to accurately report the resulting condition of the corporation to shareholders and potential investors. Unless such responsibilities are enforced with very stiff penalties for noncompliance, as many now recommend, our accounting systems and other elements of corporate governance will function in a less than optimum manner.

Already existing statutes, of course, prohibit corporate fraud and misrepresentation. But even a small increase in the likelihood of large, possibly criminal penalties for egregious behavior of CEOs can have profoundly important effects on all aspects of corporate governance because the fulcrum of governance is the chief executive officer. If a CEO countenances managing reported earnings, that attitude will drive the entire accounting regime of the firm. If he or she instead insists on an objective representation of a company's business dealings, that standard will govern recordkeeping and due diligence. It has been my experience on numerous corporate boards that CEOs who insist that their auditors render objective accounts get them. And CEOs who discourage corner-cutting by subordinates are rarely exposed to it.

I recognize that I am saying that the state of corporate governance to a very large extent reflects the character of the CEO, and that this is a very difficult issue to address. Although we may not be able to change the character of corporate officers, we can change behavior through incentives and penalties. That, in my judgment, could dramatically improve the state of corporate governance.

Our most recent experiences clearly indicate, however, that adjustments to the existing structure of regulation of corporate governance and accounting beyond addressing the role of the CEO are needed. In designing changes to our regulatory framework, we should keep in mind that regulation and supervision of our financial markets need to be flexible enough to adapt to an ever-changing and evolving financial structure. Regulation cannot be static or it will soon distort the efficient flow of capital from savers to those who invest in plants and equipment. There will be certain areas where Congress will choose to provide a specific statutory direction that will be as applicable 30 years from now as it is today. In other cases, agency rule-making flexibility under new or existing statutes is more appropriate. Finally, there are some areas where private supervision would be most effective, such as that of the New York Stock Exchange, which requires certain standards of governance for listing.

Above all, we must bear in mind that the critical issue should be how to strengthen the legal base of free market capitalism: the property rights of shareholders and other owners of capital. Fraud and deception are thefts of property. In my judgment, more generally, unless the laws governing how markets and corporations function are perceived as fair, our economic system cannot achieve its full potential.

Talking Points

A market-based solution to the current scandals has much to recommend it. Markets work most effectively where there is accurate information readily available, a reliable enforcement mechanism for contracts, honesty in dealings, and a choice for buyers about what to purchase. Securities markets today do not make accurate information readily available, nor offer much honesty. And they don't give buyers much of a choice about what to buy when it comes to how a company is run and what its stated objectives are.

It would be well if the market offered investors different approaches to corporate governance from which to choose. Instead, today by ideology the securities market imposes a standard approach on companies. The market could be better utilized, with more reliance on investor choice. Some companies might retain an imperial CEO; others might use a management board, with greater independence for the CEO and CPO. Some companies might take a direct route to shareholder wealth-building by stressing it as the company's mission without qualification; others might approach shareholder wealth-building indirectly via a primary commitment to customers, suppliers, employees, and communities (the stakeholder approach). If there were a variety of approaches, then investors could evaluate how different companies with different approaches perform, and the market could value each accordingly.

16 Ethics Can Make the Market Work

"In my day those of us who went to business school did so because we were interested in business; if we'd wanted to make money, we'd have gone to medical school to become doctors."

—Graduate, Harvard Business School, Class of 1954

President George W. Bush, Fed Chairman Alan Greenspan, and investor spokesman Warren Buffett tell us that the core problem in the corporate scandals is the ethics, or lack thereof, of top executives. Presumably, therefore, improving the ethics of corporate leadership would reduce the problems that investors have been having. There are several aspects to improving ethics. For every executive and manager below the rank of the CEO, the most important influence on his or her own behavior is the standard set by the CEO. Research shows clearly that people in an organization, for better or worse, take their cues on how to behave from those in highest authority. There can be isolated incidents of unethical behavior in a firm in which the CEO sets high moral standards, but nothing more. On the other hand, in a firm in which the standards are low, massive fraud is possible. So the first place to go to improve ethical behavior is the office of the CEO, both to get him or her to hold others to high standards and to hold the CEOs themselves to high standards.

In trying to improve the standards of CEOs, business schools can play an important role, and so can continuing education, which is not required of top executives and directors of publicly-held firms, but which might be. The role of the market is to support efforts to encourage higher corporate ethics by rewarding those firms that exhibit ethical behavior via the price of their shares. This is part of a market-based solution to the crisis of the securities industry.

Corporate Leadership's Role

Psychological and sociological evidence are compelling regarding the strong influence of the ethical culture of an organization on its members. Similarly, the organizational behavior evidence is compelling about the strong influence of a CEO on the ethical culture of an organization.

In situations involving authority, as in a corporation, people sometimes do things they wouldn't otherwise do. Since the leadership of a company is responsible for its ethical culture, the leadership bears a direct responsibility for what is done at lower levels in the organization. In this light, the protestations of top executives that they were not responsible for unethical behavior below are not credible, except in circumstances where the behavior is clearly an aberration in the firm. Where, however, the unethical behavior is a key element of the business and goes on for quite a while and on a large scale, there would seem to be no question of top executive responsibility.

The subject of obedience to authority is linked inextricably to Dr. Stanley Milgram's obedience experiments of the 1960s. His conclusions were: "The results as I observed them in the laboratory are disturbing. They raise the possibility that human nature cannot be counted on to insulate men from brutality and inhumane treatment at the direction of malevolent authority. A substantial proportion of people do what they are told to do irrespective of the content of the act and without limitations of conscience so long as they perceive that the command comes from a legitimate authority. If in this study an anonymous experimenter could successfully command adults to subdue a 50-year-old man and force on him painful electric shocks against his protests, one can only wonder what government [or other authorities] with ...vastly greater authority and prestige can command of its subjects."

In a corporation, as an employee rises through the levels of a corporate hierarchy, loyalty and obedience are likely to be rewarded with a promotion. If at any level conscience interferes with loyalty, or obedience, then the employee likely won't be promoted. So we have an employee screening process that has tended to select *for* ability, loyalty, and obedience but *against* conscience. Subtle influence on what people believe to be proper behavior is as important as any other approaches to improving ethics and honesty in corporations. For example, for the moment companies are being much more careful about whom they hire. "The nation's major corporations...are responding by vetting candidates for top positions as never before, looking into all aspects of their professional and private lives with an intensity usually reserved for major criminal investigations."[242] The ethical character of the leader of the firm—good or bad—is amplified via authority so that its consequence is far greater than the behavior of the executive him- or herself. Hence whatever influence the CEO's ethics have is a magnified effect, and this is why business schools potentially might do some good if they could affect the attitudes of people who will someday be CEOs of great firms.[243]

Business Schools' New Role in Teaching Ethics

Ethics is not merely about private and individual behavior. At its core, ethics is about how people should behave with respect to other people—ethics is a matter of social norms of behavior. This is especially true in the financial marketplace in which strangers interact in a market, making possible deception and dishonesty on a large scale. In American colleges and universities, almost 2 million students each year take introductory economics courses, which stress markets and belittle institutions, and which treat the economic system as largely amoral. There are no statistics on the number of students who take courses in ethics, in part because the number seems to be very small, according to people who teach in ethics. So many students get a vocabulary and conceptual apparatus for economics, but only some get one for ethical behavior.

Even if we take the position that ethics are something a person learns early in life and cannot be inculcated when a person reaches his or her mid-20s, there remains a strong case for ethics instruction in business schools. First, people who are being trained to go into business will be encountering ethical challenges in a context different from school or the military and can benefit from preparation for the new challenges. Second, people being trained for leadership roles in business will not only be encountering business anew but will be learning a new role for themselves, one beset by the ethical challenges that confront any leader. Again, there's a strong case for preparing people for these challenges. The function of the school is to help people understand what their role-related responsibilities will be.

In Chapter 12 we saw how business schools are limited in their ability to draw the attention of their students to courses about ethics, and in their ability to improve the moral standards of the investment marketplace. These limitations originate in the frequently indifferent attitudes of the rest of the American community to ethical issues. But at the moment, in the midst of the current corporate scandals, indifference has turned to concern. In this environment efforts by the schools are likely to be more successful than in the past. The following sections discuss the key issues about how to teach ethics, and the new initiatives that might be successful.

What the schools should turn out are capable, well-trained people who are ambitious but not greedy. Our society has the right to expect schools of business to aim for this. One way of achieving such a product is through instruction; another way is by more carefully choosing who is admitted to business schools.

A business school student expressed it this way: "What do junior people like me in a company do when faced with watching senior management falsify the books? I think it's critical to continuously have courses in which immoral and unethical actions end up being penalized. It's our responsibility to ourselves and society to understand what is ethical and what is not, and our school's responsibility to help us understand this. I was on a panel for a reception recently when a potential applicant asked what our school has been doing in response to events such as WorldCom and Enron. I answered that it's our responsibility to send out leaders that are not only well-rounded in academics and business capabilities, but well-rounded as people."

Should Ethics Be a Separate Subject or Part of Other Courses?

Faculty and administrators at America's business schools have debated how best to present ethics to students. There are two different opinions. Some support separate courses for ethics, arguing that ethics involves a moral system that needs to be addressed as a whole and on its own merits. Others support including ethics in the regular curriculum of the business program, so that ethical issues in finance or marketing or leadership are addressed in their context. People who support separate courses for ethics fear that if ethics is addressed in each course, then it will get short shrift. People who support including ethics in other courses fear that if it's addressed separately, it won't have the immediacy and practicality to cause students to take it seriously.

What would appear to be a straightforward solution, to teach ethics both ways, is rarely done. In part this is a result of disciplinary jealousies; if a school has a faculty that teaches ethics solely, it won't want professors in other fields teaching ethics in their courses and their own way. They won't seem qualified to specialists. And if faculty in other courses teach ethics they won't want a specialized department in ethics which is likely to criticize what they're doing in their classrooms. A good solution would be specialized ethics courses, with ethical issues addressed in other courses by faculty who have been taught how to integrate them. This doesn't happen much because it's unusual for schools to teach instructors what to teach.

Schools that teach by the case method (including especially Harvard) have a special opportunity to address ethical issues in their classrooms, because ethical issues tend to arise in student discussions of cases, while they might not arise in an instructor's lecture. And in fact, when ethical issues are raised in classroom discussions by students, the way the instructor responds is critical to what a student learns about ethics.

The CEO of a medium-sized firm once described to me the first encounter he had with e-marketing, and one of the first classes in the program. The students were just getting to know each other and the professor, a very well known and admired expert in marketing. The class was discussing a case. The future CEO raised his hand and commented, "I see that you could do what is being suggested, but would that be right? Is it fair to the customer?"

The professor gave him a look as if astonished that such a question would be asked, and responded, "Well, do we want to make money or not?" The rest of the class burst into laughter, and no one again raised a question of ethics in the course. The CEO-to-be had gotten what he thought was the school's message about ethics.

Sometimes, of course, when a student raises an issue of ethics, an instructor welcomes the comment and invites the class to discuss it, adding his or her own positive views. Still, the experience recounted above, in which ethical considerations are minimized in favor of a cynical supposed practicality, appears all too common in America's business schools. Perhaps this false practicality is how many academics who teach in business schools pretend to their students that they are practical people, men and women of affairs. They seem to confuse cynicism and amorality with practicality.

There even appears to have developed the notion that freedom in our country grants one a right to act amorally. A good deal of intellectual authority apparently has provided support for this idea. A professor of business law at the University of Texas at Austin wrote in the *New York Times*, "Finance professors have told me that insider trading rules and financial disclosure requirements simply undermine the efficiency of the markets."[244] If the purpose of the markets is to fleece investors, then insider trading rules and disclosure requirements do undermine their efficiency. But if the purpose of the markets is to build our economy by providing investment support for businesses over the long term, then rules of this nature are crucial to the efficient functioning of the markets.

Where a school has courses devoted to ethics only, instructors in other courses can refer issues about ethics as they arise to instructors in the specialized course. The current tendency in MBA programs is to have specialized courses in ethics. In part this reflects the leadership of Harvard Business School. About 15 years ago, Harvard debated whether or not to have ethics courses, or courses with ethics mixed in with other subjects. Derek Bok, then president of Harvard, took a personal interest in the issue and argued strongly for specialized courses, insisting that ethics is a separate discipline with its own internal logic, which students learn best by addressing it directly in a course limited to ethics. Responding to Bok's leadership, the Harvard Business School established courses in ethics, and many other business schools followed suit.

What is important is that business school students get an opportunity to discuss with well-trained and supportive instructors ethical issues such as the use of off-balance sheet financing to disguise debt from investors. Ideally, this should be done in courses devoted entirely to ethics and also in courses devoted to other topics when ethical issues arise. Certainly the current scandals are providing a wealth of examples of manipulation of the investor and of the sometimes seriously adverse consequences of it.

Better Selection of Business School Applicants

Schools can also do a better job of screening applicants for moral standards. It's not uncommon for some students to falsify applications. For example, recently a second-year student at Wharton Business School was expelled for submitting fraudulent information on an application, which was not verified until the student's second year.

Improved Course Content

The current scandals provide much material for demonstrating to students the adverse consequences of unethical behavior. Jeff Skilling, former CEO of Enron and a partner at McKenzie Consultants, a Harvard Business School graduate, is now begging people to believe his version of events at Enron. During the time he was CEO, he was widely perceived as arrogant and bullying. Now he is said to be humble and contrite.[245] Going through the dynamic of unethical and/or illegal behavior, getting caught, being or feigning contrition, is exactly the danger that business school students face, and how this dynamic occurs, and how to avoid it, are exactly what courses in ethics might successfully teach.

There is plenty of significant content for courses in ethics. For example, suppose that an executive is negotiating a deal for his company with another company. What is his proper objective? Is it to gain the most advantage for his company, or to work toward the best win–win situation for both companies? As another example, should an executive distort the truth in financial reporting to gain advantage for current shareholders (and him- or herself), and hope to make it up in the next quarter; or should he or she stick closely to the actual figures? In these two instances, what is the right thing to do? And is there a single answer, or does it depend on circumstances? For example, if the deal being negotiated is one of a series, is a win–win solution more attractive, more ethical, because the other firm is likely to retaliate in future negotiations if it lost out in this one? Or does ethics take no notice at all of the firm's gain or loss in how it handles such a situation?

A second topic seems ideally made for business school ethics courses: how to deal with whistle blowing in the corporate environment. Unethical behavior can sink a company and a whistle-blower's career. If a person observes such behavior, how should he or she react? What are the potential consequences of being a whistle-blower; or having the whistle blown on you? The point is to prepare students for such situations when they arise in the work environment.

In other courses, there are similarly significant opportunities for identifying ethical content. But one critic noted that "ethics teaching…is hollow.… The evidence is not even clear that honesty pays."[246] This is the notion that unless ethics and honesty pays, most people will pay no attention to them. But it's dangerous to suggest that ethical conduct will be more financially beneficial than unethical conduct. That idea makes ethics merely an instrument to success, which is likely to be abandoned if a greater temptation arises, such as unethical behavior that promises faster, greater success. Often ethics requires a sacrifice of financial success for morality. Business schools will always struggle with the question of ethics if they deal with it from a pragmatic and not from a moral point of view.

In addition to having courses in ethics, mainstream business subjects should also be strengthened with ethical issues. In accounting, instead of teaching only technicalities and how to use imaginative devices such as a "cookie jar" (for which Microsoft got into trouble), the ethics of these approaches should also be discussed. In finance, the ethics of financial engineering should be discussed: What is the motivation behind certain maneuvers—is it to deceive investors, and if so, what are the ethics of that?

The Importance of Continuing Education about Ethics

We've been discussing means of including ethics in business curricula at the MBA and undergraduate levels. But what about continuing education for executives? There are, after all, requirements for most professionals to take continuing education courses in their fields.

It's ironic that the people who are leading great businesses and making the decisions that determine where shareholders' money goes have no such requirement. It would not hurt these people to have a reminder about fundamentals they should have had from their religious or secular education.

It's not that top executives need a reminder—they know what's right and wrong. But there are always new complications in business. Suppose that when off-balance sheet financing began to be popular, it had been pointed out to CEOs that this would be seen as deceiving investors. Would that have had an impact? Probably. Or if there'd been a discussion of the way the American people and the nation's political process would have reacted to the spectacle of former executives walking away rich from firms collapsing in bankruptcy and from tens of thousands of people who'd lost their pensions, would it have caused some executives to think twice about fraud? Perhaps.

But surely, it might be objected, CEOs did think about these things; surely they were aware of them but chose to ignore them. Any other conclusion would be naive. However, it's important to remember the rarefied atmosphere in which American imperial CEOs exist, in which few people are prepared to give them bad news or dispute their opinions. If the CEO sees benefit in something, then other people are likely to encourage him, not challenge him. And CEOs tend to look to other companies' CEOs (especially those who sit on their boards) for any guidance they seek, so there is a circle of reinforcement, not of challenge. A required outside course in ethics from time to time might be helpful in breaking into this closed chamber of opinion.

What I am proposing here are not ethical awareness programs for middle-level managers, which many firms already have. The scandals we're discussing in this book arose at the top of the companies involved, not in the middle. So top executives and directors need to be included, not just the middle-level people who may be involved in carrying out unethical schemes.

Will Society Reinforce Courses in Ethics?

We shouldn't be naive. Courses in ethics will not compel people to act ethically, it merely helps them understand what is ethical behavior. This is an important contribution, but to get more ethical behavior, more is necessary

The securities industry is closely interconnected to our political and social systems. Hence, we cannot expect to have major changes in our securities industry occur in a vacuum. Changes in the securities industry have to be reinforced by political and social changes. The major political change necessary is to lessen the dependence of political campaigns on corporate and personal giving, which corrupts the political and business processes. The major social change necessary is an increased respect for ethical behavior. Only if society as a whole reinforces ethical training can that training have an impact—if society produces ethical leaders, and if it punishes the thousands of people who participated in the frauds, especially those who led the companies in which these things happened. But both these responses seem difficult for American society today.

Where do people find moral leadership in our society? Where do they find examples of people who trade off financial gain for morality? It's hard to find moral leadership among sports figures concerned with their own pay; or politicians who are continually raising money from the very businesspeople enmeshed in scandal; or from university presidents and religious leaders who are continually seeking contributions from them. If the money is tainted because it was taken from investors by fraud, then should leaders of other institutions be flattering the defrauders to get money from them? Should they try to have it both ways: condemn the fraud and yet receive the contributions? Where is the moral leadership in this? So our society offers little today to reinforce morality positively.

A specific example involves the president of the State University of New York at Stony Brook who sat on the board of directors of Computer Associates, now being investigated for accounting and securities fraud, and who received for the school from the firm's founder and CEO gifts totaling some $40 million. The president of the school was at the time one of three outside directors on the company's seven-person board and a member of its Audit Committee. The company in its financial statements described the university president as a nonemployee rather than a member of its board, thereby possibly remaining within the letter of the securities laws when it failed to disclose the gifts by its CEO to the school. The intent of this slight of classification was to mislead investors by failing to disclose the gifts, which, of course, created a conflict of interest for the university president.[247]

Nor does our society offer much in the way of punishment to dissuade unethical behavior. If there is no punishment for the guilty, or it's directed at too small a proportion of the guilty, or is too limited in severity, then ethical training will be wasted on many people who will still pursue the temptation to get rich at their investors' expense. In the first two years of the scandals only a handful of people pleaded guilty to securities fraud, a handful were indicted, and none were convicted. This flimsy record doesn't provide much support for courses in ethics.

If people were actually going to jail, if they were having to make restitution for what they took, if there were triple damage penalties as there are under the antitrust laws, then we could say to the class, "Ethics are these things you have to do in part to keep yourself clean and out of these problems." Then ethics courses might do some real good.

American society has a penchant for admiring money, no matter how it's been made. This undercuts ethical instruction in the schools, because it assures people that even if they get rich via fraud, others will accept and admire them. This characteristic of American society is one of the sources of the temptation to steal that has driven the financial scandals of recent years. Yet will Americans do any differently? Will Americans learn to despise rich crooks?

It's often argued that a person is innocent until proven guilty, and so if a person has made off with the money successfully, and there's no prosecution or there's no conviction, then the money is his or hers by right, and that should be accepted. But this isn't a moral position at all. It's merely a rule of a justice system so imperfect by way of technicalities and the whims of judges and juries that almost no moral judgment can accompany a legal judgment—that is, the guilty are released and the innocent convicted in about equal measure.

So when Americans accept business leaders who have defrauded investors on the grounds that they were not tried and convicted, this is not a moral position, but a rationalization for a longstanding tendency of American culture to admire the clever rascal.

This attitude is reinforced by a sophisticated cynicism that effectively dismisses any effort to improve ethics in American business. "The real lessons to take away from Enron and Worldcom..." wrote the editors of *The Economist*, "are ...that managers will be as greedy as they can get away with."[248]

To these attitudes: that the thief is to be admired when he or she succeeds in getting rich, and that there will never be effective self-restraint, there are two responses. First, that if these attitudes are justified, then those, including President Bush, Chairman Greenspan, and investor Buffet, who argue that a lack of ethics is at the root of the corporate scandals, are merely naive and mistaken. Second, only in the law can an investor find any protection and, American law being imperfect as it is, that is little consolation.

But cynicism may be wrong-headed. After all, our economy continues to operate, and that's largely because there are enough ethical people around maintaining the minimum amount of trust needed to allow transactions to take place. The flaw in the cynics' view is that it doesn't explain the persistence of a necessary level of honesty that remains in our economic life. Hence, if the cynic is wrong about that, he or she may be wrong about it generally. In fact, our society cycles through periods of greater and lesser corruption. There was a general decline of business morality in the period after the Civil War, and then a period of reform; there was a decline in business morality in the 1920s and a period of reform in the 1930s and 1940s. There's now been another, larger decline in the 1990s, and perhaps, if we make an effort, a substantial reform can be made to follow—that would certainly involve a resurgence of individual ethics. But such a resurgence will occur only if we work hard to cause it to do so.

Talking Points

Improved ethics can play a key role in resolving the crisis of honesty in our financial markets. Corporate leaders and business schools can do much to turn business behavior in the right direction. A new generation of corporate, banking, and accounting leaders with a greater commitment to honest disclosure than their predecessors can help improve ethics in their companies.

Business schools can teach ethics both as a separate subject and in the context of courses in marketing, finance, and so on, but only if they're prepared to help instructors learn how to teach it effectively. But business doesn't exist in a vacuum, and substantial change can't occur without support from other elements of American society, which must reinforce the importance of ethical behavior by rewards and penalties, and most importantly by abandoning our collective willingness to admire people who make money, whatever the means.

VII *Getting Your Money Back*

An Adelphia cable installer, immediately after the company's bankruptcy and the arrest in handcuffs of its top executives for securities fraud, shook his head in astonishment and told me, "My 401(k) is so low that I only hope that I can get back what I put in by the time I retire."

Lots of people are in this position, and it's fair that they try to get their money back. It wasn't the ordinary risk that accompanies investment that caused them to lose their money—it was fraud.

17 Freezing and Seizing: A Direct Route to the CEO's Pocketbook

"We're taking the mansion. We're draining the bank accounts. And we're coming after the yacht."

—Tom Delay, House of Representatives, Republican, Texas.[249]

Three Routes to the Money

The key question is whether Americans feel strongly enough to go get their money back from the people who took it, and if they do, whether our political system is responsive enough to make it happen. There are three avenues to getting the money back, each of which is currently of little value but might be made significant if there is sufficient investor activism:

- Complaints to brokers and mutual funds
- The courts
- Congressional action to establish a compensation fund

The government is currently making limited changes intended to do two things:

- To try to prevent a reoccurrence of fraud (reform)
- To try to punish executives who engage in fraud (retribution)

The government is doing almost nothing to help people get their money back (restitution). But it might if voters pressed strongly enough. That is the topic of this chapter.

Getting the Company to Sue for You

It's useful for investors if a company brings suit against the executives and directors who defrauded them. It may be especially valuable if the suit is filed against the auditors, because then the standard of judgment is whether the auditor has been negligent, not whether it has engaged in fraud.[250] But many companies lack the resources to bring suits, and any suit is stressful to a management team that may be trying to resurrect a weakened company—so ironically investors may lose from the company bringing the suit. Furthermore, if an investor has sold his or her stake in the firm, then a successful suit by the company that gains money for the company and thereby for its investors provides no gain to those investors who have sold out.

Also, a board of directors can rescind or otherwise modify a golden parachute (that is, a severance package) if it has a proper reason and acts properly. For example, if the parachute were awarded under improper circumstances, or if the board's vote were not properly conducted, it can be rescinded. As usual in American law, the matter seems to turn on the validity of the procedures used by the board to fashion and approve the severance package, not whether the executives walked away with large amounts while shareholders took losses on their shares. But perhaps, in light of the extreme size of many severance packages, and the extreme losses meted out to shareholders, the suitability of the parachute might itself become an issue under a standard of reasonableness. Whether this is possible will, of course, have to be tested in our courts.

Appropriate Limitations

As suits against companies, executives, and directors increase in number, there should be some reasonable limitations on what is recoverable lest the baby be thrown out with the bath water. Suits for fraud at one company should probably not be permitted reach to all the assets of a director, especially those derived from other employment. Otherwise, it will become very difficult to get people to serve as directors since the risk–reward ratio will be tilted too much toward risk. It's important to remember the imperfections of our legal system—many judgments are reached that are not justifiable. In the case of CEOs, however, legal reach should be to every asset gained with the assistance of the company, including, for example, sale of IPO allocations received from banks in return for banking business from the company.

Filing a Claim against Your Broker

If you have a claim against your broker, there is an arbitration procedure under the NASD that must be utilized before going to court. It's a fairly quick procedure. If your claim is less than $25,000, you don't need an attorney. According to a study by the GAO, you have a 60% chance of recovering 60% of your claim, coming to a probability of getting back 36% of your claim.[251]

Going Directly to the Courts

We pointed out in Chapter 7 that most of the actions that misled and damaged investors were illegal. In that chapter we explained in detail what the law provides. Can investors benefit from the law to get their money back? The answer ought to be a simple yes, but it turns out to be much more complicated, and uncertain.

In civil suits such as investors would bring (criminal cases can be brought by the U.S. Department of Justice or the attorneys general of the states), the standard for conviction is negligence by the executives involved. Negligence is easier to prove than the standard for conviction under criminal law. There is also a useful concept called "unlawful blindness." By this standard a CEO who does not see fraud he should have seen or claims he didn't know about when he should have, has breached his fiduciary duty of care and is therefore guilty.

Under the Federal Corporate Accountability Law of 2002:

- Top executives are required to forfeit bonuses if their companies restate financial results.
- Defendant executives are denied the use of bankruptcy laws to avoid paying fines or surrendering bonuses or insider-trading profits.

Both these changes strengthen the hands of investors in litigation against top executives.

The law also requires a complainant to show that an executive or director participated in failing to disclose or misstating material information to investors. This is called "culpable participation." If it's proven, then the defendant is liable for a proportion of the claim as decided by a jury. This is the path to the pocketbook of executives and directors.

Can Investors Get the Law Enforced?

Robert Monks, a shareholder activist, summarized the situation this way: "It's simple. No new laws.... It just requires the executive branch to decide they are going to enforce the law as it stands."[252] Since so much of what has happened is already illegal, if the courts expedited these cases, if they imposed substantial financial penalties on violators, if they forced those convicted to disgorge what they've taken from investors, then investors might find some real relief in the courts.

But this will not happen on its own. So investors must ask, can trial lawyers or the SEC get my money back for me? The answer is maybe. If fraud is the issue, then the laws are in place to recover investors' money; but the standards of proof are so strict, and processes of the American legal system are so imperfect, that ordinarily little of the money lost can be recovered.

We've seen in Chapter 10 that prosecutions for security fraud are rare in the United States, and convictions even more rare. When a conviction is won and violators are ordered to disgorge their ill-gotten gains, not much is recovered. For example, the SEC collected only about 14% of the $3.1 billion in fines and penalties levied against individuals in the years 1995 to 2001.[253] In the first half of 2002, the SEC won orders forcing executives to disgorge $632 million, of which $73 million has been retrieved. In the last 5 years, 935 suits alleging securities fraud recovered an estimated 7.2% of estimated shareholder losses (up from 948 suits and 5.1% in the preceding 5 years).[254]

In 1995 Congress passed the Private Securities Litigation Reform Act, making it more difficult to sue corporations and professional service firms like accounting firms for securities fraud. But it didn't make it impossible. Corporations whose stock fell in value were getting sued for securities fraud, and financial services firms that assisted them, and often had deeper pockets, were getting stuck with large claims when the companies had no money to pay shareholders. Now financial services firms can be held liable for only a portion of the claim—that which is directly attributable to their misconduct.[255]

Through civil suits, the attorney general of New York, Eliot Spitzer, is seeking to recover more than a billion dollars for investors from CEOs who steered their investment banking business "to Citigroup in return for inflated ratings of their companies' stocks and new shares in other companies."[256] Some large public pension funds have begun to sue to recover their losses from the executives who led the companies that defrauded them. In some instances they are even offering a percentage of what's regained as a bounty to the attorneys. They are seeking the real estate of the top executive of WorldCom and the Impressionist painting collection of the top executive of Tyco International.

"Part of the idea is to recover as much as we can, but part of the idea is also deterrence," said Christopher W. Waddell. "We're going to go after the paintings, the yacht, the apartments—everything," said Jay W. Eisenhofer, a lawyer at Grant & Eisenhofer in Wilmington, Delaware, which represents the Teachers' Retirement System of Louisiana and the Louisiana State Employees' Retirement System in a lawsuit against Tyco.[257]

A recent ruling in a Federal District court in Houston may allow investors wider recourse in the courts for investment losses. It allowed investors to sue advisors to corporations, for example, banks, as primary participants in a fraud if they helped corporations conduct transactions intended to mislead investors about the companies' finances.[258]

What Happened to Chainsaw Al

We visited Al Dunlap's tenure at Sunbeam in Chapter 2. In 2002 he agreed to pay $15 million to settle a shareholder suit. Later that year an attorney for Mr. Dunlap "pointed to a decision by a federal judge accepting the settlement of the shareholder suit for a fraction of the billions lost by investors in the Sunbeam collapse. In explaining why they settled for so little, class-action lawyers said they had 'no direct evidence' that Mr. Dunlap 'had any actual knowledge of Sunbeam's improper accounting techniques.'"[259]

This result says a great deal about our legal system. The fraud ended in 1998, and the litigation continued late into 2002; no criminal charges have yet been filed and may not be. Had there been quicker action, fraud in other companies might have been deterred.

Proving that CEOs Were at Fault

As mentioned in Chapter 5, there should be no need to prove direct knowledge by a CEO of improper accounting techniques in his firm; yet even in a fraud of this magnitude a highly paid CEO can claim he didn't know what was going on in the company, that he was ignorant of the very things that stood to make him a fortune! A CEO who does not know that large-scale fraud was occurring in his company, and got a substantial pay package, has already perpetrated a fraud on investors, who were paying him a great deal to know exactly those things.

The sort of defense that says, "I didn't know what was happening in the company of which I was the CEO," should be denied. Rather than investor plaintiffs having to prove that a CEO knew what was going on in his company, the CEO ought to have to prove he didn't know—after all, he's being paid to know what's going on. Perhaps this is in part what Congress had in mind when in the summer of 2002 it required CEOs of large public companies to personally certify their companies' financial reports. This would seem to make it more difficult for CEOs to claim they were unaware of irregularities. But a CEO's signature on financial reports only indirectly proves that he knew what was going on. The law has now sought to establish the presumption directly by requiring CEOs to personally sign financial reports.

There are circumstances, of course, in which a CEO might truly be ignorant of a financial fraud in his company. For example, he may have just entered his position; the managers involved in the fraud might have been chosen by a predecessor; the fraud might be in a nonstrategic unit that is small and distant and even unlike the core of the business. In these circumstances, a CEO might be caught off guard. But when fraud occurs after the CEO has been for a year or more on the job; when it's committed directly by people he chose for their jobs or by people chosen by his own choices; when it's in the core of the business, then it's ridiculous to permit a CEO the defense that he didn't know about it. Yet this is how Chainsaw Al escaped having to make more significant restitution to the investors who lost out on Sunbeam.

The new Corporate Responsibility legislation requires executives whose companies restate their accounts because of misdeeds to disgorge bonuses and stock option gains, and it strengthens the government's hand by not requiring the SEC to connect the executives directly to the misdeeds. But it remains a bit unclear whether an executive had to have knowledge of the misdeeds in order to have to disgorge, and the SEC is given the authority to waive this provision. Assuming the provision is not watered down or waived regularly, then it's a substantial step forward, because it adopts the principle that those in charge when the frauds occurred are responsible and denies them the claim, usually false but difficult to prove, that they knew nothing about what was occurring and so bear no responsibility.

Individual Suits

No matter how much damage has been done to an investor, there is no easy answer to the question whether he or she should sue. It's necessary—if the investor is to have a hope of recovery—to get an attorney who is effective and energetic. This isn't easy. Then there are questions about the cost of litigation and whether the investor will be able to collect if the suit is won.

In general, where the company is bankrupt, small, or financially weak, there's not likely to be anything to recover. If there were executives who pocketed a lot before it went down, they can be pursued. Their money can be flushed out of the Cayman Islands or the Isle of Man, or possibly even Switzerland. But it's expensive and time consuming and the race is to the swift.

Money buys good legal talent, and executives who have defrauded investors often have a great deal of it. Unfortunately, although trial attorneys may go after fraud at WorldCom and Enron, it probably won't help small investors who took brokers' advice to buy shares. They have often lost less than $100,000, and with attorneys' fees at one-third, that's likely to be too little incentive.[260]

Class Actions

Because of the high cost of litigation, investors who have had small losses are not likely to get into court on their own. But they might find a way via class action suits. Class action suits are often initiated by trial lawyers who know about a situation involving possible defendants (like companies or executives) and who then seek a "representative plaintiff"; that is, someone who has a case against the defendant and is like other people who have similar cases against the defendant. A representative plaintiff is key to a class action suit because only one person is necessary to bring the suit, and others can enter later at their will. If the case results in a successful recovery, either through settlement or trial, all class members receive their portion of the amount paid by the wrongdoers. The attorneys will be paid if the suit is won via a contingency, usually about 30% of the award. Contingency fees are generally illegal abroad, so this is an aspect of American law that potentially favors investors in their quest to recover their money.

When a company's share price has dropped, investors' losses may be due to fraud when:

- Company executives misrepresented facts relating to important aspects of the business or held off revealing "bad news" that should have been disclosed earlier.
- The company or its accountants "restate" financial results to reflect the true state of the company's financial affairs.
- The stock drops rapidly on a disclosure of wrongdoing by the company or its executives or employees.
- Before bad news is revealed, insiders engage in insider trading by selling their shares at inflated prices.[261]

Fraud may have been involved not only when the share price drops, but when the company has made deals with insiders or related companies that are unfair to shareholders. Such deals may represent a type of improper conduct usually referred to as "breach of fiduciary duty." This wrongdoing includes waste of a company's assets, unfair business transactions with insiders or related entities, agreeing to a sale of a company at a price that doesn't reflect its true value, or any other act that improperly robs a company or its shareholders of value. In such cases, a suit can be brought on behalf of the company and/or its shareholders to recover damages or to ensure that shareholders are treated fairly.[262]

Interestingly, a shareholder can participate in a class action even if he or she never sold the stock for a loss. In almost all cases, so long as a person held the stock when the stock dropped in reaction to bad news, the person may bring a case. What matters is that the investor bought his or her stock at a fraudulently inflated price. The investor's rights are the same whether he or she later sold at a loss or held some or all of his or her shares in the hope that the price would recover.[263]

Some class action suits result in substantial recoveries for shareholders and their attorneys. The largest corporate settlement in response to class action securities fraud litigation in recent years has been with Cendant, in the amount of $3 billion. The settlement with Waste Management involved $677 million. A settlement with Bank of America involved $490 million. Strong cases can and do yield strong recoveries.[264]

Class action lawsuits are common in America and cover a wide range of matters. By some accounts, about 10,000 class action lawsuits are filed annually. Many class action suits involve product liability, but some are about investors' complaints. More than 200 class action suits were brought against U.S. corporations in 2001 for violations of equitable limitations (or duties) toward investors, and in 2002 in the first 6 months another 112 were filed.

But it's not easy to know whether a class action suit has been filed, or won, that affects an individual investor. The court tries to reach those affected; so if you're on a list of shareholders, you may get a letter telling you about the suit and what you stand to gain if it is successful. But the court may not find each investor. Can an investor find a class action suit?

The Internet makes this easier. "Consumers can run online searches on just about any class action suit. A growing number of websites—including Findlaw.com from the American Bar Association, Classactionsonline.com, and Classaction America.com, along with those from individual law firms—provide information on pending cases. The National Consumer Law Center also keeps its clients informed about pending class action cases online, at *www.consumerlaw.org*.[265]

Unfortunately, class action suits have serious limitations, some of the most important of which arise out of conflicts of interest. The greater the award or settlement, the more both attorneys and investors would make. But attorneys also have an interest in getting a larger share of the total settlement for themselves—and the courts control what that amount is. Hence, some areas in the country are much more popular for filing class action suits than others. The courts of Madison County, Illinois, are said to be especially popular because they allegedly approve whatever class action attorneys propose, no matter how unfair to the class of complainants.[266]

Getting Money if You Win the Suit

In the past, settlement of security fraud cases was usually via payments by companies and their insurers. But today many companies are out of reach of petitioners in bankruptcy, and where there was outright fraud, no insurance may be available. In addition, executives have taken so much more out of the companies than in the past. So, complaints on behalf of 401(k) holders at Enron and Global

Crossing have named individual executives as defendants. Settlements without payments by individuals no longer make sense.[267]

In the past complainants didn't get much of individuals' money. A company's insurance firm used to make offers of settlements contingent on the plaintiffs' dropping claims against individuals, and people with money had it well hidden abroad or transferred to family members.[268] However, this practice is changing in the investors' favor. For example, in the Sotheby's price-fixing scandal, former CEO Alfred Taubman put up $30 million to settle shareholder litigation and another $156 million to settle customer complaints.

Talking Points

Many of the activities that caused great losses to shareholders were illegal. There are several means of trying to recoup losses through the law. It's useful for investors if a company brings suit against the executives and directors who defrauded the company and investors. It may be especially valuable if the suit is against the auditors, because then the standard of judgment is whether the auditor has been negligent, not whether it engaged in fraud. Also, a board of directors can rescind or otherwise modify a golden parachute (that is, a severance package) if it has proper reason and acts properly. It's possible to take a broker to arbitration, a process that is better in practice than in reputation. It's possible to join a class action suit, though many investors may recover only a little of their money. It's possible to sue directly yourself, though this is time consuming and expensive.

18 Getting Congress to Get it for You

Congress can provide some restitution to investors for money stolen from them. But will it? There are two primary ways for Congress to provide money directly:

- It can give investors the money it gets from civil and criminal defendants.
- It can allocate funds to provide restitution to investors and tax, if desired, to refill the government's coffers.

This chapter reviews both methods.

Taking Money from Perpetrators and Giving It to Victims

We've seen in Chapter 10 that under current law the government can seize the assets of an executive only when it has proven a violation of the law. This provides great comfort to guilty executives and reinforces the temptation to defraud investors. But in a few cases in which the government has obtained convictions, it provides access to ill-gotten gains.

For example, in the Enron matter in the summer of 2002 the government obtained guilty pleas from managers who reported to Andrew Fastow, CFO of Enron. Using the pleas, it went to court and asked for the forfeiture of millions of dollars in bank accounts and other assets of Fastow's. Furthermore, it asked for the forfeiture of accounts of his brother and of a family foundation, each of which, according to the government, had received funds stolen from Enron. The court refused to grant forfeiture, but it did freeze the accounts sought by the government. The freeze order restricts the Fastows and others from moving or withdrawing the funds while the courts determine whether or not the government can obtain the money permanently.[269]

Sometimes Congress can get some money back for investors directly just by grilling the guys who took it. Global Crossing's chairman pledged to contribute $25 million to offset some of the pension-fund losses sustained by employees. He made the promise under fierce questioning during a Congressional hearing.[270]

A Restitution Fund

The government could, if so persuaded, establish a fund that would compensate investors for some of their losses. Congress took a step in this direction via the Federal Corporate Accountability Law of 2002, which requires the SEC to give investors, not the government, what it collects from violators. But, as we've seen, historically the SEC doesn't collect very much.

Congress might usefully go further on behalf of investors by passing a bill to make equitable adjustment of investors' claims, calling it something like the American People's Pension and Savings Restitution Act. Its objective would be to return to investors in fraud-tainted companies some of the money they lost.

Congressional action is merited by the large scale of the problem, which threatens to swamp the courts if all legitimate claims are pursued in litigation. Congress might do something like what was done for victims and survivors of the World Trade Center attack—a fund was set up (the Victim Compensation Fund) to provide benefits. To receive an award from the fund, in an amount determined by the fund's administrators, the recipient must agree not to sue.

Something similar might be done for people who were victims of investment fraud—not on the same scale of loss or benefit, but similar in principle. A person's quality of life, including length of life itself, are related to the adequacy of his or her pension, so that when pensions are stolen, a crime has been committed that requires special restitution. Following this logic, the government should cover losses in pensions, 401(k)s, college savings, and annuities.

What should the victims of investment fraud get as recompense? Only the original value of their investments. That is, if a person had a bank savings account and put it in the market (via stocks, mutual funds, or annuities) during the bubble and scandals and lost it, he or she should get it back; and the same for life insurance benefits, divorce settlements, pension lump sum payouts (from IRAs, for example), the money corporations paid into 401(k)s, and so on. So they'd get back their money without appreciation. This is a tight, minimal standard, but it would still do some real good.

Not all investment losses due to fraud need be covered, but only those arising in the current scandals. This is consistent with the government's action in the World Trade Center matter. Various sorts of disasters that take human life occur all the time, but Congress addressed only the World Trade Center victims in this manner. Similarly, not all victims of fraud need have access to the fund, but only those defrauded in this especially large and grievous group of scandals.

The objective of the fund should be to restore investors' status quo ante—to restore to investors their real capital before the bubble distorted all measures. A BTB—before the bubble—objective could cover losses in pensions, annuities, and for-college savings. If such a fund were established, it would require an administrative mechanism, possibly in the Department of Labor, which already handles pension security. Claimants would make application showing amounts lost, dates, times, and so on. Congress or the fund administrators should prescribe standards governing eligibility, and the agency should implement them.

Voluntary Assumption of Risk

Some people are bound to argue against a proposal for a restitution fund, saying there are crucial differences between the WTC survivors and people who were defrauded by corporate executives and their associates. Loss of life and loss of comfortable retirement are not the same, but, with respect to the WTC disaster, government aid doesn't go to those who died but to survivors; while in the investment scandal it would go primarily to the actual victims. People lose their lives every day under circumstances in which the government fails to protect them, and the government does not pay compensation. For example, women who are supposedly protected from their spouses by court orders are nonetheless murdered by husbands violating those orders. Yet Congress established a fund for WTC survivors, but not for women murdered while under court protection. Why? Perhaps because of the size and exceptional nature of the WTC disaster.

A similar logic exists for the victims of the investment fraud of the last few years. It is not proposed that all investors who lost money at any time be compensated, only those in this especially glaring occurrence, like the WTC disaster. There are difficulties determining amounts to be paid to WTC survivors, and the difficulties will be no different in determining amounts to be paid to fraud victims. The benefits of the WTC fund go not to the dead but to their survivors, as we've noted, and this reflects in part a judgment that the quality of survivors' lives has been so damaged as to require government restitution. The same may be said of the victims of corporate fraud who lost their pensions and savings.

Some may object that investors assumed risk voluntarily and so are not entitled to restitution from the government, though they may be entitled to it from the perpetrators of the fraud. People assumed the risk. But why did the investors assume the risk? Because they relied on the assurances of those in authority (analysts, brokers, financial advisors) that there was reasonable safety in the investment choices they made, and they relied on other authorities (the SEC and other regulatory bodies whose duty was to protect investors) to do a proper job and protect them. In both the investors were disappointed. An underlying justification for a compensation fund for victims of the financial disaster is that the government of the United States is complicit in their losses due to its failure to exercise due diligence in protecting them.

In other words, both WTC workers and investors knowingly assumed more than just an ordinary amount of risk, but they did it on the assurances of authorities that it was safe and in the knowledge that the government was there to protect them. In both they were disappointed and they suffered grievous loss. Both are entitled to recompense from the government, and the government is entitled to retrieve money from the perpetrators—from the terrorists by seizing their assets and from the financial defrauders by seizing their assets or taxing them.

Paying for a Fund

In the case of the World Trade Center disaster, the government chose to provide benefits to survivors because victims couldn't recover from the perpetrators. There's a difference in the case of the securities market swindles: much of what was lost can be recovered from individuals and companies, and should be. Recovery should be from companies, executives, investment banks, mutual funds, and accounting firms. Thus the fund might be financed by penalties and disgorgement of illegal gains that the government takes in under securities fraud law, but also from general revenues or a specific tax levied on financial service institutions.

A bill was introduced in the House of Representatives (by Richard Baker, Republican of Louisiana) that would put all money recovered by the Federal government—including civil and criminal penalties for security fraud, and disgorgement of ill-gotten gains by executives—into a fund for swindled investors. But some object that it would be complex to determine who gets it. So the bill hasn't passed. The White House might require the task force on securities law enforcement that it established in the spring of 2002 to place a high priority on recovering money stolen.

Without some very substantial restitution package (a fund or much help with litigation), Congress can do no more than close the barn door after the horses have been stolen. It can hardly be surprising if investors who are victims of the frauds respond, "Thanks a lot; my horses are gone. This is of no value to me."

Idle Redress—Excessive Legalism

Whether or not Congress will help investors get their money back is uncertain, but it is certainly getting involved in how investors' companies are managed, and in so doing is preparing the ground for more and more lawsuits. In Chapter 13 it was argued that what is needed is not more regulation, but better, smarter regulation. Unfortunately, today Congress and federal and state regulators are beginning to micromanage the securities and accounting industries, and not doing it well. Business executives and the securities industry brought intrusive regulation on themselves by switching from disclosure to concealment, and from transparency to deception in dealing with investors. But the form that regulation is taking is not good for executives, the securities industry, or investors. The problem is not individual regulations or rules, which may make sense, but that the overall system is increasingly complex, litigation-prone, and leads not to more transparency and disclosure, but often to less.

We're wandering into a maze and down a blind alley by substituting detailed rules for principles, so that the large picture is no longer visible and what we do see makes no sense.

American accounting used to be based on the application of generally accepted accounting principles, America's GAAP. Its intent was to provide to investors a fair representation of the financial status of a business. But over the years GAAP has become loaded down with detailed rules. A condensed version of U.S. GAAP rules now fills more than 1,000 pages and full rules may reach 5,000 pages. There are 800 pages on derivatives, and about 450 pages on leases. This complexity reflects a general trend in American society. For example, Congress has now provided us with the most complex tax code in the world, and the responsibility of individuals and companies is to adhere to the code explicitly, no matter how absurd the result in a particular circumstance. The same is now true of our accounting system, which has evolved from general principles, intended to guide ethical people in reporting openly and honestly the financial status of a company, into something very different—a system of complex rules that companies attempt to manipulate to their advantage, just as they attempt to manipulate the tax code to their advantage. (An example of difference between rules and principles: The U.S. has hundreds of pages of rules about SPEs, versus a principle that the company must not control the SPE if the items are not to be listed on its balance sheet.)

In effect, with both the tax code and our accounting system, we've now trained a generation of American businesspeople and financial professionals to focus on numerous detailed rules and ignore the larger picture. We've imposed a rule mentality versus a report to my shareholders mentality. We've made ourselves a nation of people who see only trees, not a forest. So frankly we're lost in the forest, wandering aimlessly among the trees.

What are the results of this? The major consequence is that our increasingly rule-based law is being carried to comical extremes as Congress and the courts micromanage our securities industry. Some examples are small but telling.

The CEO of a long-standing and very successful private equity firm has a business school degree and has served on the boards of dozens of companies, private and publicly traded, and is an expert in reading balance sheets and income statements and in understanding the accounting judgments that underlie financial reports. Under new federal securities legislation, it appears that he is no longer qualified to serve on the Audit Committee of a publicly traded firm. This is an absurdity.

A main instance is that in a system in which what matters is adhering to rules, not applying principles, auditors have changed their role. No longer do they ask, "How do I fairly represent the status of the business?" but instead, "How do I structure a transaction to accommodate a specific set of rules?"

The result is that investors cannot make sense of financial reports, and the securities industry breaks down.

The problem Congress seems to be trying to solve by detailed regulation may not be resolvable in that manner. The small investor may not be made secure by increased regulation of this sort. Already the accountants are trying to circumvent the new rules on SPEs. And "America's tort system has become one of the most costly and inefficient methods of dispute resolution in the world…"[271]

America has a large number of retail brokers whose role is to help investors choose particular stocks and bonds and other investment vehicles. But the overwhelming evidence is that individuals who try to pick stocks in which to invest lose money. To try to make investors safer we try to regulate the brokerage houses more and more aggressively. Currently, regulators are seeking to force brokerages to pay large sums to provide unbiased investment analysis to investors. So we have the regulators trying to get the brokerages to pay for analysts to help small investors lose money in the market, all the while thinking they're doing something very different—making the market safe for small investors.

It isn't safe, and small investors shouldn't be in it, except on a very limited basis—the same basis on which a person plays the lottery or gambles in a casino.

In pursuit of making the market safe for small investors we're lawyerizing the accounting and the securities industry. People know that this is happening, and there is a reaction against it. For example, the U.S. is moving toward the less rules-based approach of the International Accounting Standards Board, via an agreement between the IASB and the U.S. Financial Accounting Standards Board announced October 29, 2002.[272] The trouble is, positive though this may be, it's a countercurrent in a much stronger flow of increasingly detailed regulations and rules.

Recent Congressional legislation perpetuates the illusion that we can resolve these matters by passing more laws. This legislation and the additional rule-making that will follow at the SEC do not get us out of the maze into which we've wandered. All it really does is to add more paths, and we continue to wander among the maze, going up one blind alley after another.

The danger in thinking that resolving the current crisis in our financial markets by dealing with detailed issues, no matter how important the issue, has been well stated by William Sahlman of Harvard: "The furor over expensing [of options] is … a sideshow distracting us from deeper flaws in accounting standards, compensation philosophy, and professional standards in the financial service industry. If the advocates of expensing win their small point and the spotlight on corporate America fades away as a result, I fear that we will end up having done nothing at all to prevent unscrupulous executives from yet again stealing their investors' money."[273]

Yet we have great difficulty addressing the broader and more important concerns. For example, when we address issues of financial reporting, we're afraid of the issue of right or wrong except in the context of a specific rule. (Not surprisingly, we are in a similar situation with respect to moral issues generally, as we discussed in the chapter on ethics.)

Unfortunately, there is no solution in a retreat into rules; instead we are trapped by our timidity because not even Congress can write enough rules to cover every eventuality and circumstance. We're getting into a situation where we place too much reliance on law. Investors have lost large amounts, but much of the action in the courts is idle redress—attorneys going after convenient targets, not the real perpetrators.

The consequence is an explosion of litigation. In 1991 suits were filed on behalf of shareholders against 164 companies. By 1998 it was 236 companies. Did investors gain more protection as a result of this? It's hard to see that they did, since in the years immediately following 1998 occurred many of the scandals we listed in the second chapter of this book. But in 2001 suits were filed against 486 companies (Bob Keefe, "Number of Shareholder Suits During Past Decade," Cox News Service, January 31, 2002. The source of the data is the Stanford University Securities Class Action Clearinghouse).

It's tempting to conclude, as many do, that the reason there is more litigation is that there is more corporate chicanery, and there is some truth in this, as previous chapters in this book have shown.

But the increasing litigation doesn't seem to be eliminating the wrongdoing. In fact, security law violations by companies and litigation are locked in an increasing spiral of cause and effect. That is, violations of law cause suits, and suits cause violations of law.

This is because suits in America encourage an overly technical response from the companies that are their potential targets. To protect themselves companies seek to be in compliance with the law in a technical way, by adhering to specific rules. Firms that are in reality blameless cease to deal honestly with investors, and instead look to abide by detailed rules to avoid suits or convictions.

Shareholder suits brought on a class action basis have become an industry for trial lawyers. Many of the most handsome new mansions rising in America's playgrounds belong to this new breed of litigant. Because of the imperfections of America's legal system, it cannot be assumed that attorneys who win large settlements for themselves and their clients have actually righted a wrong; nor can it be assumed that investors on whose behalf no one brought a suit were in fact not actually victimized.

In the end, investors don't want litigation against their companies, and they don't want to be forced into litigation themselves. They want profitable and growing companies that report fully and honestly—not companies hobbled by complex regulations and the subject of suits, some of which are meritorious and some little more than extortion.

Talking Points

Congress can provide some restitution to investors for money taken from them. It's proper for it to do so, since Congress acted in many ways to make it easier for the money to be stolen. There are two primary ways for Congress to provide money directly to investors who have lost out: it can give to investors the money the government gets from civil and criminal defendants, and it can allocate funds for the purpose of providing restitution.

Congress is writing increasingly detailed legislation regulating the securities markets and is encouraging private regulatory bodies to provide increasingly complex requirements for accounting, securities registration, security analysis, and so on. Yet it is not obvious that this is going to benefit the small investor. What it is doing is creating an increasingly legalistic environment in which companies try to toe the letter of the law, not its spirit or intent, and in which there is more and more litigation. On balance, this is not an approach that is likely to increase the security of investors.

VIII *Protecting Yourself from New Dangers*

"Broke, busted, disgusted, you know they can't be trusted."

—Lyrics from a song in the 1960s
by The Mamas and the Papas

19 How Should I Invest?

MORE MODERN FINANCIAL DEFINITIONS:

MOMENTUM INVESTING—The fine art of buying high and selling low.

VALUE INVESTING—The art of buying low and selling lower.

BROKER—What mine made me.

STANDARD & POOR—Investor's life in a nutshell.

MARKET CORRECTION—The day after you buy stocks.

INSTITUTIONAL INVESTOR—Investor who's now locked up in an asylum.

A Tough Time for Investors

Recent years have been very difficult for American investors. There have been two major threats to their financial security: the conflict of interest between investors and the CEOs of the companies in which they have invested, and the conflict of interest between investors and the financial service firms of which they are clients. Ironically, in most circumstances both CEOs and financial service firms have fiduciary responsibilities toward investors. Financial service firms provide expert advice to investors, and CEOs are agents of investors whose primary role is to increase shareholder wealth. Unfortunately, in recent years these obligations haven't seemed to matter—both corporate executives and financial firms have enriched themselves at investors' expense.

In this environment, it hasn't been possible for investors to do well in the stock market. Investors who tried to pick stocks themselves failed because companies didn't report their financial situations honestly—instead there was fraud, misleading information, and nondisclosed information.

Investors who didn't trust themselves to pick stocks unaided and instead relied on professional analysts to provide guidance were intentionally misled by the analysts who, with the financial service firms who employed them, had nondisclosed conflicts of interest, which caused them to act against investors' interests. Investors who relied on their brokers for guidance in picking stocks were frequently misled because of nondisclosed conflicts of interest in the brokerage firms. Investors who let professionals (like mutual fund managers) make stock selections for them failed to succeed due to nondisclosed conflicts of interest in the management firms—often the mutual fund companies used volume trades from their mutual funds to gain leverage with investment banks for trades done on their own behalf, not that of their customers.

No part of the system has been working for investors the way it should have been. But the dangers this created for investors should have been largely mitigated by the supposed checks and balances in the American securities industry. In general, it's the role of the regulatory agencies to keep investment professionals honest, and the role of corporate boards of directors to keep CEOs honest. In neither case in recent years have these checks and balances worked effectively.

Despite some 70 years of rule-making by the SEC, which was intended to protect investors largely by providing information about companies, we still have considerable obscurity in financial statements. In Chapter 2 we saw that the financial accounts of companies like General Electric and IBM remain subject to misrepresentation and manipulation. So we haven't solved the riddle of disclosure. If an investor can't figure out the accounts of blue-chip firms like these, what chance does he or she have against a corrupt CEO and board in another firm? In consequence, everywhere a person looks, every way he or she turns to try to make sensible investments, the deck is stacked against the investor. There's no way to win. And the only way not to lose seems to be not to invest at all.

In these pages we've seen what went wrong with the American financial system, and we've seen what can be done to correct it. But until these things are done, until the government and the financial services industry admit that the scandals were not merely a matter of a few bad apples but were instead indicative of a massive failure of the system as a whole, and until the system is fixed by comprehensive reform and restitution to those investors who were swindled in the 1990s, then all but the largest and most sophisticated investors are well advised to avoid the nation's equity markets. The promise of gain is an illusion. Even if there appears to be wealth creation by companies, the investor can be sure the wealth will be taken by the professionals who move the markets. Investment seems a sucker's game—like gambling in a casino where the games are fixed. Only the people who run the casino are certain to win; the odds are all in their favor. The same is true of today's equity markets—only the professionals who manipulate the markets win. Casinos provide fine entertainment—they are a place to spend one's money—but they are not a place to make an investment. Similarly, today's equity markets are no place to make investments.

Investment advisors are having a great deal of difficulty accepting the logic of the tale they tell and investors are understandably suspicious. After explaining to their readers how today's system is distorted and exploited against investors, advisors tell working people "first and foremost" to enter their companies' self-managed pension plans [401(k)s].[274] This is remarkable advice. An investor wonders, "If the money is going to be stolen from me, what's the point of investing? Then I'll get my hopes up for a decent retirement, only to have them dashed. Isn't that what's happening to everyone else? Wouldn't I do better to save what I get for a pension in a bank account, even if the return is low? So what if I lose my company's matching contribution, if it's not coming to me anyway in the end?"

Advising people to seek a big return that causes them to lose capital is providing them no gain at all, while a small return that preserves capital is much. In today's security markets the pension investor cannot be confident that he or she will retain capital, so it makes no sense to jump in. It's understandable that a common opinion is that Congress authorized companies to set up these plans, encouraged working people to enter them, then permitted executives and financial service professionals to loot them.

Professionals in the financial markets know this, and in their own way, they acknowledge it. They tell the public that the equity markets will be slow to recover. Why? Because, they say, the current generation of investors must either have time to forget what has happened to them, or must be replaced by a new and naive generation before investors will again enter the markets strongly and provide a basis for broad share price advances. There has to be time before investors can be lured into the markets again by promises of gain—promises that today ring hollow.

How to Invest

Peter Lynch, years ago a successful mutual fund manager in a different kind of equity market, tells us that if an investor stays out of a whole category of investment vehicles—such as corporate stock—he's likely to have less opportunity to make gains. This is true, but if one vehicle, such as stocks, is so arranged that the investor's almost certain to lose his money, then he'd be a fool to invest much in it.

The basic rule is that investors must not put the short-term rate of return above long-term safety of capital. This was the basic mistake made by investors in recent years. Rates of return seemed high, but risk was grotesquely underestimated by misleading statements from corporations and financial service firms. Furthermore, risk itself was poorly understood, despite all the formal studies that have been done about the topic in investment houses and universities in recent years. These studies assess two categories of risk: market risk and firm-specific risk. But there was an entire and significant category that was largely ignored: the risk of fraud and deception driven by conflicts of interest—and these were the most important risks investors faced during recent years.

What should be the role of equities in an investment portfolio? Are stocks a good long-term investment? They are said to be. But when deliberate deception is factored in, it changes the formula; we are then investing in a different world. Unless there are big changes in the way the stock market works, equities should play a much smaller role in investor portfolios. Diversification is always appropriate, but it means buying different types of investments, not just buying different stocks.

It's unfortunate that investors have to be so wary today, even to the extent of staying out of the stock market, because when the markets are fair, corporate equities are especially attractive to people saving for retirement or college or other long-run objectives. While all markets carry risk, some are a natural home to speculation (like international currency markets and commodity markets) and some are better suited for investment. The difference is that in equity markets we anticipate a long-term upward trend (driven by economic growth), which lowers the downside risk and makes equities suitable vehicles for long-term investors trying to finance retirements, college tuition, and so on. That is, a long-term investor should be able to take a position in corporate equities with the expectation that over the long term the value of the securities will rise due to economic growth. There is no such presumption in other sorts of markets.

Stocks are more risky than bonds, however, because bond holders own a promise from a corporation or a government to pay, while shareholders do not. So there's thought to be a long-term premium of about 5% per year on equities compared to bonds, which is supposed to compensate the equity holder for the higher risk. But it may not be so high. Much of the premium historically is due to dividends, which are disappearing.[275] It is this supposed premium that investors are encouraged to obtain through investments in equities.

The equity risk premium over bonds is mathematically equivalent to two separate concepts: the excess return that people require in order to take on the higher risk of owning equities and (therefore) the expected excess return of equities over the long-term return of less-risky products. When one assumes that in the future equities will be fairly valued, a higher equity risk premium implies higher returns because fewer people are willing to take on the risk of owning equities. That drives down the current prices and drives up expected returns. Lower equity risk premiums provide the opposite case—people flood money into equities, driving up valuation and driving down expected returns. In short, a lower equity risk premium does not imply that people are "gambling" on equities, just that they perceive the risk of equities as lower and are therefore willing to purchase them for a smaller expected return. In short, this points out that the argument made at the top of the boom that "the equity risk premium is lower than ever, therefore the market is actually fairly valued at these levels" and "buy now—equities outperform bonds by X% over the long run" were contradictory.

But the premium for equities over bonds or other types of financial investments can't be obtained by investors in a stock market that is stacked against them, so stocks are losing their advantage over other types of investments. Hence, the best bet is to stay out of equity markets for the moment, except for a small investment that hedges the possibility that the markets will be better than reasonably expected and safer. None of us can perfectly predict the future, so we hedge, but we should do it on the proper scale, which is small. We should stay as much diversified among different types of investments as possible; we probably should not select individual stocks but rely on mutual funds and funds of funds, and stay in safer investments, accepting the likelihood of lower returns. But don't risk much of your nest egg.

The Fundamentals of the Market: The Economic Environment

As if the difficulty with the integrity of the markets were not enough to deter investors from equities, the economy in the next several years is likely to be rough. There will be only slow growth with periodic downturns. It's an environment in which it will be difficult for companies to develop a winning strategy. The overall equity market indices will be volatile but within a certain range and with little trend, so that investors cannot count on the averages improving their investments; instead they'll want to pick specific stocks despite the high risk. This is difficult enough, but the incentive will remain for CEOs to enrich themselves at the expense of shareholders, and for accountants, banks, brokerages, and mutual funds to assist them, so that investors are likely to again and again be enticed into what look to be attractive investments only to see their value collapse. It will, in short, be an economy without the excitement of the great bull market, but with all its dangers—an even less attractive environment for the investor than before.

Learn How the Game is Played

The first thing investors should learn is how the investment game is played. How enthusiasm is built by banks, brokerage houses, companies, and the business press; how earnings are exaggerated, how brokers press an investor to buy; how arguments are made for classes of stock, for whole industries, as a basis for buying; and how the rise in the price of a stock is argued to be the best reason to buy it. By understanding these devices of salespeople, an investor can recognize the signs of a bubble and either stay out or invest carefully and get out at the first sign of a bust.

Set Your Expectations Reasonably

In the aftermath of the scandals, investors must be happy with a smaller return—if you decide you want more, then speculate knowing what you're doing. Don't pursue someone who sells you a dream of riches, it's too likely to be false. If you run into a really great thing that works out, be pleased; but recognize that most people won't have this kind of luck.

What is a reasonable expectation? Many commentators say that investments are going to yield very little in the next decade or so. For example, William Wolman and Anne Colamosca advise investors to load up on high dividend stocks and bonds, expecting only 2%/year appreciation in equity averages over the next two decades.[276] But this seems a bit low. Even national economic growth is likely to exceed 2% per year on average and there will be much more rapidly growing companies. But there's no basis for expecting long-term returns in the double-digit range, as some leading CEOs insisted in the 1990s were achievable.

Deciding Whether the Market as a Whole Is Becoming Less Dangerous for Investors

We've seen that the stock market remains stacked against investors, but that could change if the reforms discussed previously occur. So investors much watch the news—if the government tightens regulations, if boards of directors begin to oversee more closely, if imperial CEOs lose some of their power over boards and executive compensation packages are tied to real performance, if accountants return to disclosure rather than concealment as their purpose, and if banks cease to support corporate subterfuges, then the markets may become safer for investors and it will become sensible to raise the allocation of investment that goes to equities.

Though it's hard to keep abreast of all this, especially changes in accounting rules and in what banks will and won't do for a company, there are more obvious indications of whether the wind is blowing for investors or against them. The wind is strong against them now, so we're really looking for change—changes that will benefit investors. If they occur, then investors should go more strongly into the market; if they don't, then it's prudent to stay out. Keeping abreast means more than assessing the direction of the market as a whole—whether it's a bull or a bear market, whether the economy's growing, or whether corporate profits as a whole are rising or falling. These things remain important, but more critical is the question whether an investor wants to be in the market at all, and that depends on whether the game is fair and an investor can win.

This is a new concern. It hasn't been a critical issue for American investors since the new regulations adopted in the 1930s made the market safe for investors until the 1990s. Because the market could largely be trusted to provide honest and sufficient information, and financial firms to treat investors fairly, this set of threshold issues was safely ignored. Reflecting the relatively secure investing environment, investment guides advised investors, rightly, to begin by assessing the economic fundamentals of the market, then pick particular stocks or funds in which to put their money (or invest in the market as a whole via an index fund). These are steps one and two in the traditional model. But the scandals of the present require that a new first be added. We must assess whether or not the system is fair enough for us to invest safely. It's rather like deciding whether to invest in the bonds of an underdeveloped country—the investment return that is promised may look good, but will the investor be able to get his or her money back?

If the system as a whole seems more fair, then an investor must ask with whom it is safe to deal—who are honest and reliable brokers, mutual funds, stock analysts, and so on. This is a step investors have always had to take, but one that is more significant now. In the past it was the odd exception to the rule who might cheat an investor. Now it's the odd exception to the rule who might deal fairly and openly with an investor.

This decision is similar to deciding from whom to buy a car. A buyer has to ask not only who has the best deals, but whom it's sensible to buy from. A few years ago when I was trying to buy a used car, I found a great deal advertised on the sort of car I wanted. I went to the person's home and looked at the car. It was very nice; the price was great. But I decided to check out the seller before buying. I discovered that he was an enforcer for organized crime who bought damaged vehicles and restored them on the side. I was told, "For gosh sakes, don't deal with him. What if you get in a dispute—he'll break your arms." I was glad I hadn't given the man my name, and I bought a car elsewhere. An investor isn't likely to get a broken arm by dealing with the wrong financial services firm, but he or she is likely to lose his or her investment.

There are places investors can put their money other than in equities, and as long as the stock market is stacked against the equity investor, he and she should stay out. So the first step in making investment decisions is to assess the market as a place to be—only then should we go on to asking whether this is the right time to be there and in what we want to invest.

We're assessing the market as a whole, or the system as a whole, to see whether or not it's getting safer and fairer for investors. In the next list we'll be assessing the risks of individual companies. The key point is that it's going to be very difficult to do well on individual companies (except perhaps as a short-term speculator) when the overall system is stacked against the investor. So we need to assess the system's favorability, then try to decide on individual investments.

This is a hard thing to do, because it's a market of stocks as well as a stock market—meaning that individual stocks go different ways, and so you should be able to get a good return by picking the winners. But look at what happened in the 1990s—almost everything went up; and beginning in 2000, almost everything went down. If this was a market made up of individual stocks, why did this pattern occur? The answer of course is that it's a stock market first and then a market for individual stocks. So we start by assessing the favorability of the market as a whole, and only thereafter is it a market of individual stocks.

Three Steps to Making an Investment

1. Decide whether the market will treat investors fairly—if not, stay out.
2. Decide whether the economy and the market trends are rising or falling—if falling, hold back.
3. Pick particular mutual funds or stocks—if you can't find a likely winner, hold back.

While there's risk at every step, it's the failure to pay sufficient attention to the first of the steps above that caused so many people to lose so much money in the aftermath of the bull market of the 1990s.

How should an investor decide whether the market will treat investors fairly? Here are the key indicators.

Key Things to Watch for

- Are top executives from the worst offending companies, Enron, and so on, going to jail? If it's only middle-level people who are being charged, then the incentives for fraud at the top haven't changed and the game is still being stacked against the investor.
- Are top executives from the worst offending companies returning large sums of money to the government and to investors? If they're not, then the incentives to cheat remain very high and the investor is likely to get taken again.
- Are investors like you beginning to get some of their losses back from the executives and companies who misled them? They should be getting money back; if not, it's the same game and the same incentives to cheat are in place, and investors are likely to get taken again.
- Are CEOs giving up being the chairs of the boards of directors of their companies? If not, then too much power is still centered on the CEO; the board can't really oversee the company objectively, and the potential for an investor to lose out to fraud and greed in the executive suite remains very high.
- Are stock option grants to executives from their companies being made seriously contingent upon real performance? If not, then the incentive

remains for top executives of companies to pop up the stock in the short term by any means, then sell their shares and go, leaving long-term investors holding the bag.

- Is CEO pay as reported in the business magazines coming down? It should. If it's not, the system hasn't changed and it's still stacked against you.
- Do the stock analysts you follow recommend selling as well as buying? They should, or they're not being balanced and objective.

How to Pick Individual Stocks

Generally people who try to pick individual stocks lose. There are enough instances, however, of people making big gains on individual stocks, or saying that they did, for most of us to be unable to resist the temptation, and when a broker calls with a hot tip, most of us buy at least once in a while. But even if companies clean up their accounting act, so that more and more reliable financial information is available, still more is needed than favorable income statements to make a company a good investment.

An investor should look for measures of leverage—less debt is better than more debt. He or she should look at cash flow, perhaps as a percentage of earnings. This is a way of determining whether the earnings are real or not; the higher cash flow is, as a percentage of earnings, the better. It's wise to look at the company's credit rating, and its Standard and Poor's common stock rating.

Then, of course, there is the question not of the company's present and past financial performance, but of its future prospects. This is where analyst's reports could be especially valuable, with information that it is hard for an investor to obtain himself or herself. Only if the current conflicts of interest that have caused analysts to mislead investors in the past are resolved, however, should analysts' reports be trusted.

Which Way Will the Market Go?

Above we noted that it's proper for someone who's decided to invest to any degree in the stock market to assess the likelihood of the market's direction. There are always conflicting currents that could carry the market either way. It's useful to look at the case for a bull market, and then for a bear market, and decide which seems most likely.

The long-term upward trend in the value of stocks is said by most commentators to reflect increasing corporate profits and dividends. But the data don't support this—both earnings and dividend growth have been modest over the long term. Instead, the long-term upward trend in the price of equities has reflected a growing multiple of earnings. People pay more in the price of a stock; that is, for the same amount of profit per share. Some people have referred to this as the triumph of the optimists.

Is the long-term increase in multiples justified? It may seem strange to say so in a time of crashing stock values, but the answer is probably "yes." Stocks are less risky because companies are larger and better managed. Interest rates have fallen dramatically so that the return on other kinds of investments has fallen and made equities more attractive (it can also be said that capitalization ratios have risen greatly for stocks); and the world is much safer geopolitically for investors in stocks than before. During the 20th century, America fought two world wars and then was engaged in the Cold War. We continually faced the threat of major disruptions to commerce and even defeat. The situation today is very different. America is militarily dominant; there is no immediate major threat to our country or its commerce. Terrorism itself is not comparable in the significance of its threat to World War II or the Cold War.

The danger to investors today are not coming from economic weakness (we're not facing a great depression), or from geopolitical dangers (we're not facing another world war), but from fraud and conflicts of interest within our own markets. In view of this, what are the prospects in the near future for equity markets? Here are the key considerations about the future of the stock market.

The Case for Another Bull Market

- Higher than usual price/earnings ratios for stocks are justified by low interest rates and low inflation, so that current valuations on the whole are justified.
- Underlying fundamentals are good for the U.S. economy.
- Chinese production keeps a lid on world inflation by supplying increasing volumes of goods at low prices.
- There are tremendous technological opportunities to be exploited.
- There's much investable money in the world that will sustain an upward trend once it starts.

The Case for a Bear Market

- The market has been significantly overvalued in the recent past.
- The hangover from the great bust is still painful (the failure of confidence in the market hasn't been restored).
- A double-dip recession is possible.
- The risk of a disruptive war is high.

What is ironic about the case for a bear market is that the weakness of the economy (the possible double-dip recession) is a direct result of the loss of confidence in the share market—the market wasn't forecasting a double dip except in the circular logic of a self-fulfilling prophecy. America came out of the first quarter of 2002 at a 5% real growth rate and with good fundamentals, but the fall in the stock market (largely due to loss of investor confidence in the integrity of financial markets) caused consumers to hold back and investment to remain moribund, resulting in an economic slowdown. More vigorous government action would have prevented this. The Fed and White House thought the economy would be expanding at 3.5–4% in the second quarter and so nothing much more was needed to stimulate the economy. They thought the stock market was an isolated problem, so they didn't act with boldness. They were wrong. The economy slowed to a 1% growth rate in the second quarter and was slowing again thereafter.

Special Considerations for Investing Pension Money

The worst tragedy of the stock market collapse was the loss of people's pensions and savings for retirement. So it's important to address directly how people should consider the stock market and their nest eggs.

The best advice is:

- If the stock market is not significantly reformed, stay out.
- If the stock market is reformed—there is real retribution and restitution—then
    - participate because tax advantages remain strong and the yields in the long term are likely to be better than other investment vehicles
    - know your own objectives and stick to them
    - try not to borrow—the money won't grow if it's not there
    - limit exposure to shares of any single stock, including those of the company for which you work
    - allocate carefully (across classes of stocks, bonds, cash)
    - reallocate from time to time as circumstances change
    - don't panic; If you've decided the market is reasonably safe for you, stay there

A common and sad spectacle is the person who sells on the worst news and buys on the best, which usually means selling into falling values and buying on the rebound. It's the opposite of buying low and selling high, and it's a sure way to lose money in the market.

Picking Individual Companies in Which to Invest

Tip-offs that a company is very risky to invest in:

- The company doesn't disclose assumptions that underlie its financial statements and consequences if they're wrong.
- The company is reporting rapid growth but management has no experience in the business.
- The management team is getting paid megabucks regardless of business performance.[277]

Beyond these new matters, which have been added to an investor's list of concerns by the recent scandals, there remains all the advice about investing that an investor can obtain from the literature about how to invest, including such matters as the financial health and prospects of the mutual fund or individual companies that are considered for investments. But what is crucial, and different, today is what has been stressed in this chapter—the importance of determining at the threshold whether the market is safe for investors, or whether any investment at all in the stock market puts the investor's capital at risk from fraud and deception.

Talking Points

There've been two major threats to the financial security of American investors: the conflict of interest between investors and the CEOs of the companies in which they have invested, and the conflict of interest between investors and the financial service firms of which they are clients. In consequence, everywhere a person looks the deck seems stacked against the investor. There's no way to win. For many of us the only way not to lose is not to invest at all. Still, if an investor can diversify and is careful, the stock market may be a place to put some of his or her money. Key rules are:

- Learn how the game is played
- Set your expectations reasonably
- Be cautious of the new, new investment

Today's new four steps to an investment are:

1. Decide whether the market will treat investors fairly—if not, stay out.
2. Pick a particular financial advisor or firm with whom to do business—if you can't find someone you're sure is honest and reliable, stay out.
3. Decide whether the economy and the market trends are rising or falling—if falling, hold back.
4. Pick particular mutual funds or stocks—if you can't find a likely winner, hold back.

20 Hedge Funds That Don't Hedge

While investors are still learning what happened to them in the 1990s and are trying to get their money back, they find themselves facing a new set of dangers—in some cases from the same people who victimized them before. And while it's been difficult for all investors, smaller investors have had a particularly tough time. During the 1990s small investors lost out to professional financial firms that manipulated the market; this time they're likely to lose out—if they're not careful—to other sophisticated investors as well.

The Next Big Thing—The Fund of Funds

Most investors got badly burned in the Internet and telecom bubbles. Those who have money left, or who have new savings coming in and are seeking investments have heard that hedge funds have done well. For example, they've heard that Julian Robertson's Tiger Fund has made money, so they are looking for that kind of smart investment management themselves.

Sensing this demand, which is what they do best, investment banks are now creating funds, which then are invested in other funds. This is the big new thing, the fund of funds. People who managed funds during the Internet and telecom bubble, and then saw those funds go under, now emerge as managers in hedge funds. But investors who lost their shirts in the Internet and telecom funds managed by these people no longer give them their money. So how can the money managers (once of Internet mutual funds, now of hedge funds) get it? The answer is to entice investors to entrust their money to one of the big investment banks or brokerages—Citibank, Chase, Merrill Lynch, or Bear Sterns—which then invests it for them in hedge funds. Funds of funds, the word is on Wall Street, are the next bubble—the next place for financial market professionals to make a killing.

In many instances the banks are accepting investments from qualified individuals—people with a net worth of more than a certain amount. But the net worth measure is somewhat elastic, and smaller investors are creeping into these funds. Are these investments suitable for pensions, college savings, IRAs, and 401(k)s? We have yet to see the answers to these questions. The likelihood is that if the investments are laundered, so to speak, through a big bank that pretends to impose some prudence in management on the hedge funds in which investors' money ends up, then until another collapse, funds of funds will be considered suitable investments.

The bank is an intermediary between the investor and the hedge fund. The bank pretends to place a cordon of safety, of conservative investing, around its investors' funds, but in reality it simply transfers them to a hedge fund for management. For a percentage of the assets managed, or a percentage of the investors' gain, the bank places investors' money in other funds for management. The fee the investor pays the bank is for expertise the investor lacks in choosing hedge funds in which to invest, and which the bank claims to have but really doesn't—any more than the mutual funds had expertise in picking dot-com stocks. The banks argue that they have expertise allowing them to pick the better hedge funds in which to invest. And they provide statistical models that supposedly allocate investors' risks properly. But little reliance should be placed in these. Banks might be able to steer investors away from the most fly-by-night of the hedge funds, but beyond that threshold protection, the expertise necessary to impose prudence on the investments being made by a hedge fund is not available to the banks.

All this the investor has seen before. Statistical models of risk and reward, supposedly prudent investment management coupled in bizarre and undisclosed fashion with the most extremely risky investments, were characteristic of the Internet bubble. And here, less than 3 years later, is the whole concoction emerging again in a slightly different disguise. Again, salespeople for the banks and brokerages are telling investors that they have a safe haven for investments at high returns and are placing investors' money in extremely speculative investment vehicles.

So we are turning full circle. During the Internet and telecom bubble, investors placed money in mutual funds, believing it was being managed carefully, only to discover that it was placed in dot-com and telecom stocks. When the bubble burst, the money was mostly lost. Disenchanted with many mutual funds, for good reason, investors are turning to the banks, which are directing investors' money into places as speculative as dot-com and telecom stocks. But this time the destruction of investors' value isn't likely to take the form of a large run-up in share prices followed by a collapse; that is, of a bubble in share prices that gets punctured in a spectacular bust. Instead, market averages will not move very much, while value is consumed in the hedge funds as they speculate up and down, long and short, on the movement of prices in the markets.

During the bubble, it was easy to see where an investor's money went—it was invested in stocks or in a mutual fund, and as stock prices rose so did his or her account, and when they fell, so did his or her account. With hedge funds money is going to be made, and lost, in arcane positions trading with or against the market, sometimes in so complex a fashion that not even the fund managers will know exactly what caused an investment to be a success or a failure. From the point of view of most investors, including the banks that claim expertise when they intermediate investors' money, invested funds go into a black box at a hedge fund in which it's not possible to see why the fund grows or declines. The investor is further away from the actual management of his or her fund than during the Internet bubble. The outcome is not likely to be much better.

Despite the temptation to think so, an investor can't protect him- or herself in this market just by finding a way to join a hedge fund. There are now thousands of them, and most perform very badly. In a period of starvation, some wolves get eaten by the others. This is happening among the hedge funds.

Hedge Funds

The increasing number of small investors who have entered the market now face the hedge funds, the big, new sophisticated players in the investment world into which not only wealthy individuals but large pension funds and endowments have poured money. Big investors like hedge funds are secretive, and small investors aren't sufficiently protected. It's a setup for a small investor to get killed.

Hedge funds don't really hedge; mainly they sell short as well as buy long; and they are very aggressive in the marketplace, taking strong positions and moving money very quickly. A news report is issued at noon, moments later hedge funds are buying or selling. They've added a new dynamic to the market that is reflected in the enormously increased volume of stock transactions and in the very greatly shortened period of time for which shares (on average) are held by investors. The market is made much more volatile; there are spikes of trading on any news.

It is important for investors to realize that the stock markets in the first years of the 21st century are not just down, but down in a particular way, as a result of the new forces at work in the market, the most important of which is the hedge fund. A hedge fund investor must have at least $1.5 million in net worth to invest. The funds are regulated little and do not report their activities, trades, and balances. The smaller investor cannot play this game successfully. He or she can only go long in the market, hoping for sustained rallies, while through the hedge fund a richer investor is free to go either long or short. The ordinary investor can make money in only one way—an up market—while the larger investor can make it coming or going, up or down.

Hedge funds are a much bigger part of the market than they used to be. They follow a herd mentality, as do most fund managers of any sort. When they all go long, the market rises—when they all go short, it falls. They tend to go one way, then the next—and the market experiences violent shifts from day to day, but in a narrow range without much of a trend. Hedge funds have increased in number in the past decade from about 2,000 to 6,000, and assets managed have risen from about $69 billion to about $600 billion.[278] Funds differ in investment strategy—some go long, some short, some both; some use leverage, some don't. Europe has about 450 hedge funds managing the equivalent of some $65 billion and their number and the amount invested are growing quickly (more than a fourfold increase in the past 3 years).[279] More funds mean more competition, and some funds are now closing.

Investment banks run sessions for investors (high net worth individuals and pension funds) to introduce them to hedge funds. Here's a description of one such session. "Suddenly the lights went out and two Morgan Stanley hedge fund marketers appeared on giant television screens. The comely pair—both men—sported blunt-cut blonde wigs and cheerleader outfits with pleated skirts.…This pep squad launched into an arm-waving cheer, 'Chilton, Chilton, he's our man; if he can't short it, nobody can!'" This is an account of the Morgan Stanley hedge fund conference held at the Breakers Hotel in Palm Beach in January 2002. The pep squad's reference was to Richard Chilton of Chilton Investment Company, a Connecticut-based hedge fund.[280]

Banks rarely take a fee for this sort of entertainment. They make their money on trades and other services that are now a big source of revenue to the banks.

Hedge funds began in 1949, and were fashionable in the late 1980s, then were tarnished by the failure of Long Term Capital Management, then in the late 1990s became major drivers of the market, having grown enormously. They are often close partners to the investment banks, because the funds are small money-management units with no credit ratings and little infrastructure, so they need to rent the clearing and settling capabilities, the stock loan inventories and balance sheets of the banks.

The hedge funds claim to be able to provide substantial returns regardless of the direction of the market. Like mutual funds and traditional money managers, most hedge funds probably can't beat a market index, but a few do very well. Hedge funds are now becoming respectable investments for pension funds, as did venture capital firms about 15 years ago. Major colleges and universities have 20 to 30% of their endowments in hedge funds, and so have become major contributors to the way in which the market is changing against the interest of most investors.[281] In 2001 the California Public Employees Retirement System,

America's largest pension fund, put $1 billion into hedge funds. It was a major stamp of approval. Yet this is an industry about which *Institutional Investor* writes, "Secretive and far from pristine, the industry [hedge funds] has long been notorious for providing scant information (if any at all) and for suspect fund-raising practices."[282]

Research indicates that long-term investors should reduce their portfolio allocation to equities when volatility increases, as it has recently. But it also shows that there isn't sufficient volatility to justify a big increase in demand for stocks for hedging purposes.[283] In today's market, long-term investors should be pulling out of equities and have little need for buying stocks to hedge volatility.

There is thus no justification for the enormous growth of the hedge funds. It follows that the hedge fund mania is simply the latest of the securities industry's new, new things" for investors—another sales gimmick.

Regulating Hedge Funds

Hedge funds, like venture funds, do not reveal performance. But they should be required to do so. They should be required to report activities and positions to regulatory authorities frequently so that the regulators know what is going on. When the Long Term Credit Management crisis broke, it caught the Fed flat-footed because the Fed hadn't known of the developing problem. Yet years later the quality of the information available to the government to avoid even larger crises has not improved at all, although the number of hedge funds and their significance in the markets have increased dramatically.

We need a study as to the impact of the funds to see what, if any, new regulations are required. On July 26, 2002, the SEC wrote to major hedge funds asking them to fill out a questionnaire about such things as background of fund managers and valuation processes. The SEC seems concerned about conflicts of interest (such as mutual funds owning hedge funds) and possible fraud and the increasing availability of hedge funds to retail investors. The SEC may be getting ready to regulate hedge funds.[284]

The Impact of Hedge Funds on the Market

Hedge funds sell short. Short selling is always speculation, not investment. The growth of hedge funds thereby injects a much larger speculative element into the market. This makes the market much more dangerous for investors who are trying to finance pensions and retirements, college tuition, and so on, by appreciation on their stock market investments.

Some speculation via short-selling is necessary and appropriate; it adds liquidity to the market and limits excessive optimism. But too much speculation turns the markets from an investment vehicle into a casino. Hedge funds most likely affect the performance of the market by making it more volatile and limiting its upside potential (via much larger amounts of short-selling). Most commentators about the market ignore this. When the market suffers big losses on a single day, they find some small piece of bad economic news and attribute it to that. When the market gains a lot on a day, they look at the overall upward direction of the economy and attribute it to that. When the market stalls and seems to move aimlessly, they say the American economy is stagnating like that of Japan. The point is that even though the market is behaving in unfamiliar ways, it is explained as if it were behaving in traditional ways. Nowhere is the change in the players in the market recognized. The change in the means by which large players seek to profit and the greater role of the hedge funds and of speculation via short-selling is ignored.

Hedge funds had their origin in speculating in international currency markets. Currencies have trends, crises, and turnabouts, all of which makes them ideal for speculation. But rarely does one invest directly in currency markets expecting long-term appreciation. Currency markets are speculative markets, not investment markets. The same is true of commodity markets. Hedge funds are now very active in equity markets and are making equity markets much more like currency markets; that is, speculative markets rather than investment markets.

Talking Points

Hedge funds are the emerging giants in securities markets. Most sell short as well as buy long. Until recently they were the arena of wealthy individuals, but now college endowments, corporate pension funds, and moderately wealthy people have much money invested in them.

The best hedge funds are very sophisticated investors, and they make it even more dangerous today for an individual investor trying to pick stocks. But there are many more hedge funds than there used to be, and many don't seem to have a good investment record. There is little known about the funds because by and large they do not yet report to regulators.

The big new thing in investments for many people is the fund of funds, by which an investor pays a bank to find hedge funds in which to place the investor's money. The fees for investing in this way are high, and the banks that take a fee for placing investors' money rarely have any expertise in the selection of hedge funds, so the investor is again taking a large chance with his or her capital, whatever the promised return.

21 Do Investors Dare Return to the Market?

"There is no equity in the equities markets."

—Michael G. Oxley, Republican, Ohio, House Committee on Financial Services, October 2, 2002

A Bear Market, Yes, But Not *Only* a Bear Market

What will restore investors' confidence in our financial system? Some observers believe that we have merely entered a bear market, akin to many we've had in the past, and that as share prices fall and the economy strengthens, stocks will begin to look cheap, people will reenter the market to buy, and the bear will again give way, in the time-tested manner, to the bull.

But things are different today. The equity market collapse this time did not originate in a business downturn, but in the sudden recognition by investors that things were not what they seemed. The financial losses are on an enormous scale, and because of increasing share ownership and the placement of pension funds in stocks, they reach further into our society than ever in the past. Revelations of fraud are on such a scale as to undermine confidence in the system as a whole.

What we have experienced is unlike anything since the Great Crash of 1929, and what we are now doing is trying to avoid another Great Depression. Restoring confidence in equity markets after 1929 took many years and a complete reform of the system. We again require a complete reform of the system, but if we go about it quickly and effectively, we may be able to avoid a collapse of the economy like the depression of the 1930s.

The decline of American participation in the market has begun. People held on for a long while, believing that the market would turn around, that their losses would be temporary. But as the share price declines continued, and the market began to exhibit the new behavior associated with the hedge funds (e.g., huge volume of trades, rapid and strong reaction to any news, large price swings within a wide band of value with no apparent trend), people began to give up and get out.

In 2002 the number of Americans owning stocks *outside* retirement plans declined from its peak in 1999. But because people are still being drawn into retirement plans that invest in the market, the number of American households with a stake in the market had actually risen from 49.2 million to 52.7 million between the 2 years.[285] Thus, left to themselves without the lure of tax-sheltered retirement savings, people are getting out of the market. It won't be long before they seek from the government and their employers other places to put their pension money than in the stock market.

The core of the current problem is that many of our business institutions have been gravely compromised by these scandals. There is a compelling need to clean the system, but also a danger that if already weakened confidence is further undermined by additional revelations and strong action, the economic system as a whole can be tipped into a serious downturn. But the danger of such a result should not be a reason for inaction. We should not try to cover up the problems in order to try to avoid further economic downturn—we need to find a way to bring about disclosure of past misdeeds and reform without tanking the economy.

While it is not true that the problems of the American financial system are merely the consequence of a few bad apples among our corporate leaders, it is best to act as if that were the case. But many more than a few apples need to go in order for us to restart the system in an ethical manner—because there were far more than a few bad apples. The proper route is to approach the problem calmly while making major changes in the leadership of major firms and financial institutions.

There will be a tendency to accept the current leadership's words of contrition and promises to abide by more ethical standards. These statements cannot be regarded as honest and should not be accepted. The ethical stripes of a CEO are no more easily changed than the colored stripes of a tiger.

A careful reform can best be achieved by cleaning the leadership, by getting rid of the top people on whose watch these things have occurred. The scandals are in large part a matter of the lack of ethics, and disregard of ethics on the scale we've just experienced starts at the top of large companies. The scandals are also a matter of abuse of the system, of converting it entirely to private interest—and that also must have been tolerated at the top to have occurred on so large a scale. The proper response is therefore to make major firms' leadership go. In the case of the banks this can be easily achieved by the Fed, acting directly or in concert with revitalized boards of directors. It is more difficult in the case of industrial firms, where changes in top leadership must come from boards, many of which are currently subservient to the very CEOs they should replace.

If Americans in droves are to return to our equity markets, we must do at least one of the following well:

- Have a rebirth of ethical behavior in the world of finance.
- Have much more rigorous enforcement of legal standards by the government and the courts, including punishment and effective restitution so that current incentives to steal are greatly reduced.
- Have a much more rigorous system of checks and balances in the corporation.

Any of these three will do, but each has a limitation:

- We are a complex and cynical society that hasn't been willing to take ethics seriously.
- Our government is much influenced by the wealthy and powerful among us and is easily corrupted or enfeebled, so that enforcement of our laws is not strict enough and the incentives to steal remain enormous.
- We have an ideology of the dominant or imperial CEO that makes it almost impossible for in-company checks and balances to work effectively.

Diagrammatic Summaries of CEO and Investor Conflict in the Securities Markets

Much of what has been described in this book can be displayed in two diagrams, each representing wealth creation in American securities markets. The first diagram (Figure 21.1) shows the securities markets as they are intended to function, and the other (Figure 21.2) as they actually function under the influence of the imperial CEO. The diagrams are somewhat simplified in order to make them intelligible to readers, the major simplification being the omission of many of the federal regulatory agencies with their specific roles and the influences on them. Instead, the SEC, the most important of the agencies from the point of view of most investors, is given prominence in the diagrams.

Figure 21.1 shows wealth creation in the securities markets as the law intends them to operate, protecting investors via transparency, disclosure, and active regulation. Investors purchase shares in companies (directly or via interme-

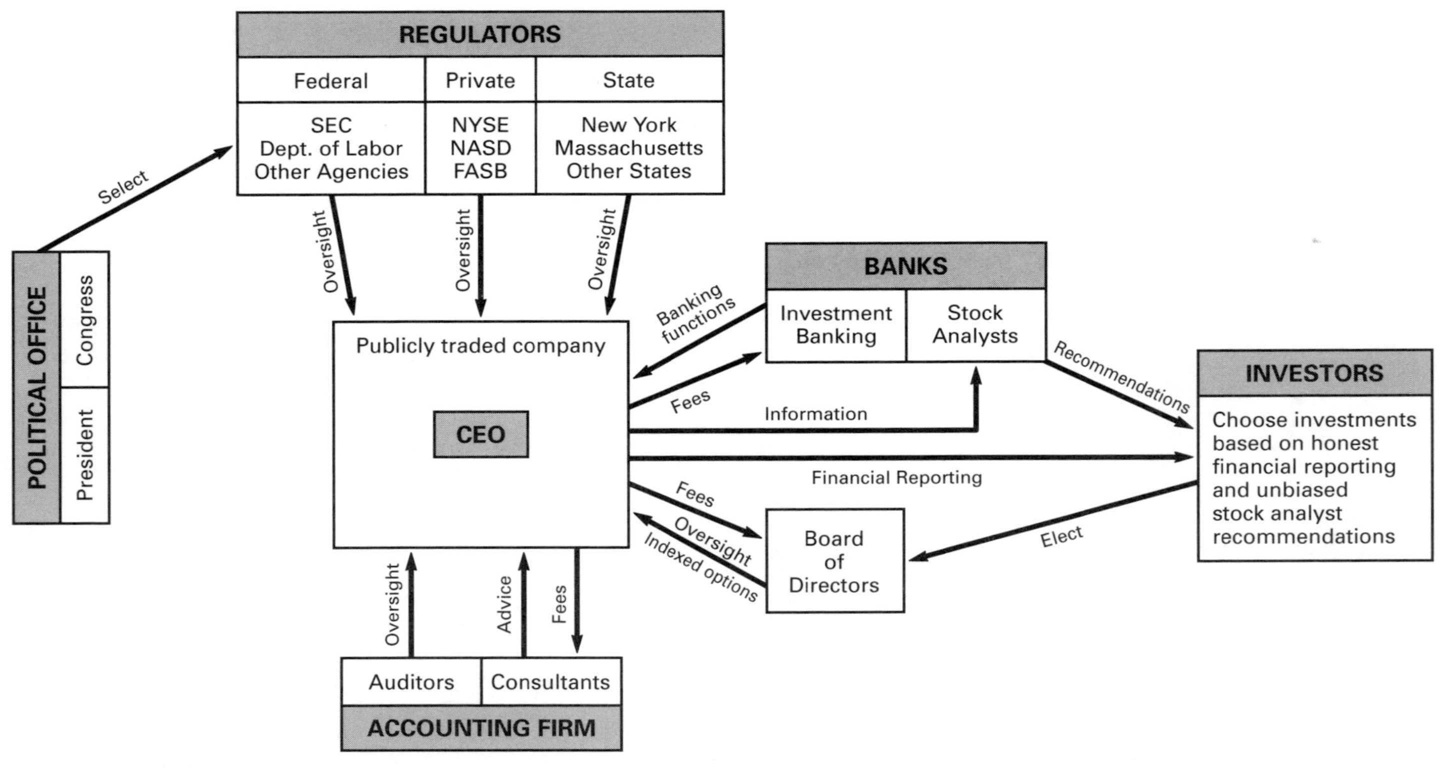

Figure 21.1 Investor wealth creation and securities market.

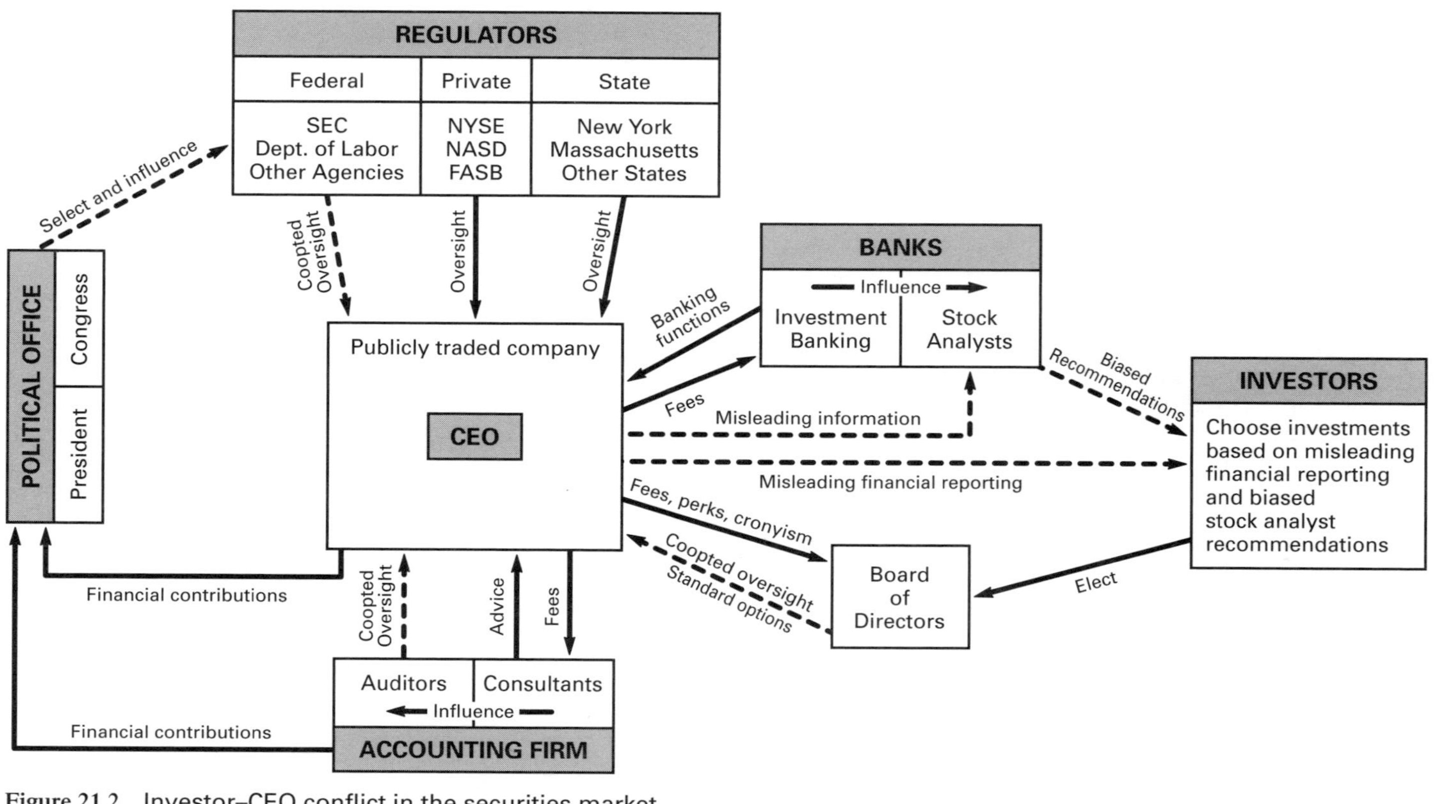

Figure 21.2 Investor–CEO conflict in the securities market.

diaries like mutual funds) and the CEOs of those companies act as the agents of their shareholders to build financial wealth for shareholders. A major function, many people would say the primary function, of a CEO as shareholder agent is to so manage a firm that wealth is created for the investor. Employees of the firm assist the CEO in this purpose. The CEO obtains assistance from banks and consultants to improve the performance of the firm. The board of directors of the firm is elected by shareholders to see that the CEO and other employees of the firm act in the shareholder's interest. The board fashions executive compensation packages that provide incentives for outstanding financial performance, measured against peer companies (indexed options). Auditors are engaged by the board to monitor the actions of executives of the firm. A company may also purchase consulting services from an accounting firm, but within the accounting firm consulting does not affect the actions of auditors. Federal regulators closely oversee the financial reports of a firm and act to correct securities violations. Private regulators (the stock exchanges and the accounting standards boards) require that corporations be run with appropriate protections for investors. State regulators watch for violations the national authorities might miss, but generally defer to federal authorities. Congress legislates as necessary to protect investors and funds the federal regulatory agencies, all with the purpose of facilitating the effective operation of our securities markets via protecting the investor. Firms may buy investment banking services (including underwriting of shares and bonds, and assistance in doing mergers and acquisitions) from banks, and may also be the subject of reports to investors by financial analysts who are employed by banks. But so-called "Chinese walls" between investment banking and financial analysis prevents investment bankers from influencing analysts' recommendations. Banks and brokerage houses issue reports to investors via financial analysts whom they employ advising investors to buy, hold, or sell the shares of companies. It is a handsome conception, and when it works, gives investors confidence that they are protected from fraud and conflicts of interest when they invest.

Figure 21.2 depicts the securities market system as it has actually operated in recent years, as described in the preceding chapters of this book. It reflects the conflict in interest between investors and CEOs, who in this depiction manipulate checks and balances in their own favor and against investors. In this picture most of the key participants, private firms, and governmental bodies, have pursued conflicts of interest in their own behalf and against the interest of investors. In this circumstance CEOs and bankers have gotten rich, accountants have waxed prosperous, and politicians have been elected and reelected in large part due to generous campaign contributions, but many investors have not done well at all.

In this very different picture the imperial CEO of the large, publicly traded company has come to exert a dominant influence. The objective of the system has ceased to be the creation of shareholder wealth, and has become the enrichment of corporate executives, accountants, bankers, and the reelection of politicians. These objectives are accomplished via the co-option of most, though not all, overseers and regulators. At the center of this perversion of the securities markets is the CEO because he or she has both the personal incentive and the means at hand to co-opt the other participants in the system. In Figure 21.2 co-option is depicted by dotted lines showing oversight of the CEO.

For example, as Figure 21.2 illustrates, the CEO co-opts the board by choosing who is on it, by providing board members with attractive compensation and perks, and by drawing into the status of the CEOs cronies key members of the board. The board in return fashions a pay package for the CEO (focused on the standard stock option) that makes it virtually certain that he or she will become rich, regardless of what happens to the wealth of investors. The CEO emasculates both federal and private regulatory agencies via campaign contributions to politicians as they seek to gain or retain office and by board memberships, consulting and speaking fees, and other perks when they are out of office. The CEO is assisted in this by contributions to public officials from accounting firms and banks. Successful politicians, favored by contributions from companies and their executives, then reduce the effectiveness of the regulators in various ways via their oversight and funding authority. State regulators, largely unaffected by Congress and the White House, particularly those of New York State who have Wall Street itself in their jurisdiction and who possess the strongest state statute for pursuing securities violations (the Martin Act), recently have stepped into the breach left by the weakness of federal regulators on behalf of investors. Auditors are co-opted via consulting contracts to the accounting firms of which the auditors are partners or employees. Consultants in the accounting firms now influence auditors in how they conduct audits of the firms so that key interpretations are made in favor of the CEO. CEOs award lucrative investment banking contracts to banks in return, in part for investment bankers influencing analysts to make favorable recommendations to investors on behalf of the CEO's companies. The Chinese wall between investment banking and financial analysis is pierced. In consequence, the advice offered investors via financial analysts at banks and brokerages is falsified in the interest of corporate executives via CEOs purchasing investment banking services from the banks and requiring in return that the banks influence analysts' reports favorably.

This second system is one in which almost everyone benefits except the investor, who is systematically misled about the real financial status of companies. Still, an investor may benefit also, if he or she is able to invest with sufficient suspicion and cynicism and for the short term, like professional speculators. But the long-term investor, managing pension or college savings, whether as an individual or through a fund, is almost certain to be a loser in this system, for it is designed to exploit such an investor.

A brief review of the economics of the late 1990s makes it clear how effectively the system shown in Figure 21.2 worked. The system created a bubble in the shares of large, old economy companies. For example, corporate profits adjusted for inflation peaked in 1997, but the stock market peaked in 2000. The continued, rapid run-up of share prices after profits had peaked represented something quite different than the ordinary operation of equities markets—it was a classic asset price bubble in which asset prices grew increasingly disconnected from underlying asset values. A measure of the bubble was that the market capitalization of industrial (nonfarm, nonfinancial) corporations as a percent of gross national product averaged from 1947 through 1995 about 60%, then jumped to 147% in 1999–2000. By 2002, during the stock price bust, the ratio had declined to about 80%.

There's more. In 1999 the share prices of firms were at an all-time high, yet merger and acquisition activity was also at an all-time peak (this can be measured technically by Tobin's Q ratio, that we needn't explain further here). CEOs were buying other firms when they were most expensive, wasting shareholder dollars and pouring transaction fees into investment banks, which were in turn issuing falsely favorable recommendations about the shares of the buying companies. With share prices high, CEOs were getting rich via the exercise of standard options in their compensation packages. By 1999 the ratio of CEO pay to manufacturing worker pay in the European Union was about 20 (that is, the CEO made about 20 times what an average production worker made); in Latin America it was about 45. In the United States it was 475—off the chart, so to speak. Finally, the Fed accelerated real monetary growth (adjusted for inflation) in late 1999, permitting credit to feed the bubble. The CEOs and the banks had a tidy little system—inflating share prices via misleading financial reporting and dishonest analysts' recommendations, then using inflated stock and cash to acquire other companies with inflated share prices, generating large investment banking fees and high paydays for CEOs either via their companies being bought out or cashing in standard options. The system benefited CEOs and banks very well.[286]

The Temptation Remains

This book's story of executive greed and investor loss is about an opportunity to get rich by doing wrong, the temptation it has exerted on powerful people, and how many business leaders succumbed to the temptation and in so doing despoiled investors. It's a story about how some powerful business executives found willing accomplices and then stopped at nothing to seize the prize. It's a story played out in company after company, but it's not primarily a story about individual firms and their top executives. Instead, it's a story echoed in so many companies that it's about the entire system. This is perhaps the biggest surprise of all. What distinguishes the story from all previous situations is that it was so widespread.

The indecisiveness of the government about whether to prosecute the boards at Enron and Tyco and other firms involved in the scandals, or the top executives at the banks and accounting firms, or even worse its decision not to prosecute anyone at all in some cases, reveals more dramatically than anything else the sorry state of our laws and enforcement. The government might choose not to prosecute because it lacks the resources to pursue all the perpetrators and must choose to let some go free; or current standards of evidence may be so peculiar that the guilty cannot be convicted; or what is apparently illegal may not be so, which would be the worst explanation of all. Whatever the explanation, the result is terrible for investors, that those who cheated shareholders for their own benefit go free, and others, seeing that misrepresentation was a route to great riches for many, have the incentive to use their energy and imagination to defraud investors in the same or novel ways.

The core of today's dangers for investors in America's large, publicly held companies is that the top executives of the firms have enormous temptation to defraud investors, making the fraud look as legitimate as possible, and that they are able to find valuable allies in doing this—including accountants, banks, attorneys, and boards of directors. To eliminate this danger, the temptation to CEOs must be drastically reduced. Their reward (stock options) must be reduced and the penalty increased. But while these things are easy to imagine and discuss, they are hard to implement. Reducing the rewards to CEOs for nonperformance requires truly independent and assertive boards, but these are hard to imagine in the age of the imperial CEO. Will the power of CEOs be restrained? In addition, increasing the penalty CEOs pay for fraud requires much more vigorous securities law enforcement. Will Congress support and pay for that? If the imperial CEO is not restrained, and there is not far more vigorous law enforcement, then today's powerful incentive to steal will remain.

So long as the incentive remains, powerful people will be attracted to it, and so long as they can find willing accomplices, then the scandals will continue. In this book we've examined what needs to be done to remove the incentive, and to dissuade accomplices—and though these things could be done, they are not yet done and may not be. Without them, investors cannot be confident that they will get a fair shake in the investment market and they are better off outside it, except for very limited exposure.

This is the unfortunate conclusion of our inquiry—it doesn't matter how much research into companies an investor does, nor how carefully he or she tries to choose investment vehicles, because the system as a whole is set up to cause an investor to lose.

This doesn't have to be the case—real and comprehensive reform is possible. What is lacking is the political will. But to be lacking political will is to be lacking a very great deal. So the unfortunate conclusion for investors is that the need for reform, retribution, and restitution to protect investors is clear, but these things have not yet been done.

It's Still Going On

How have companies reacted to the public concern attending the accounting scandals? Some superficial change has been widely touted as significant reform. In reality, all the methods of deceiving shareholders, and all the conflicts of interest played against them, are still in general use.

Let's begin with what little has changed. Auditors, for example, are much more vigilant when they review firms that look like an Enron, WorldCom, or Global Crossing; that is, that are growing rapidly; have complicated, esoteric business models; report high profit margins; have large noncash revenues; and use off-balance sheet financing. Many of the firms that fit these characteristics are small, even startups, but the auditors watch them very carefully. For other firms, especially those with established relationships with accounting firms, there's little evidence that anything has changed. Firms continue their long-standing auditing relationships and pay their accountants more for consulting than for auditing.

Similarly, boards of directors are widely reported to be watching CEO compensation more carefully and generally being more diligent. But there's little evidence that anything of significant importance has changed. For example, boards of directors at the investment banks, challenged about the behavior of the firms and about the credibility of CEOs who have presided over the scandals and fines levied by regulatory agencies, routinely give the CEOs strong endorsements and fail to mention the scandals.

The imperial CEO continues to rule the corporation, going to conferences of his and her peers and listening to panels on leadership address questions like "What went wrong?" But the conferences are in fine hotels and lovely resorts, the participants are carefully screened, and within the company the CEOs remain surrounded by sycophants, so that they wring their hands together, reassure each other that it's only a matter of a few bad apples among their group, and continue the practices that created the scandals.

In Chapter 3 we identified a whole series of accounting dodges used by executives and their accountants and banks to artificially inflate earnings and thereby make equity investments look more attractive to investors than is merited. One of the most egregious of these devices is the statement of pro-forma earnings. Yet in a poll of chief financial officers of corporations taken in mid-2002, in the midst of the media coverage of corporate accounting scandals, more than three-quarters of CFOs insist that companies should continue to issue pro-formas. In fact, almost three-quarters deny that the United States should dramatically rethink its regulation of corporate disclosure and markets; and they assert by a two-thirds majority that for the SEC to more carefully scrutinize corporate financial statements would result in a bureaucratic nightmare rather than a fairer market.[287]

Little sympathy is being expressed by CFOs for the investors who have seen their portfolio values collapse, though these corporate executives are supposedly the agents of investors whose primary motivation is supposedly to increase shareholders' wealth. Nor do CFOs indicate any intention to reform financial reporting practices to protect the investor. They are still the agents not of shareholders, but of their CEO bosses, and the CEOs are still deeply involved in conflict of interest—seeking to make themselves rich whatever happens to investors.

Meeting late in 2002 while the accounting scandals remained very much in the public eye, top executives of major companies warned that they might be impeded in their efforts on behalf of shareholders by government attempts to protect investors. Said the chief executive of a major bank that had a significant role in many of the scandals, "I just hope we don't go too far with these things [reforms] so that we damage what's made Wall Street great and what's made this country great."[288]

Even after some of the biggest accounting firms have spun off their consulting businesses, they are still consulting. In mid-2002, for example, accounting firms are estimated to have been receiving about half their revenues from consulting services of various sorts.[289] Accounting firms continue to provide both auditing and consulting services to corporations and to be paid much more for consulting than for auditing. In effect, firms continue to pay auditors for friendly auditing via consulting fees. According to the Investor Responsibility Research Center's comprehensive annual study of 1,240 American corporations, the proportion of fees paid by companies for nonauditing consulting services came in at exactly last year's level: 72 percent of the total paid. Average consulting fees were almost three times the average auditing fees. "And while nine companies used different firms to audit their results and provide consulting services last year, only six have chosen to do so in 2002."[290]

Also, Wall Street firms continue to paint a rosy picture of investments rather than a realistic one. Analysts' reports continue to show a bias toward buy recommendations, even in a bear market. A recent study of research analysts conducted by Weiss Ratings shows that three out of four brokerage firms covering companies that filed for bankruptcy from May 1 to August 31, 2002, kept "buy" or "hold" recommendations on those companies' shares as they made their filings. Of the 62 brokerage firms studied, 34 failed to issue a single "sell" rating on any company that filed for bankruptcy in the period.[291] The diabolical linkage between analyst and banking in the investment banks continues, despite all the public representations to the contrary.

The consultants who design executive pay plans have been warning that even with current reforms, executives, with the help of compliant boards, can easily enrich themselves at shareholders' expense.[292]

Finally, the swinging door still swings. U.S. senators who have presided over Congress's gutting of the regulatory agencies retire from Congress into high positions at investment banks—to industries they've never worked in before, but whose interests they've supported while on Capitol Hill. The revolving door from business to government to business swings as well as ever, and to the disadvantage of investors.[293]

In most companies, banks, and accounting firms the same leadership who presided over the destruction of investor value remains in place, though less self-assured and arrogant now than before. They've gone underground, so to speak, waiting for an opportunity to start the old game as vigorously as before.

Despite more than two years of a falling market and more than a year of corporate financial scandals, and despite a new federal reform law, the underlying causes of the financial scandals have been addressed only a little if at all. Firms continue to buy both auditing and consulting services from accounting firms; investment banks continue to use analysts' reports to get and hold investment banking business; analysts continue to recommend nothing but buy even when companies are going bankrupt; boards of directors continue to provide large option grants and golden parachutes to executives, so that they get rich no matter how shareholders do; CEOs continue to dominate boards; companies and accounting firms continue to work together to conceal key information from investors; and, government regulatory authorities continue to let executives and bankers get rich from misleading investors. There are new regulations and settlements of suits that go in the right direction, but they affect the margin of the activities listed in the lines above. Not much has really changed.

Reform, Justice, and Restitution

"The era of low standards and false profits is over."

—President George W. Bush, signing the Corporate Reform Act at the White House on July 30, 2002

In his comment President Bush addressed the issue that most troubles American investors: can the stock market be trusted in the future? According to the President the answer is yes. But a careful look suggests that investors must be cautious about accepting such assurances.

Hard earned savings and pensions of Americans were taken by misrepresentation and outright fraud. We've seen that this was not limited to just a few bad apples among American companies. Instead, thousands of companies were involved in some sort of accounting shenanigans, and almost every CEO of a public company got share options that promised to benefit him or her at some point even if the company's shareholders did poorly.

It was, as we've seen, a failure of the system—a failure of checks and balances, of ethics and morality, of corporate governance and government regulation. The overall scandal is so great that it isn't likely to be fixed by a single, and limited, piece of legislation, even though the President said it was. Investors understand that there is risk in equity markets. But investment risk is one thing—it's another to face the likelihood that your capital will be stolen via misrepresentations and fraud, and that is what faces investors today.

Three major responses are needed from the government and the investment industry if investors are to safely return to the market: reform, justice, and restitution. Reform means that the markets won't operate without new, higher standards that are rigorously enforced. Justice requires that those who defrauded investors will be severely punished. Restitution means that those who lost their nest eggs in these scandals will get them back.

It's true that there have always been dishonest people in business and that scandals happen periodically. But what was different this time that made these scandals more serious for business? The answer is found in our history.

America was initially a nation of farmers; business was limited mainly to small town stores and the average American didn't care much about how it was done.

In the late 19th century Americans poured, as workers, into the emerging manufacturing giants and discovered practices, even exploitation, which they eventually found intolerable. Masses of Americans were now tied to the corporations and they demanded changes in what they found there. There was now a political critical mass of Americans concerned about business behavior. The result was a wave of regulation of corporations that continued for decades.

In the late 20th century, Americans were herded by changes in the law and in corporate pension funds into dependence on the securities industry for their retirements and the college education of their children. Where once only a few people owned stock, and the retirements of most Americans were benefits paid by the companies for which they worked, a revolution in savings and retirement put the money directly into securities. With most Americans now dependent to some degree on Wall Street, there was a critical mass of political support for forcing changes on the securities industry. Practices which had been tolerable when affecting only a few, became intolerable to the mass of our people, particularly when those practices resulted in massive financial losses for millions of Americans and in the enrichment of a few.

Thus today's pressure for change in corporate board rooms and on Wall Street is part of a long-term dynamic process in American society. As people left the farms to work for business, they demanded changes in how business operates. As people today become dependent on the securities industry, they demand changes in how it behaves.

Today's attempts at reforming the securities business via legislation and regulation are but partial steps and often misdirected. But with trial and error, we may do better. Winston Churchill once observed about our country that one can always trust the Americans to do the right thing—after they've exhausted every other possibility. We are probably going to prove that aphorism right once again in the area of security regulation.

Top executives of the brokerages which paid major fines in the winter of 2002 for violating the securities laws (though they never admitted the violations) were not charged personally despite paying hundred's of millions of dollars in fines to the government for securities violations. Embarrassed regulators tried to explain their failure to indict the top executives of the firms involved (all ten largest American brokerages, including the top commercial banks and investment banks) to reporters as due to their inability to "find evidence that would show definitively that [CEOs] knew the firm was releasing false or misleading ratings" to the public.[294]

This is not a persuasive reason for the failure to hold CEOs personally responsible. It is in fact the same argument that David Irving, a British historian, has employed to absolve Adolf Hitler from responsibility for the death camps; that is, that there is no evidence—no written memos or orders that have Hitler's signature—that Hitler directed the mass murder in the death camps. This is correct—there are in fact no such memos or orders with Hitler's signature—but no reasonable person believes that the death camps operated without Hitler's knowledge and direction. To believe something like that violates both common sense and the general standard of personal responsibility by which large-scale events that occur on the watch of a top executive are his or her responsibility, whatever their direct involvement.

Similarly, the notion that events like the systematic misleading of investors for the purpose of gaining large fees from corporate clients (from which a CEO benefits directly in his or her pay package) occur many times in a company, and the CEO is unaware of them, violates both common sense and the general standard of top executive responsibility for what happens in a firm.

When prosecutors fail to insist on the personal responsibility of top executives, they invite further violations of the law because they've allowed executives to benefit from the violations personally and pay no personal price for it. The incentive to steal is left fully in place.

Justice is necessary if a new generation of corporate leaders is not to prey upon investors. And the justice must be personal (both in terms of jail time and fines), not just institutional. If the regulators require no leadership changes in companies in which there have been violations of the securities laws, and make no drastic requirements for change (such as divorcing research completely from investment banking by moving research into a different company), but instead merely let the companies pay fines to the government for their misdeeds, then corporate leaders will have been allowed to use shareholders' money (the corporation's funds) to buy their way out of their misdeeds and yet retain both their positions and their ability to do the misdeeds again. Securities laws have built into them a basic inconsistency that works against investors. In product liability law, a company is held liable for damage to customers because it's presumed that the shareholders were intended to benefit from the company's action. Security law makes the same presumption, but without reason, since securities violations are generally directed at the shareholder, not on his or her benefit. Fining the company simply penalizes the shareholder a second time. It's not the company that should pay, but the executives who committed the fraud. Often the company pays and the executives walk! So fines alone are not a useful result at all. They might be, if boards were independent of CEOs and therefore can fire a CEO. But that won't happen in the setting of the imperial CEO in American companies.

Thus the temptation remains for top executives to violate the securities laws that are intended to protect investors, and then to use investors' money to buy themselves out of the crimes.

It may seem that only reform is forward looking—that justice and restitution are focused on the past. Because of that appearance, it's sometimes argued that we should just go forward leaving the past to the courts; and it's argued that investors will do so, lured ahead by the promise of future gains in a reformed market. But this is not right. The viewpoint is myopic. Retribution for past wrongs is key to the future, because without it the incentive to steal, which drove CEOs and their associates in the 1990s remains as strong as ever. It's worth repeating that when a person can get very rich via the leadership of a great corporation, with very little risk that he'll pay a significant penalty, then American ethical standards are insufficient to restrain him, and investors will again be the victims.

Restitution is also important, not only because it is justified and yet very difficult to acquire under American law today, but because without it no investor can be certain that in the future, if he or she is again victimized, there will be any recourse. That there are mechanisms of recourse for the individual investor in today's law and exchange regulations is true—that they sometimes benefit individual investors is also true—but they have been completely inadequate to the magnitude of the recent, and will prove so again in the future.

Reform, justice, and restitution are the keys to the future.

So far, the government and the investment industry have made some progress on the first, a tiny amount of movement on the second (indictments are not convictions, and there have been only a few indictments), and virtually nothing on the third. It bears repeating, investors are not well-advised to reenter America's equity markets, and probably will not do so, until there has been significant progress on all three—reform, justice, and restitution.

The Irony of the Investor as a Victim of American Capitalism

There's been an ironic change in American capitalism since the New Deal of the 1930s. Before the reform legislation of the 1930s and the benefits established in the 1940s employees were routinely cheated out of their pay, workers had no job security, there were no pensions or unemployment insurance and no health insurance, and workers were prevented from joining unions to try to better their conditions. For most American employees, all that has changed. We now have laws that are generally effective in protecting people in the work environment. In consequence, our system isn't so hard on employees any more, and cases of exploitation are exceptions rather than the rule. But American capitalism is today very hard on investors; though we have laws, we have little effective enforcement of them; and cases of exploitation of investors are the rule rather than the exception.

The threats to investors reviewed in this book are not minor matters, but matters deeply imbedded in the nation's investment markets.

What seemed as they were revealed and reported to be very different things—the Internet bubble, the telecom bust, the corporate accounting scandals, CEOs often unmerited golden parachutes—turned out to have a lot in common. Each involved substantial misrepresentation to investors, many involved overt fraud, and they were each rife with conflicts of interest. At the core of each of these occurrences was an intention to deceive investors for the benefit of corporate executives and the professionals and financial service companies that assisted them (in particular, the banks, accountants, and their attorneys). Addressing the role of the investment banks in the scandals, Felix Rohatyn, formerly a banker himself, commented, "If Wall Street knows what is good for it and what is good for the country, it will very definitely clean up its act."

The Trembling Foundations of Wall Street

The economic consequences of the great bull market and its collapse included a dramatic transfer of wealth from investors to CEOs and investment bankers; the tipping of the economy into recession; and more subtle, but perhaps more important, a dramatic misallocation of capital. This last consequence is particularly disturbing because it raises questions about the very foundations of Wall Street.

The great irony is that top corporate executives, bankers, accountants, and attorneys, all supposedly committed to American capitalism, have in fact spent the past decade doing their best to undermine it. Capitalism and free markets both require complete and honest information to work properly, to allow investors to allocate capital to the areas with the best returns, and to provide buyers with information about the best quality and best prices of the goods and services they desire. This applies to capital markets in which investors are the buyers as well as to markets for other types of goods and services. This is well known to corporate executives and financial professionals, yet they have assiduously sought to misrepresent and conceal information.

In this perverse reversal of roles—in which the supposed champions of capitalism join to undermine it—corporate executives, bankers, accountants, and attorneys devoted and continue to devote vast amounts of energy and imagination to concealing and falsifying information so that the capital market has been grievously misled about the attractiveness of different sorts of investments. Corporate executives and financial professionals have, that is, spent their time and effort trying to destroy the very markets that they allegedly support. This has been done in recent years on an even larger scale than during the boom of the late 1920s.

The economic consequences have been serious: the Internet bubble diverted huge amounts of investment to companies and technologies not yet ripe for the commercial marketplace, so the investment was largely wasted. The telecom bubble diverted even larger sums to building traffic capacity for which there was not yet a market—so even vaster sums were wasted. The accounting frauds diverted larger sums again to equities and away from other financial investments such as bonds, thereby artificially inflating interest rates. Investors' money, as we've seen in this book, largely found its way into the pockets of corporate executives and their bankers, accountants, and attorneys.

In effect, the large company accounting ruses diverted capital from productive investment by firms (which is what investors thought they were getting for their money) into the luxury consumption expenditures of corporate executives, bankers, accountants, attorneys, and consultants. The diverted money fueled our housing price bubble and the success of companies providing luxury goods of all sorts. This is an intriguing twist in which the capital markets—whose economic justification is the allocation of capital to its most productive uses—became, and still are, an engine for directing capital instead to personal consumption. When investors began to perceive that this was happening, the value of equities generally collapsed, and the process ceased for the moment.

This result goes far beyond the issue of a few malfeasant corporate executives, and strikes at the very heart of American capitalism—the effectiveness of our capital markets themselves. If capital markets don't allocate capital to the best productive uses, then the very foundations of Wall Street are challenged, and that is where America finds itself today. We need a mechanism that uses the markets to allocate capital to the most productive uses, but it isn't today's Wall Street. Either a very deep reform of Wall Street is needed, one that current leadership in the banks is not suited to provide, or another mechanism is required.

Incremental changes in the way boards run themselves, or in the rules the regulators apply within the existing framework of power and regulation, is not going to be effective. Limited changes will not be effective because the same leadership is in control at the banks, the corporations, and the accounting firms that created the scandals; the same incentives for deception are in place; and the same temptation to get rich at the expense of investors remains. The cancer is thus very deep in the current system, and American financial markets need a thorough-going reform.

The American system has been so deeply corrupted that the basic thinking about how markets work is now being challenged. The American financial markets do not properly allocate capital, they do not properly reward investment, and they do not contribute to the growth and stability of the economy. Certainly this is the evidence of the past decade. The reason is that for institutional reasons they fall far short of the requirements of strong competition that enable markets to work effectively. The American system is one of manipulated markets, not perfectly competitive markets, and the results are therefore not what strong competition predicts. The results are not optimal but perverse.

As we've indicated above, to ask for very substantial changes on Wall Street is not to threaten American capitalism but instead to try to defend it—because it's now in a circumstance in which those who profess themselves its greatest supporters are in fact doing the most to undermine it. In fact, American business leadership, through greed and lack of self-restraint, has undermined the position of U.S. capitalism as a model for the world at a critical time, just as the President is asserting military dominance and political leadership against an often resistant world. Since business has compromised American economic leadership, a harsher burden falls on the President and on our military.

Sources of Investor Risk

I have reviewed in this book five key aspects of these matters, each of which has a significant risk for investors, and each of which can be corrected. I summarize them here:

1. Accounting fraud. Investors must be concerned about whether they can trust the financial reports of companies. Accounting has been used to conceal, not reveal, through:
    - Off-balance sheet financing using special-purpose entities
    - Overt fraud
    - Not expensing options
    - Too many one-time charges
    - Smoothing earnings

    These can be fixed by:
    - Reducing the conflict of interest for auditors, in part by separating auditing from consulting in the accounting firms
    - Enforcing much stronger regulation of accounting and auditing
2. The decline of corporate ethics. President Bush, Warren Buffett, and Alan Greenspan have all told Americans that the personal ethics of corporate leaders are the key to financial markets that are reliable for investors, and they've told us that ethics and honesty can't be legislated. If that's so, then unless ethics improve, and there's clear evidence that they are, investors must be very careful about trusting corporate America with their savings and pensions. The core of the problem is that incentives to steal have overwhelmed ethical reservations.

    This situation can be corrected by:
    - Imposing stronger penalties for fraud
    - Paying attention to ethical standards
    - Maintaining closer oversight of executives by boards
    - Restricting today's imperial CEOs

3. The risk of the wrong kind of regulation. What is needed is not more regulation of our securities markets, but smarter regulation, relying on two key elements:
    - A consolidation of regulatory agencies
    - A reliance on principles-based rather than detailed rules-based regulation
4. Dangers of the future. In recent years the stock market has become the arena of even more speculative and predatory pools of capital—the hedge funds—and therefore even more dangerous for many investors. This situation can be corrected by more careful oversight and regulation of hedge funds, and increased protections for investors generally, such as are recommended here.
5. Getting investors' money back. There must be restitution for reasons that are:
    - ethical—when people have been defrauded they should be made whole, as much as possible
    - social—it's a serious error for a country to impoverish its middle class by depriving people of pensions and college for their children, and to force the elderly back into the labor market for lack of adequate pensions, yet the United States is doing these things today on a large scale
    - expedient—it is important to restore confidence in markets so that investors return to them

American Investment Markets without Investors

"People are willing to take a risk with their money, but they're not willing to gamble when the system seems rigged against them."

—Michael G. Oxley,
House Committee on Financial Services, October 2, 2002

The proper goal of reform of the securities markets is to make them understandable and honest. The crucial question is whether or not Congress and regulators will do all that needs to be done to achieve it—the right kind of regulation rather than more regulation. Abby Cohen of Goldman Sachs says she "underestimated the depth of investor fear and loss of confidence seen this year [2002]. That has had a very dramatic impact on the market."[295]

It's no surprise that Wall Street was slow to see the impact of the loss of investor confidence, and it's no surprise now that Wall Street is slow to realize that unless there are significant reforms, investors are not going to return to the market. There will be traders and speculators, but no investors. Without investors they'll be no upward trend in the market, since hedge funds drive it first this way then that, trying to profit from motion in either direction. Without an upward trend in equities, innovation is going to slow, and the economy also will slow down. The market won't be responding to the economy, but the opposite. "I didn't know the market was so important," a friend told me; and I responded, "It's not, except when suddenly it's not there."

If Americans are unable to reform the financial markets sufficiently for them to regain public confidence, the financial markets will become a casino in which sophisticated players gamble against one another while capital allocation in the economy is much damaged. This is what has been happening in our country in the past few years. It is what happened in Britain in the 1920s and provoked an outburst from John Maynard Keynes—that when the capital allocation process of an economy becomes the offshoot of a casino, the job is likely to be ill done. Keynes was right. The equity markets did become a casino, and capital allocation was so ill done that a great depression in Britain was an immediate result, and Britain's post-war sinking to the status of a lesser power was a long-run consequence.

Such a future for the United States seems unlikely now, but if, after a half-century of expanding the reach of our capital markets among our citizens and those of the world, we now so lack effective national leadership that we see them contract, then the consequences will be severe and at this time incalculable.

Responsible businesspeople who make money without exploiting the public or misrepresenting their companies' situations ought to be the leaders in seeking smart, straightforward regulation. They're under tremendous pressure to join in illegal and unethical tactics in order to survive, and ought to lobby for sensible regulation to help themselves and to save an ethical business system. Capitalism works well when it is sensibly regulated—not too little and not too much—and responsible business leaders know this and know the difference between the two.

Were our markets to be fully reformed and were reported business successes to be real rather than fraudulent, then investors would stream back into the markets immediately. This is the challenge to the financial system and the American government today—to reform the markets by instituting real protections for the investor, and to show by retribution and restitution that the resolve to reform is real so that investors feel secure in returning.

Key Ideas of This Book

- The CEOs of large, publicly traded American companies are too powerful for the good of investors. Fixing this requires much more than advocating stronger boards of directors.
- There has been a pervasive decline of top business leadership into self-seeking. In the process, much harm has been done to investors and great bitterness has been engendered. This has happened in the context of a similar decline in the quality of leadership in other American institutions.

- Corporate ethics has declined to a lowest common denominator that is so minimal that ethics hardly exert any influence at the top of many corporations at this time. With few exceptions, executives seem to think about ethics only rarely, will discuss them if asked, but don't let ethics influence their work.
- Increased regulation via detailed rule-making by Congress or regulatory authorities cannot resolve the crisis of our securities markets. Congress is already micromanaging the securities industry and doing it poorly. A shift to smarter regulation via consolidated agencies and principle-based regulation is a better answer.
- Fining companies for the securities violations of their leaders only punishes defrauded investors, already victimized, a second time. Justice and reform both require that the leaders of companies be personally punished when fraud occurs, otherwise the problems will certainly reoccur with a new generation of executives.

Talking Points

It's ironic and in many instances tragic that investors have become victims of American capitalism. After all, they were told and for a while believed that they were the primary beneficiaries of the system. Instead, our system has shown itself to be very hard on investors: the law doesn't sufficiently protect them and their supposed agents—corporate executives, accountants, bankers, and corporate attorneys—have conflicts of interest against them.

Most disturbing of all to investors is that despite their losses and the publicity that has accompanied them, all the methods of deceiving shareholders, and all the conflicts of interest arrayed against them, are still in operation. Very little has changed, and probably even that little has changed only for the moment.

Three major responses are needed from the government and the investment industry if investors are to safely return to the market: reform, retribution, and restitution. Reform means that the markets will operate with new, higher standards that are rigorously enforced. Retribution means that those who defrauded investors will be severely punished. Restitution means that those who lost their nest eggs in these scandals will get them back.

Reform looks ahead. It should be based on stronger ethics, greater penalties for violations of securities laws (this reinforces ethical standards), and regulation that is smarter, not simply more and more detailed rules.

Reform should include:

- Reliance on improved ethics
- Smarter regulation based on a consolidation of regulatory agencies and more principle-based, less-detailed rule-based regulation

- Stronger penalties for fraud and means to be sure they are implemented
- Greater attention and support for higher ethical standards
- Closer oversight of executives by boards of directors
- Restrictions that lessen the power of today's imperial CEOs

Notes

Author's note: Wherever possible when I've used original documents, I've provided a citation to a secondary source in a newspaper, magazine, or television program for the convenience of readers in looking more deeply into matters mentioned in the book's text.

1. Arthur Levitt, former chairman of the Securities and Exchange Commission, *Fortune*, 145, 4, February 18, 2002, pg. 10.
2. "Investor Self-Protection," *The Economist,* November 30, 2002, pg. 12.
3. Milton Friedman, *Capitalism and Freedom*, Chicago: University of Chicago Press, 1962.
4. Jeanne Cummings, "Small Investors Now a Big Bloc," *Wall Street Journal*, September 27, 2002, pg. A4.
5. Albert J. Dunlap, *Mean Business: How I Save Bad Companies and Make Good Companies Great*, New York: Simon and Schuster, 1996.
6. Martha Brannihan, "Sunbeam Inquiry Looks at Events of Dunlap's Time," *Wall Street Journal*, September 10, 2002, pg. B5.
7. Brian Hall, Rakesh Khurana, & Carleen Madigan, "Al Dunlap at Sunbeam," Harvard Business School, 9-899-218, December 30, 1999.
8. Brian Hall, Rakesh Khurana, & Carleen Madigan, "Al Dunlap at Sunbeam," Harvard Business School, 9-899-218, December 30, 1999.
9. Brian Hall, "Al Dunlap at Sunbeam," Harvard Business School, 5-902-135, March 8, 2002.
10. Floyd Norris, "Former Sunbeam Chief Agrees to Ban and a Fine of $500,000," *New York Times*, September 5, 2002.

11. Floyd Norris, "Will Justice Department Go After Dunlap," *New York Times*, September 6, 2002, pg. C1.
12. Kurt Eichenwald, "The Findings Against Enron," *New York Times*, September 23, 2002.
13. "Prosecutor's Dilemma," *The Economist*, August 31, 2002, pg. 55.
14. Michelle Pacelle, "Enron Report Provides Details of Deals that Masked Debt," *Wall Street Journal*, September 23, 2002, pg. A6.
15. Kurt Eichenwald, "Secret Deal Part of Tangle in Enron Case," *New York Times,* October 1, 2002.
16. Kurt Eichenwald, "Ex-Enron Official Admits Payments to Finance Chief," *New York Times*, August 22, 2002.
17. Jonathan Weil & John Wilke, "Senate Panel Chides SEC for Falling Short in Enron Regulation," *Wall Street Journal,* October 7, 2002, pg. C1ff.
18. "When Something Is Rotten," *The Economist*, July 27, 2002, pg. 53
19. "The Power of WorldCom's Puff," *The Economist*, July 20, 2002, pg. 60.
20. Susan Pulliam & Deborah Solomon, "How Three Unlikely Sleuths Discovered Fraud at WorldCom," *Wall Street Journal*, October 30, 2002, pgs. A1, A6.
21. Deborah Solomon & Dennis Berman, "Global's Winnick Is Tried to Swap," *Wall Street Journal*, August 30, 2002, pg. A3.
22. Andrew Ross Sorkin, "Two Top Tyco Executives Charged with $600 Million Fraud Scheme," *New York Times*, September 13, 2002, pg. 1ff.
23. Floyd Norris, "Is a Looted Tyco Really Worth $36 Billion," *New York Times*, September 13, 2002.
24. Floyd Norris, "Tyco Took Profit on Bad Deal, Then Paid Bonuses to Executives," *New York Times*, September 25, 2002, pg. C1.
25. Geoffrey Colvin, "Liar, Liar, Pants on Fire," *Fortune*, September 16, 2002, pg. 60.
26. Geoffrey Colvin, "Liar, Liar, Pants on Fire," *Fortune*, September 16, 2002, pg. 60.
27. Gretchen Morgenson & Andrew Ross Sorkin, "Tyco Rewarded an Executive During a Grand Jury Inquiry," *New York Times*, September 26, 2002.
28. Geraldine Fabrikant, "Indictments for Founder of Adelphia and Two Sons," *New York Times*, September 24, 2002.
29. See, for example, Andrew Pollack, "Ex-Drug Executive Faces U.S. Charges of Insider Trading," *New York Times*, August 8, 2002.
30. David Leonhardt, "Qwest Officials Made Millions in Stock Sales," *New York Times*, July 30, 2002.
31. Deborah Eckert, "Warnaco Settles Wachner's $25.1 Million Claim," *Wall Street Journal*, November 19, 2002, pg. B4.
32. Geraldine Fabrikant, "GE Expenses for Ex-Chief Cited in Divorce Papers," *New York Times*, September 6, 2002.
33. James Bandler, "Xerox Faces Criminal Charges," *Wall Street Journal*, September 24, 2002.
34. "Xerox Says U.S. Attorney Probing Accounting," *New York Times*, September 23, 2002.
35. Rebecca Buckman, "SEC Still Investigates Whether Microsoft Understated Earnings," *Wall Street Journal*, February 13, 2002.
36. Henry Norr, "SEC Slaps Microsoft for Books," *San Francisco Chronicle*, June 4, 2002, pg. B1.

37. Kathleen Day, "SEC Says Microsoft Broke Law," *The Washington Post*, June 4, 2002, pg. E1.
38. Roy Olofson, testimony, Federal Document Clearing House, September 24, 2002.
39. See, for example, Howard Schilit, *Financial Shenanigans, 2nd Edition*, New York: McGraw-Hill, 2002. Schilt's book was first published in the early 1990s and describes many of the accounting dodges described in this chapter.
40. For example, in December 2001, shortly after Enron filed for bankruptcy, a senior vice president of the American Institute of Certified Public Accountants (AICPA) said that, with respect to all of the financial statements filed with the SEC, "99.9 percent of those audits are high quality" (Alex Berenson, "Watching the Firms that Watch the Books," *New York Times*, December 5, 2001).
41. "Huron Consulting Group Research Reveals Leading Causes of Financial Restatements," U.S. Newswire, July 19, 2002; conversation with Huron Consulting Group on August 28, 2002; Ianthe Jeanne Dugan, "How Decade of Greed Undid the Proud Respectability of a Very Old Profession," *Wall Street Journal*, March 14, 2002. According to the Huron Consulting Group's figures, moreover, from 1999 to 2001, the number of restatements increased 25%, while the number of public companies decreased 7%.
42. Stephen Barr, "Misreporting Results," CFO, December 1998; James Surowiecki, "The Dirty Little Truth about Corporate Lies," *Slate*, July 6, 1998; Lisa I. Fried, "Accounting Abuse," *New York Law Journal*, January 14, 1999.
43. See, for example, John Kenneth Galbraith, *The Great Crash 1929*, Boston: Houghton Mifflin, 1979.
44. Floyd Norris, "Is a Looted Tyco Really Worth $36 Billion," *New York Times*, September 13, 2002.
45. John Cassidy, "The Greed Cycle," *The New Yorker*, September 23, 2002, pgs. 64–77, at pg. 74.
46. Warren Buffett, "Who Really Cooks the Books," *New York Times*, July 24, 2002.
47. Floyd Norris, "Siebel Systems Salvaging Sunken Options," *New York Times*, September 10, 2002.
48. Warren Buffett, "Who Really Cooks the Books," *New York Times*, July 24, 2002.
49. Floyd Norris, "Pension Woes," *New York Times*, August 9, 2002, pg. C1.
50. Mark Maremont, "Tyco Inflated Cash Flow of Acquisition," *Wall Street Journal*, March 19, 2002, pg. A3.
51. For example, John Manley, a senior equity analyst with Salomon Smith Barney, was asked in early 2002 about questions that had been raised regarding some of the accounting practices at Tyco International. He strongly defended the company. "There is strong cash flow there," he said, "and you cannot fake cash flow" (*Nightly Business Report*, February 4, 2002).
52. Mark Maremont, "Tyco Inflated Cash Flows of Acquisition," *Wall Street Journal*, March 19, 2002, pg. A3.
53. David Leonhardt, "It's Called A 'Loan,' But It's Far Sweeter," *New York Times*, February 3, 2002.
54. Michael Schroeder, "SEC List of Accounting-Fraud Probes Grows," *Wall Street Journal*, July 6, 2001.
55. Michael Schroeder, "Accounting for Enron: Enron Reports Weren't Reviewed Fully by SEC for Several Years before Collapse," *Wall Street Journal*, January 18, 2002.

56. Transcript of program "Bigger Than Enron" (http://www.pbs.org/wgbh/pages/frontline).
57. Michael Schroeder, "SEC Gets a Raise, but Will It Be Enough?," *Wall Street Journal*, August 12, 2002.
58. Quoted in *New York Times*, July 8, 2002.
59. CNBC, August 6, 2002 (Ms. Siebert heads a financial services firm in NYC).
60. Warren E. Buffett, "Who Really Cooks the Books, "*New York Times*, July 24, 2002.
61. Warren E. Buffett, "Who Really Cooks the Books?" *New York Times*, July 24, 2002.
62. "Lou Takes the Gloves Off," *Business Week*, November 18, 2002, pgs. 64–70 at pg. 70.
63. Gretchen Morgenson, "Does the Rot on Wall Street Reach Right to the Top?" *New York Times*, November 11, 2002, pg. BU3.
64. Lawrence J. McQuillan, "Just Send Scoundrels to Jail," *USA Today*, July 10, 2002, pg. 10A.
65. David Leonhardt, "Anger at Executives' Profits," *New York Times*, July 9, 2002, pg. C6.
66. KPMG, Integrity Management Services, "2000 Organizational Integrity Survey," KPMG US Web page (2002), November 18, 2002, cited in the Conference Board, op. cit).
67. Steven Rosefielde, *Comparative Economic Systems*, Chapters 1, 3, and 4. Malden: Blackwell Publishers, 2002.
68. See D. Quinn Mills, *eLeadership*, New York: Prentice Hall, 2001.
69. See D. Quinn Mills, *Rebirth of the Corporation*, New York: Wiley, 1991, *The Gem Principle and Six Steps to Creating a High Performance Organization*, New York: Wiley, 1994.
70. Laura Citron & Richard Walton, "International Comparisons of Company Profitability," *Economic Trends,* 587, October 2002.
71. An investment banker, interview, August 2, 2002.
72. Julie Creswell, "Banks on the Hot Seat," *Fortune*, September 2, 2002, pg. 79ff.
73. Joseph L. Bower, "When We Study M&A, What Are We Learning," Harvard Business School, Division of Research, Working Paper No. 03-026, June 1, 2002, pg. 8.
74. Spencer Ante, "Big Blue's Boardroom Bind," *Business Week*, October 14, 2002, pg. 14.
75. Kurt Eichenwald, "For WorldCom, Acquisitions Were Behind Its Rise and Fall," *New York Times*, August 8, 2002.
76. Matthew Boyle, "The Shiniest Reputations in Tarnished Times," *Fortune*, March 4, 2002.
77. Kenneth F. Broad, Transamerica Investment Management, quoted in David Leonhardt, "Anger at Executives' Profits," *New York Times*, July 9, 2002, pg. 1.
78. Louis Uchitelle, "Will a Deck of Options Always Be Stacked?" *New York Times*, April 7, 2002.
79. John Kenneth Galbraith, *The Great Crash 1929*, Boston: Houghton Mifflin, 1954.
80. A. A. Berle, Jr., & G. C. Means, *The Modern Corporation and Private Property*, New York: Macmillan, 1932.
81. See Brian J. Hall & Jeffrey B. Liebman, "Are CEOs Really Paid Like Bureaucrats?" *Quarterly Journal of Economics*, XCII, 3 (August 1998), pgs. 655–691.
82. Brian Hall, "Incentive Strategy II: Executive Compensation and Ownership Structure," Harvard Business School, N8-902-134, May 8, 2002, pg. 5.

83. Brian Hall, "Incentive Strategy II: Executive Compensation and Ownership Structure," Harvard Business School, N8-902-134, May 8, 2002, pg. 25.
84. Ronald I. McKinnon & Huw Pill, "Credible Liberizations and International Capital Flows: The Overborrowing Syndrome," in T. Ito & A.O. Krueger, eds., *Financial Deregulation and Integration in East Asia*, Chicago: Chicago University Press, 1996, pgs. 7–42.
85. These figures were compiled by Pearl Meyer & Partners, a compensation consulting firm, and reported in "Executive Pay: A Special Report," *New York Times*, April 7, 2002.
86. Mark Gimein, "You Bought, They Sold," *Fortune*, September 2, 2002.
87. These figures were compiled by Kevin Murphy of the University of Southern California, who has done a lot of work on executive pay; cited in Jim Collins, "Emphasis on CEO Pay Outweighs Focus on Results," *USA Today*, June 10, 2002.
88. Peter Schwartz, "The Relentless Contrarian," *Wired Magazine*, August 1996.
89. Gretchen Morgenson, "When Options Rise to Top, Guess Who Pays," *New York Times*, November 10, 2002, reporting a study by Joseph R. Blasi and Douglas L. Kruse of Rutgers University.
90. John Kador, "Just Rewards; CEO Pay Is Outrageous—But Is It justified? And Will It Ever Change?" *Electronic Business*, June 1, 2001.
91. Tracie Rozhon & Joseph B. Treaster, "Insurance Plans of Top Executives Are in Jeopardy," *New York Times*, August 29, 2002.
92. Brian Hall, "Incentive Strategy II: Executive Compensation and Ownership Structure," Harvard Business School, N8-902-134, May 8, 2002, pg. 25.
93. Brian Hall, "Incentive Strategy II: Executive Compensation and Ownership Structure," Harvard Business School, N8-902-134, May 8, 2002, pg. 26.
94. See for an example of this view, Matt Murray, "Options frenzy: What Went Wrong?" *Wall Street Journal,* December 17, 2002, pg. B1ff.
95. Diana B. Henriques and Geraldine Fabrikant, "Deciding on Executive Pay: Lack of Independence Seen," *New York Times,* December 18, 2002, pg. 1ff.
96. This is the view of Warren Buffett, Alan Greenspan, and Arthur Levitt, former chairman of the SEC, the CFOs of certain companies like Dell Computer and Coors Brewing; various academicians; and many other analysts. The academician who is perhaps the strongest advocate of indexing stock options is Alfred Rappaport ("New Thinking on How to Link Executive Pay with Performance," *Harvard Business Review*, March-April 1999). Even people who strongly endorse the use of conventional, fixed-price stock options more or less acknowledge that indexing stock options would do a better job of linking pay to performance (e.g., Brian J. Hall, "What You Need to Know About Stock Options," *Harvard Business Review*, March-April 2000).
97. John Kador, "Just Rewards; CEO Pay Is Outrageous—But Is It Justified? And Will It Ever Change?" *Electronic Business*, June 1, 2001.
98. Brian J. Hall, & Thomas A. Knox, "Managing Option Fragility," NBER Working Paper #9059, National Bureau of Economic Research, July 2002.
99. Floyd Norris, "Option Absurdity: Hoping for Lower Prices," *New York Times*, March 15, 2002.
100. Executives typically do this by making use of "zero-cost hedge collars." This involves simultaneously buying a put and selling a call on the company's stock,

thus locking in a price range for it. This takes much of the risk out of holding the stock.

101. Louis Lavelle, "Undermining Pay for Performance," *Business Week*, January 15, 2001.
102. This was the basis of the $100 million fine that Credit Suisse First Boston agreed to pay the government in January 2002. A lot of good material about this is available on the PBS website for its Frontline program, "Dot.con" (*www.pbs.org/wgbh/pages/frontline/shows/dotcon/*). The article by John Coffee, of Columbia Law School, and the interview with Joseph Nocera, executive editor of *Fortune* magazine, explains a lot of the dynamic behind what went on.
103. Interview with Sarah Teslik, available on the PBS website for its Frontline program, "Bigger Than Enron" (*www.pbs.org/wgbh/pages/frontline/shows/regulation/*).
104. David Leonhardt, "Enron's Way: Pay Packages Foster Spin, Not Results," *New York Times*, January 27, 2002.
105. Gregory S. Miller, "Earning Performance and Discretionary Disclosure," *Journal of Accounting Research*, March, 2002.
106. Floyd Norris, "An Old Case is Returning to Haunt Auditors," *New York Times*, March 1, 2002, pg. C1.
107. Scott J. Paltrow, "Accounting for the Fall: Accounting Scandals Have Some Peering at Industry's Self-Policing," *Wall Street Journal*, January 14, 2002; Jonathan Weill & Scott J. Paltrow, "Peer Pressure: SEC Saw Accounting Flaw," *Wall Street Journal*, January 29, 2002.
108. Transcript of program "Bigger Than Enron" (http://www.pbs.org/wgbh/pages/frontline).
109. "Alan Greenspan Testifies before the Senate Banking, Housing, and Urban Affairs Committee," Federal Document Clearing House, July 16, 2002.
110. Daniel Kadlec, "Who's Accountable?," *Time*, January 21, 2002.
111. This kind of activity was in fact encouraged by the American Institute of Certified Public Accountants (AICPA), the primary trade association for the accounting profession. In 1999 it published for its members a manual titled "Make Audits Pay: Leveraging the Audit into Consulting Services." The president of the AICPA, Barry Melancon, in 1998 described the "certified public accountant" designation as a marketing liability (David S. Hilzenrath, "After Enron, New Doubts About Auditors," *Washington Post*, December 5, 2001).
112. Ken Brown & Ianthe Jeanne Dugan, "Sad Account: Andersen's Fall from Grace Is a Tale of Greed and Miscues," *Wall Street Journal*, June 7, 2002.
113. Mark Maremont, "Lawsuit Details Rite Aid's Accounting Woes," *Wall Street Journal*, February 8, 2001.
114. Associated Press, "Bush Seeks More Tax Cuts," *Newsday*, March 20, 2002.
115. Melody Petersen, "Consulting by Auditors Stirs Concern," *New York Times*, July 13, 1998.
116. Much of the following detail about Andersen and Enron comes from Ianthe Jeanne Dugan, Dennis Berman, & Alexei Barrionuevo, "On Camera, People at Andersen, Enron Tell How Close They Were," *Wall Street Journal*, April 15, 2002; Thaddeus Herrick & Alexei Barrionuevo, "Were Auditor and Client Too Close Knit?," *Wall Street Journal*, January 21, 2002.
117. "America is No Japan," *Financial Times*, July 23, 2002, pg. 13.

118. Andrew Ross Sorkin & Jonathan D. Glater, "Some Tyco Board Members Knew of Pay Packages, Records Show," *New York Times*, September 23, 2002.
119. See "How Ebbers Kept the Board in his Pocket," *Business Week*, October 14, 2002, pg. 138.
120. Robin Sidel, "Board Compensation becomes a Balancing Act," *Wall Street Journal*, August 30, 2002, pg. C1.
121. Robin Sidel, "Board Compensation becomes a Balancing Act," *Wall Street Journal*, August 30, 2002, pg. C1.
122. "Prosecutor's Dilemma," *The Economist*, August 31, 2002, pg. 55.
123. Sol M. Linowitz, *The Betrayed Profession,* New York: Charles Scribner's Sons, 1994, pp. 228–230.
124. Warren E. Buffett, "Who Really Cooks the Books," *New York Times*, July 24, 2002.
125. Christine B. Whelan & Tom Hamburger, "IPO Largess Flowed to Capitol Hill," *Wall Street Journal*, September 6, 2002, pg. A4.
126. Jonathan Fuerbringer, "Computer Associate Trips Up Directors on Disclosure," *New York Times*, August 27, 2002.
127. Richard W. Stevenson, "To Greenspan, 90's Bubble Was Beyond Reach of Fed," *New York Times*, August 31, 2002.
128. Stephen Cecchetti, "The Perils of Ignoring Bubbles," *Financial Times*, September 4, 2000, pg. 11.
129. Heather Timmons, "Surprise! The Little Guy Loses," *BusinessWeek*, July 8, 2002, pg. 42.
130. Jacob M. Schlesinger, "Did Washington Help Set Stage for Current Business Turmoil?" *Wall Street Journal,* October 17, 2002, pg. A1.
131. Alan S. Blinder and Janet L. Yellen, *The Fabulous Decade: Macroeconomic Lessons from the 1990s,* Twentieth Century Fund, 2001.
132. David Barboza, "U.S. Said to be Investigating Another Enron-Merrill Deal," *New York Times*, September 12, 2002, pg. C2.
133. Paula Dwyer, Laura Cohn, Emily Thornton, & Wendy Zellner, "Merrill Lynch: See No Evil?" *BusinessWeek*, September 16, 2002, pgs. 68–76.
134. William B. Harrison, Jr., of JP Morgan Chase on deals with Enron, quoted on CNBC, August 2, 2002. See also Gretchen Morgenson, "Banks are Havens (and Other Myths)," *New York Times*, July 28, 2002.
135. Paul Beckett, "Citigroup Changes Policy on Options, Enron-type Deals," *Wall Street Journal*, August 8, 2002, pg. A3.
136. Julie Creswell, "Banks on the Hot Seat," *Fortune*, September 2, 2002, pg. 79ff.
137. Paul Beckett & Jathon Sapsford, "Gigantic Headaches: Citigroup's Vast Reach Brings It Trouble From Many Quarters—Sandy Weill's Financial Titan Is Mired in Woes of Enron, Grubman and Argentina—Still, 'the Postman' Delivers," *Wall Street Journal*, July 26, 2002, pg. A1ff.
138. Paul Beckett & Jathon Sapsford, "Gigantic Headaches: Citigroup's Vast Reach Brings It Trouble From Many Quarters—Sandy Weill's Financial Titan Is Mired in Woes of Enron, Grubman and Argentina—Still, 'the Postman' Delivers," *Wall Street Journal*, July 26, 2002, pg. A1ff.
139. Paul Beckett & Jathon Sapsford, "Energy Deals Made $200 Million in Fees for Citigroup, J.P. Morgan," *Wall Street Journal*, July 24, 2002, pg. A1.
140. Paul Beckett & Jathon Sapsford, "Energy Deals Made $200 Million in Fees for Citigroup, JP Morgan," *Wall Street Journal*, July 24, 2002.

141. David Barboza, "Ex-Executives Say Sham Deal Helped Eron," *New York Times*, August 8, 2002.
142. "Unburdening," *The Economist*, September 28, 2002, pg. 70.
143. Patrick McGeehanpar, "Wall St. Banks May be Fined for Discarding E-Mail Traffic," *New York Times*, August 2, 2002.
144. Tom Hamburger, Susan Pulliam, & Suzanne Craig, "Salomon IPO Deals Provoke Congress," *Wall Street Journal*, August 20, 2002, pg. C1ff.
145. Randall Smith, Anne Grimes, Gregory Zuckerman, & Kara Scannell, "Something Ventured and Something Gained?" *Wall Street Journal*, October 17, 2002, pg. C1ff.
146. Gretchen Morgenson, "Ebbers Got Million Shares in Hot Deals," *New York Times*, August 28, 2002. See also Patrick McGeehan, "Panel's Report Offers Details on 'Spinning' of New Stocks," *New York Times*, October 3, 2002.
147. Andy Serwer, "Conseco's Colorful Crash," *Fortune*, September 16, 2002, pg. 197.
148. Emily Thorton, Heather Timmons, et al., "How Corrupt is Wall Street," BusinessWeek, May 13, 2002, pg. 39.
149. Michael Siconolfi, "Incredible 'Buys': Many Companies Press Analysts to Steer Clear of Negative Ratings; Stock Research Is Tainted as Naysayers are Banned, Undermined and Berated; Small Investors in the Dark," *Wall Street Journal*, July 19, 1995.
150. Patrick McGeehan, "The Crux of Reform: Autonomous Stock Rating," *New York Times*, October 7, 2002.
151. Patrick McGeehan, "Lawyer Says Ex-Merrill Analyst Traded Gifts with Tyco Chief," *New York Times*, September 14, 2002; Charles Gasparino, "Merrill Replaced Its Tyco Analyst after Meeting," *Wall Street Journal*, September 17, 2002; Phua K. Young, "The Skies Remain Very Clear," Merrill Lynch report on Tyco International, October 5, 1999.
152. By Jessica Hall, June 20, 2001, Reuters.
153. Rob Hotakainen and Steve Alexander; "Executives Testify in Qwest Hearing; Global Crossing Also Accused of Duping Investors," *Star Tribune*, September 25, 2002.
154. Susan Pulliam, "Analysts to Tell Congress That Skepticism Gets Them Abuse," *Wall Street Journal*, March 19, 2002; Jeffrey M. Laderman, "Wall Street's Spin Game," *BusinessWeek*, October 5, 1998.
155. Scott Cleland & John Eade, "Follow the Money to Wall Street's Big Secret," *Financial Times*, October 8, 2002, pg. 14.
156. Data from Zacks Investment Research, reported in Jeffrey M. Laderman, "Wall Street's Spin Game," *BusinessWeek*, October 5, 1998.
157. The total market capitalization of stocks traded on the New York Stock Exchange represents the large majority of the market capitalization of all stocks traded in the United States. Therefore, one can reasonably use the figures for stocks with advancing and declining prices on the NYSE as a proxy for the market as a whole. (The percentages of advancing and declining stocks on the NASDAQ and the AMEX, in any case, aren't dramatically different.)
158. The study is described by Robin Sidel, "Bullish Ratings May Hold Bearish Truths," *Wall Street Journal*, September 13, 2002.
159. Jeffrey M. Laderman, "Wall Street's Spin Game," *BusinessWeek*, October 5, 1998.
160. "Wall Street Prophets," *60 Minutes*, January 30, 2001.
161. "Wall Street Prophets," *60 Minutes*, January 30, 2001.

162. Excerpts from e-mails obtained by the office of the attorney general of New York: "Affidavit in Support of Application for an Order Pursuant to General Business Law Section 354" (*www.oag.state.ny.us/press/2002/apr/MerrillL.pdf*).
163. "Wall Street Prophets," *60 Minutes*, January 30, 2001.
164. Direct testimony about this is provided, for example, by Michael Schroeder & Randall Smith, "CSFB Analysts Felt Pressured on Stock Reports," *Wall Street Journal*, September 6, 2002.
165. "Wall Street Prophets," *60 Minutes*, January 30, 2001.
166. Jeffrey M. Laderman, "Wall Street's Spin Game," *BusinessWeek*, October 5, 1998.
167. Gretchen Morgenson, "Regulators Find More Red Flags in Another Analyst's Optimism," *New York Times*, September 12, 2002.
168. Jeff D. Opdyke, "Guidelines Aim to Polish Analysts' Image," *Wall Street Journal*, June 13, 2001.
169. Gretchen Morgenson, "Pressuring Analysts: Hard Habit To Break," *New York Times*, August 11, 2002.
170. David R. Francis, "New Rules May Temper Stock Touts," *Christian Science Monitor*, July 8, 2002; Jeff D. Opdyke, "Should You Trust Wall Street's New Ratings?," *Wall Street Journal*, July 17, 2002.
171. Susanne Craig, "Securities Firms Do the Soft Sell in Their Ratings," *Wall Street Journal*, September 13, 2002.
172. Rebecca Smith, "The Analyst Who Warned about Enron," *Wall Street Journal*, January 29, 2002.
173. David Rynecki, "The Price of Being Right," *Fortune*, February 5, 2001.
174. Gretchen Morgenson, "Pressuring Analysts: Hard Habit To Break," *New York Times*, August 11, 2002.
175. Lee Gomes, "That Glowing Report on Company X Isn't What You Might Think," *Wall Street Journal*, June 24, 2002.
176. Daniel Eisenberg & Laura Bradford, "It's an Ad, Ad, Ad, Ad World," *Time*, September 2, 2002.
177. Landon Thomas, Jr., "Board Stiffed," *New York Magazine*, August 19, 2002, pg. 14ff.
178. Ien Chang, "Executives in Biggest U.S. Collapses Made $3.3 bn," *Financial Times*, July 31, 2002, pgs. 1, 8.
179. Lawrence J. McQuillan, "Just Send Scoundrels to Jail," *USA Today*, July 10, 2002, pg. 10A.
180. Mark Gimein, "You Bought, They Sold," Fortune, September 2, 2002, pgs. 64–65.
181. Alex Berenson, "Lucrative Years as C.E.O., Despite Average Performance," *New York Times*, December 10, 2002.
182. Russell Wild, "The Grand Illusion," *AARP*, September-October, 2002, pg. 40.
183. David Kirkpatrick, "Key Figure in Homestore Inquiry," *New York Times*, September 27, 2002.
184. David Kirkpatrick, "Key Figure in Homestore Inquiry, "*New York Times,* September 27, 2002.
185. Simon Romero, "Memo Indicates Global Crossing Chief Knew of Troubles," *New York Times*, October 2, 2002.
186. Simon Romero, "Qwest Deals Are Added to Inquiry," *New York Times*, September 13, 2002.
187. Michael Jensen, quoted in John Cassidy, "The Greed Cycle," op.cit.

188. Greg Ip, "New York Fed President Chides CEOs on Hefty Compensation," *Wall Street Journal*, September 12, 2002, pg. A2.
189. Andrew Hill, "Rich Bosses Start to Feel Squeeze," *Financial Times*, September 14/15, 2002, pg. 7.
190. Warren Buffet, "Who Really Cooks the Books?" *New York Times*, July 24, 2002.
191. Testimony of Chairman Alan Greenspan, Federal Reserve Board's semiannual monetary policy report to the Congress before the Committee on Banking, Housing, and Urban Affairs, U.S. Senate, July 16, 2002.
192. Peter Singer, ed., *Ethics*, New York: Oxford University Press, 1994.
193. Michael R. Rion, *Ethics and Management in the Corporate Arena*, pg. 541.
194. Manuel G. Velasquez, *Business Ethics*, Englewood Cliffs, NJ: Prentice-Hall, 1992 (third edition), pgs. 2–8.
195. "Have Ethics Disappeared from Wall Street?" *Christian Century*, 15, July 22, 1987.
196. This may be reprinted in Max L. Stackhouse, et al., *On Moral Business*, Grand Rapids, MI: W. B. Eerdman, 1995.
197. Walter Shapiro, "Enron's Slogans," *USA Today*, February 8, 2002.
198. Hearing of the Oversight and Investigations Subcommittee of the House Energy and Commerce Committee, October 1, 2002, Federal News Service.
199. United States Sentencing Commission, "The Federal Sentencing Guidelines for Organizational Crimes: Questions and Answers," 1991, pg. 6.
200. Enron's code of ethics is on sale on eBay, perhaps illegally by former employees, for $20, and WorldCom's code of ethics is bringing $0.99 at the same site.
201. The Conference on Science, Philosophy and Religion, recounted briefly in Charles Colson and Nancy Pearcey, *How Now Shall We Live?* Wheaton, IL: Tyndale House Publishers, 1999, at pgs. 374–376.
202. See Bridget O'Brian, "Socially Responsible Funds Get Nicked, Too—Some Investment Firms Find They Can't Always Detect Problems with Accounting," *Wall Street Journal,* August 9, 2002.
203. Janice Farmer, December 18, 2001, Congressional Testimony, Federal Document Clearing House.
204. Profile: Penalties for street vs. white-collar crime, July 8, 2002, Minnesota Public Radio: Marketplace.
205. "Bush Seeks More Rules to Protect 401(k) Plans," *New York Times*, October 20, 2002.
206. Mara Der Hovanesian, "The Buyback Boomerang," *BusinessWeek*, September 23, 2002, pg. 100.
207. Tim Burt, "A Multi-million Mogul Gets Mad," *Financial Times*, September 23, 2002, pg. 8.
208. "Corporate America's Woes, Continued," *The Economist*, November 30, 2002, pg. 60.
209. Scot J. Paltrow, "SEC Isn't Likely to Discipline Enron Board," *Wall Street Journal*, September 25, 2002, pg. C1.
210. See, for example, Louis Lavelle, "How to Halt the Options Express," *BusinessWeek*, September 9, 2002, pgs. 74, 76.
211. See Daniel Altman, "How to Tie Pay to Goals, Instead of the Stock Price," *New York Times*, September 8, 2002.
212. Editorial Board, "Stock Option Excess," *New York Times*, March 31, 2002.

213. Zvi Brodie, Robert S. Kaplan, & Robert C. Merton, "Options Should Be Reflected in the Bottom Line," *Wall Street Journal*, August 1, 2002, pg. A12.
214. Financial Accounting Standard 123, paragraphs 8–10.
215. Jeffrey Skilling, Testimony before the Senate Commerce Committee, February 26, 2002.
216. At press conference, August 1, 2002.
217. Richard Katz, "America is No Japan," *Financial Times*, July 23, 2002, pg. 13
218. Jonathan Weil, "Should J. P. Morgan Set Rules for J. P. Morgan?" *Wall Street Journal*, October 8, 2002, pg. C1ff.
219. Patrick McGeehan, "Wall St. Banks May Be Fined for Discarding E-Mail Traffic," *New York Times*, August 2, 2002.
220. See, for example, "Policing Wall Street," *New York Times*, Editorial, August 5, 2002.
221. Trebor Banstetter, "Nation's Busiest SEC Office Strained by Caseload, Enron," Fort-Worth Star-Telegram, March 3, 2002.
222. Greg Ip, "White House Is Expected to Recommend Only a Slight Boost in Funding for SEC," *Wall Street Journal*, February 4, 2002, pg. A5.
223. Trebor Banstetter, "Nation's Busiest SEC Office Strained by Caseload, Enron," *Fort-Worth Star-Telegram,* March 3, 2002.
224. Robert Barker, "Will the SEC Bless This Masquerade?" *BusinessWeek*, August 5, 2002, pg. 110.
225. Interview with Arthur Levitt, on "Frontline" program, first aired in Spring 2002 *www.pbs.org/wgbh/pages/frontline/shows/regulation/interviews/levitt.html*
226. Simon London, "How to Bring U.S. companies under Control," *Financial Times*, August 7, 2002, pg. 7.
227. See Klaus Gugler, ed., Cor*porate Governance and Economic Performance*, Oxford: Oxford University Press, September 2001.
228. See Lorsch (1989), pgs. 170–171.
229. See especially, Jeffrey A. Sonnenfeld, "What Makes Great Boards Great," Harvard Business Review, September 2002, R0209H.
230. These recommendations are those of Robert Crandall, former CEO, AMR, on CNBC, July 15, 1992.
231. Cynthia Montgomery & Rhonda Kaufman, "Put Directors on the Record," *Financial Times*, August 8, 2002, pg. 7.
232. McKinsey & Company's Global Investor Opinion Survey was undertaken between April and May 2002, in cooperation with the Global Corporate Governance Forum. The survey is based on responses from over 200 institutional investors, collectively responsible for some US $2 trillion of assets under management (their organizations manage an estimated US $9 trillion AuM). For further information, contact Mark Watson (tel: (212) 446-8021) or Paul Coombes (+44 20 7961 5493).
233. Lori Verstegen Ryan & Marguerite Schneider, "The Antecedents of Institutional Investor Activism," *Academy of Management Review, 27*, 4, (October, 2002), pgs. 554–573.
234. Bernard Condon, "Mickey Mouse Math," *Forbes*, May 13, 2002, pg. 48.
235. Quoted in Jerry Useem, "In Corporate America It's Cleanup Time," *Fortune*, September 16, 2002, pg. 64.
236. Quoted in Richard W. Stevenson, "Greenspan Says Enron Cure Is in Market, Not Regulation," *New York Times*, March, 27, 2002, pg. C 5.

237. Quoted in *Financial Times*, July 22, 2002.
238. Daniel Dombey & Bertrand Benoit, "Brussels Tries to Quell German Criticism," *Financial Times*, August 29, 2002, pg. 3.
239. David Leonhardt & Andrew Ross Sorkin, "Reining in the Imperial CEO," *New York Times*, September 15, 2002.
240. Kopin Tan, "The Striking Price," *Barrons,* December 30, 2002, pg. MW13.
241. See, for example, Alfred Rappaport, "Show Me the Cash Flow," *Fortune*, September 16, 2002, pgs. 192, 194.
242. Alex Kuczynski, "Screening Applicants for Ethics at Companies," *New York Times*, August 19, 2002.
243. See Lynn Sharp Paine, *Value Shift*, New York: McGraw-Hill, 2003.
244. Robert Prentice, "An Ethics Lesson for Business Schools," *New York Times*, August 20, 2002.
245. David Barboza, "Friends Say Ex-Chief Despairs, Seeking Someone to Believe Him," *New York Times*, August 22, 2002, Online edition.
246. Dan Seligman, "Oxymoron 101," *Forbes*, October 28, 2002, pg. 160.
247. Alex Berenson, "A Gift Raises Questions on Computer Associates," *New York Times*, December 3, 2002.
248. "Corporate America's Woes, Continued," op cit., pg. 61.
249. *BusinessWeek,* August 12, 2002, pg. 34.
250. Jonathan D. Glater, "Suing the Accountants: Vitriol and Paperwork," *New York Times*, August 7, 2002.
251. Daniel Solin, "Does Your Broker Owe You Money?" Fox Cable Network, September 28, 2002.
252. Simon London, "How to Bring U.S. companies Under Control," *Financial Times*, August 7, 2002, pg. 7.
253. So reported Congress' General Accounting Office in July 2002. See Richard B. Schmitt & Henry Sender, "CEOs' Wealth May be At Stake in Investor Suits," *New York Times*, August 9, 2002, pg. B4.
254. Data: Stanford Law School, Cornerstone Research, reported in Dan Carney, "Don't Toss This Stock Fraud Law: Just Fix It" *BusinessWeek*, August 5, 2002, pg. 86.
255. Dan Carney, "Don't Toss This Stock Fraud Law: Just Fix It," *BusinessWeek,* August 5, 2002, pg. 86.
256. Patrick McGeehan, "Spitzer Sues Executives of Telecom Companies," *New York Times*, October 1, 2002.
257. Lynnley Browning, "Shareholders Rise Up (In Wild West Fashion)," *New York Times*, October 20, 2002.
258. Kurt Eichenwald, "A higher Standard for Corporate Advice," *New York Times,* December 23, 2002, pg. 1.
259. Floyd Norris, "Former Sunbeam Chief Agrees to Ban and a Fine of $500,000," *New York Times*, September 5, 2002.
260. Mike France, "Don't Kill All the Trial Lawyers," *BusinessWeek*, August 26, 2002, pg. 156.
261. See ClassActionOnline.com.
262. Adapted from ClassActionOnline.com.
263. Adapted from ClassActionOnline.com.
264. Adapted from ClassActionOnline.com.

265. Dina Temple-Raston, "Class-Action Lawsuits Gain Strength on the Web," *New York Times*, July 28, 2002.
266. See Adam Liptak, "Court Has Dubious Record as a Class-Action Leader, Critics Say," *New York Times*, August 15, 2002.
267. Richard B. Schmitt & Henry Sender, "CEOs' Wealth May be At Stake in Investor Suits," *New York Times,* August 9, 2002, pg. B4.
268. Richard B. Schmitt & Henry Sender, "CEOs' Wealth May be At Stake in Investor Suits," *New York Times*, August 9, 2002, pg. B4.
269. Kurt Eichenwald, "Freeze Reportedly Applied to Accounts in Enron Case," *New York Times*, August 24, 2002.
270. *Wall Street Journal*, October 2, 2002.
271. C. Boyden Gray, "Damage Control," *Wall Street Journal,* December 11, 2002, pg. A18.
272. Andrew Parker, "Accounting Standards Move Toward Compatibility," *Financial Times*, October 30, 2002, pg. 8.
273. William A. Sahlman, "Expensing Options Solves Nothing," *Harvard Business Review*, December, 2002, pg. 96.
274. See, for example, Arthur Levitt, *Take on the Street*, New York: Pantheon, 2002, pg. 282.
275. Daniel Fisher, "The Great Stock Illusion," *Forbes*, July 22, 2002, pgs. 194, 196, citing work by Peter Bernstein & Robert Arnott.
276. William Wolman & Anne Colamosca, *The Great 401(k) Hoax*, New York: Perseus, 2002.
277. Emily Thornton, "A Yardstick for Corporate Risk," *BusinessWeek*, August 26, 2002, pg. 106ff.
278. See *Institutional Investor, 36,* June 6, 2002, in which the magazine reported its first survey of the hedge fund industry.
279. *The Economist*, July 27, 2002, pg. 63.
280. Hal Lux, "Who Wants to be a Billionaire*?"* *Institutional Investor, 36,* June 6, 2002, pg. 55ff.
281. Gregory Zuckerman, "Hedge Funds May Give Colleges Painful Lessons," *Wall Street Journal*, October 7, 2002, pp. C1ff.
282. Hal Lux, "Who Wants to be a Billionaire?" *Institutional Investor, 36,* June 6, 2002, pg. 62.
283. G. Chacko & L. M. Viceira, "Dynamic Consumption and Portfolio Choice with Stochastic Volatility in Incomplete Markets," National Bureau of Economic Research Working Paper 7377, 1999; J. Y. Campbell & L. M. Viceira, *Strategic Asset Allocation: Portfolio Choice for Long-Term Investors*, Oxford: Oxford University Press, 2002, Chapter 5.
284. Robert Chow, "Hedge Funds Up Against SEC Deadline," *Financial Times*, August 9, 2002, pg. 21.
285. Floyd Norris, "Outside 401(k) Plans, Stock Ownership Declines," *New York Times,* September 28, 2002.
286. Thomas S. Mondschean & Bruce R. Scott, "Corporate Renewal in America," Harvard Business School, 5 703 023, November 7, 2002.
287. "Clean Report—Most CFOs See No Need to Prohibit Pro Forma Results—or Overhaul Earnings Reporting," *Institutional Investor*, September 2002, pg. 24.

288. Andrew Hill, "CEOs Hit Back over Reforms," *Financial Times*, October 3, 2002, pg. 1.
289. See Cassell Bryan-Low, "Accounting Firms are Still Consulting," *Wall Street Journal*, September 23, 2002, pg. C1.
290. Gretchen Morgenson, "On Reform, It's Time to Walk the Walk," *New York Times*, October 6, 2002.
291. Gretchen Morgenson, "On Reform, It's Time to Walk the Walk," *New York Times*, October 6, 2002.
292. See David Cay Johnston, "Designers of Executive Salary Plans Fear More Abuses," *New York Times*, October 5, 2002.
293. Gary Silverman, "Gramm to Join UBS Warburg as Vice Chairman," *Financial Times*, October 8, 2002, pg. 18.
294. Charles Gasparino, "Citigroup's Weill Might Avoid Charges Over Faulty Research," *New York Times,* December 18, 2002, pg. 1.
295. Vincent Boland, "Wall Street Analysts Feel Pain," *Financial Times*, July 27, 2002, pg. 8.

Index

C

D

E

F

G

H

I